BEYOND THE RISK PARADIGM IN CRIMINAL JUSTICE

BEYOND THE RISK PARADIGM

Series Editor: Nigel Parton

This important new series argues that a risk paradigm has come to dominate many human services in Western countries over the last twenty years, giving the impression that the social world is calculable and predictable. Each book critically engages with this paradigm, demonstrating the intended and unintended consequences of such an approach for those using and working in services, as well as for wider society, in order to open up new ways for taking policy and practice forward. Designed to challenge readers to think critically and creatively about risk, this fascinating series will develop the understanding and knowledge of students and practitioners alike.

Forthcoming titles:

Beyond the Risk Paradigm in Child Protection, edited by Marie Connolly
Beyond the Risk Paradigm in Mental Health Policy and Practice, edited by Sonya Stanford, Nina Rovinelli Heller, Elaine Sharland and Joanne Warner

Nigel Parton is Professor of Applied Childhood Studies at the University of Huddersfield, UK, and has been writing about and researching these issues for over 20 years.

BEYOND THE RISK PARADIGM IN CRIMINAL JUSTICE

EDITED BY

CHRIS TROTTER, GILL McIVOR

FERGUS McNEILL

macmillan education   palgrave

First published 2016 by
PALGRAVE

Palgrave in the UK is an imprint of Macmillan Publishers Limited,
registered in England, company number 785998, of 4 Crinan Street,
London, N1 9XW.

Palgrave Macmillan in the US is a division of St Martin's Press LLC,
175 Fifth Avenue, New York, NY 10010.

Palgrave is a global imprint of the above companies and is represented
throughout the world.

Palgrave® and Macmillan® are registered trademarks in the United States,
the United Kingdom, Europe and other countries.

ISBN 978–1–137–44132–4 paperback

This book is printed on paper suitable for recycling and made from fully
managed and sustained forest sources. Logging, pulping and manufacturing
processes are expected to conform to the environmental regulations of the
country of origin.

A catalogue record for this book is available from the British Library.

A catalog record for this book is available from the Library of Congress.

Printed and bound by CPI Group (UK) Ltd, Croydon, CR0 4YY

CONTENTS

14 Changing Risks, Risking Change   239
Chris Trotter, Gill McIvor and Fergus McNeill

INTRODUCTION

This book is part of a series of three books on the risk paradigm. It emerged from a conference held at the Monash University Centre in Prato, Italy, on risk in child protection, mental health and criminal justice. The conference discussed why it is appropriate at this time to challenge some of the assumptions underlying risk assessment and some of the practices currently used around the world. The three books engage in critical evaluation of the research and practice of risk assessment and its consequences – for adults and juveniles in an international context. Each addresses the authors' concerns about the dominance of risk assessment.

This volume focuses on risk in criminal justice. It addresses the issues relating to risk assessment and risk-driven interventions in criminal justice settings from both theoretical and practical perspectives. It aims to provide a critique of the risk paradigm and to provide practical guidance for professionals, academics and students regarding how to move to a more effective way of working with offenders.

The term 'risk paradigm' encompasses the risk assessment processes, the interventions and treatment methods which flow from them and the underlying theory and beliefs which sustain them. The book is distinctive not just in its engagement with this paradigm, which is central to the administration of criminal justice programmes throughout the world, but also because it aims to offer both critique of and alternatives to that paradigm. Most youth and adult corrections departments routinely conduct risk assessments in prison and community-based settings. These risk assessments are then used to inform the nature and intensity of subsequent criminal justice interventions. This book includes chapters from the world's leading researchers on these issues. The book is unique in providing a new direction for criminal justice work, a direction which has the potential to lead to lower recidivism and, ultimately, safer societies.

The book is divided into three sections. Section 1 discusses the risk paradigm in practice; Section 2, the consequences of the risk paradigm; and Section 3, ways forward.

Chapter 1, 'The rise of the risk paradigm in criminal justice' by Gwen Robinson, sets the scene for the book as a whole in two ways. First, it charts the ways in which sociocultural perspectives on risk, the risk society thesis and the governmentality perspective have been applied in analysing the development of late-modern criminal justice, for example in relation to arguments about the 'new penology' and the 'culture of control'. Second and more specifically, it elaborates the historical development and deployment of ideas about risk in criminal justice, explaining how, why and to what extent the risk paradigm has come to prominence in this context.

Chapter 2, 'Three narratives of risk: Corrections, critique and context' by Peter Raynor, argues that attempts to measure and control risk have become a central concern in criminal justice. Critics have pointed out how the use of risk assessments can conflict with proportionality, and have also argued that it can increase the general level of punitiveness and social disadvantage. Developers and supporters of risk assessment have pointed to advantages, such as the support it offers for rehabilitative measures. This chapter discusses the development of risk assessment in British criminal justice practice and argues that its consequences, both positive and negative, have depended not simply on the use of risk-related practices but also on the policies they have been deployed to serve.

Section 2, which focuses on the consequences of the risk paradigm, opens with Chapter 3, 'Risk assessment in practice' by Chris Trotter. This chapter considers three assumptions related to the risk paradigm: first, that youth and adult actuarial risk assessment profiles are successful in predicting the likelihood of reoffending; second, that high-risk offenders benefit more from intensive interventions than medium or low-risk offenders; and third, that focusing on client issues or problems which are defined by a professional worker through a risk assessment leads to lower recidivism than working with issues or problems defined by the client. It reviews the literature relating to these assumptions and issues and refers to two projects undertaken in community corrections and youth justice in Australia which have found that the actuarial risk profiles did not achieve high levels of prediction; that medium and low-risk offenders benefit as much from good quality supervision as high-risk offenders; and that when issues or problems are defined by the client rather than the workers, better outcomes are often achieved.

Chapter 4, 'Taking the risk out of youth culture' by Stephen Case and Kevin Haines, argues that for some people risk factor research represents the most important and significant breakthrough in understanding and explaining juvenile delinquency. Unencumbered by complex, implicit or dubious social theories and free of political bias, risk factor research represents the application of science to understand social problems. Through the use of pure scientific method, the individual and social factors prevalent in the lives of young people that predict future delinquency are uncovered, and the causes and predictors of delinquency are laid bare. As if this were not achievement enough, risk factor research (RFR) also paves the way for preventing future juvenile delinquency. The list of risk factors for future offending produced by RFR provides academics, policymakers and practitioners with a ready set of targets for intervention. If the factors in the lives of young people that have been shown to predict and cause future offending can be changed or mitigated, then delinquency can be averted or prevented. This potential of RFR to identify the causes and predictors of delinquency and, simultaneously, to offer a 'cure' has proven to be irresistible. This 'irresistability' has been bolstered by the fact that both the science and the practicality of application of its main findings in concrete, predeterminable interventions are inherently logical, relatively simple and easily understood – it all makes sense. But does it? This chapter provides one example of the problems which are often associated with the implementation of risk-driven justice. It charts the emergence, rise, domination and ultimate fall of risk in youth justice in England and Wales, and the emergence of a new 'children first' paradigm focused on achieving positive outcomes for young people.

Chapter 5, 'Justice, risk and diversity' by Gill McIvor, points out that while there have been broad concerns about the centrality of risk in criminal justice and the adequacy and relevance of risk assessment technologies, there are particular concerns in relation to how concepts of risk and risk assessments engage with and accommodate diversity and how, more specifically, the risk paradigm further disadvantages marginalized groups. Drawing principally on gender and ethnicity – but including other dimensions of diversity as appropriate – this chapter draws upon international empirical evidence and theoretical debates to demonstrate how risk and risk assessment as traditionally conceptualized and operationalized have resulted in the over-classification and regulation of marginalized individuals and groups through the reconceptualization of 'needs' and structural disadvantages as 'risks'. The chapter critically discusses the limitations of the risk paradigm and its consequences in the context of diversity, and considers the potential of alternative approaches to offer a more nuanced understanding of the relationship between processes of criminalization and pathways out of crime.

Chapter 6, 'Drugs, mental disorder and risk' by David Rose, argues that a substantial proportion of the people who enter and move through the criminal justice system have substance misuse issues and/or mental disorders and are often portrayed as high-risk offenders. This chapter examines the risk paradigm as it relates to substance misuse and mental disorder within the criminal justice system. It discusses the multifaceted nature of risk at the intersection of the criminal justice and health systems, especially within the general context of an increasing focus on the identification, classification and reduction of risk. The chapter critically discusses the impact of a risk-focused paradigm on practice, as well as the relationship of risk to broader notions of recovery. Observations from work in offender support services, primarily in post release/aftercare contexts, are made and developed through a practice example. The chapter concludes by linking these practice observations to developments in offender rehabilitation such as strengths-based approaches as well as separate but complementary developments in the drug treatment and mental health treatment fields around strengths-based recovery.

Chapter 7, 'Programmes for domestic violence perpetrators' by Dave Morran, focuses on the domestic violence field, where programmes of intervention with perpetrators have traditionally been underpinned by conceptions of 'risk' (or 'relapse'), where a focus has been on enabling men to identify, and therefore avoid, situations that might serve as 'triggers' to abusive behaviour. Increasingly, however, it is becoming apparent that although the acquisition of such skills aimed at managing 'risky' situations and behaviours may be important and useful in some respects, interventions have not focused sufficiently on the ways in which abusive behaviours meet perpetrators' needs and what, therefore, may be required for maintaining and sustaining change. Instead, it will be argued that strengths-based approaches provide a more promising mechanism for recognizing and engaging effectively with the complexity of abusive men's pathways into and out of violence.

Chapter 8, 'Risk, regulation and the reintegration of sexual offenders' by Anne Marie McAlinden, considers media reporting of and public concern about sexual offending. Media reporting of and public concern about sexual offending affects and reflects political, institutional and practical responses to those convicted of such crimes. This paper sets out to chart the various ways in which the risks imagined of or posed by sexual offenders have been regulated and managed under the 'risk paradigm'; as such it addresses issues as diverse as registration schemes, public notification schemes and employment vetting, as well as the ways in which those engaged with managing sexual offenders in the community seek to do so. Ultimately, it argues that risk-based regulation is at best uncertain in its effects and at worst is counterproductive, in that it often reduces the possibilities of successful reintegration. In seeking to look 'beyond risk', the chapter explores the usefulness of restorative and related practices in supporting such reintegration at the primary and secondary levels of harm prevention.

Chapter 9, 'The collateral consequences of risk' by Fergus McNeill, explores the unintended and collateral consequences of the emergence of risk assessment and management as central preoccupations of offender supervision. Although assessing and managing risks may be necessary for any organization or form of practice that seeks to reduce crime-related harms, when risk-focused discourse becomes dominant, it can actively (if indirectly) undermine attempts to promote positive social goods and to support change. At their worst, risk-based practices may work to inflate and instantiate risks. Drawing on a series of ethnographies exploring risk practices in criminal justice and youth justice, this chapter exposes some of the mechanisms through which a preoccupation with risk can become counterproductive. Seeking a way out of this impasse, the chapter goes on to ask how and in what ways the need to reduce and manage risks can be balanced by the need to support desistance and social integration.

Chapter 10, 'Probation, risk and the power of the media' by Wendy Fitzgibbon, focuses on media issues. Media representation of offenders strongly influences community perceptions of offender-related risks as well as risk management practices within the criminal justice system. This chapter examines how, within a criminal justice system strongly framed around the risk paradigm, media reporting and subsequent community outrage can impact on the way risk is managed and in itself becomes a key target for risk management strategies. The influence of this on workers and practice within the criminal justice system will be examined, as well as broader consequences such as stigma and marginalization of offenders.

Section 3, 'Ways forward', opens with Chapter 11, 'Putting risk in its place' by Craig Schwalbe and Gina Vincent. Criticisms of risk assessment and the risk paradigm, presented here and elsewhere, are a welcome catalyst for the evolution in our thinking about risk, needs and interventions. Nevertheless, in this chapter it is argued that these criticisms should not lead to the wholesale rejection of the risk paradigm, which continues to have a rationale and place in the criminal justice arena. Until now most empirical research has focused on the comparatively easy questions of identifying risk factors, evaluating the predictive validity of risk assessment instruments and, to a lesser extent, estimating their reliability. Virtually ignored in the scholarship of risk assessment and the risk paradigm are the challenges associated with implementation of the risk assessment framework in actual practice. This chapter distinguishes between frameworks for assessment and case conceptualization (risk paradigm) and intervention models and modalities. It then proceeds to utilize critiques of the risk paradigm to formulate case-level and system-level strategies for its optimal implementation in justice settings. The chapter concludes with a discussion of unanswered questions that may serve as a springboard for further research and scholarship.

In Chapter 12, 'Dynamic and protective factors in the treatment of offenders: A reconceptualization', Tony Ward and Imogen McDonald argue that there is theoretical and practice gridlock in the correctional and forensic domains due to an increasing reliance on dynamic risk factors to guide assessment and intervention with individuals who have committed crimes. The dilemma for clinicians is that on the one hand they want to engage in evidence-based practice, but on the other, current models centred on dynamic risk factors result in formulaic approaches to working with individuals. The current trend to build protective factors into the assessment matrix does not help much, as they are conceptually almost as problematic as dynamic risk factors. In this chapter we outline the concepts of dynamic risk factors and protective factors. The ability of these concepts to function as explanations of crime (and its desistance) is then critically evaluated and their relationships to proximate causes explored. After concluding that dynamic risk and protective factors have limited explanatory or practical value in offender rehabilitation, we present the Agency Model of Risk (AMR). In the rest of the chapter, we demonstrate how dynamic risk factors and protective factors can be incorporated within the AMR, and better inform the explanation of crime and correctional interventions.

Chapter 13, 'An unfinished alternative: Towards a relational paradigm' by Beth and Allan Weaver, discusses how studies of desistance from crime – and of their implications for criminal justice practice – have begun to challenge 'the risk paradigm'. That challenge has been cast principally in terms of the ways in which desistance can be supported (and therefore risk of reoffending reduced), with research suggesting, for example, the critical importance of motivation, relationships and social contexts in the human development processes associated with leaving crime behind. However, more recently, desistance research has begun to raise questions about the end point or destination implied: What comes after desistance? This chapter argues that a focus on social relations, trust and reciprocity is essential – both practically and normatively – to processes of change and to supporting them. That focus in turn requires the development of co-productive approaches to practice that take more seriously the lived realities of the struggle for change, and the experiential expertise of those engaged in that struggle.

Chapter 14, 'Changing risks, risking change' by Chris Trotter, Gill McIvor and Fergus McNeill, draws together the themes which have been presented in the book. It summarizes the rise of the risk paradigm to become the dominant paradigm in criminal justice interventions. It identifies the problems associated with the prevalence of the risk paradigm, including the practical implementation of risk assessment and risk-driven interventions and the consequences for the recipients of those interventions. It then outlines a way forward for criminal justice interventions which does not involve risk as the predominant paradigm. We argue that a greater focus on involving the client in criminal justice interventions, on client strengths and on helping offenders to address their life goals will ultimately lead to lower recidivism and to a safer society.

SECTION 1

THE RISK PARADIGM IN PRACTICE

1

THE RISE OF THE RISK PARADIGM IN CRIMINAL JUSTICE

Gwen Robinson
University of Sheffield, UK

Introduction

In many Western jurisdictions in the twenty-first century, risk has become a taken-for-granted part of the criminal justice field, both in policy and practice. But, although ideas associated with risk have a long history in both criminal justice and other areas of public administration (O'Malley, 2004), the centrality of risk thinking in contemporary criminal justice has more particular and more recent origins, in the latter part of the twentieth century. It is there that we can locate the conditions of emergence of current forms of risk thinking. In this chapter I will consider these conditions or foundations on which risk thinking in criminal justice has developed. To begin, the chapter reviews two macro-theoretical perspectives which have been proposed to explain the rise of risk in late modern societies and have been applied to various areas of public administration to explain its purchase and spread therein. These are the so-called risk society and governmentality perspectives. Next, the chapter examines the emergence of ideas about 'crime as risk' and actuarialism as a response to crime, most famously expounded in Feeley and Simon's 'new penology' thesis in the early 1990s. It then goes on to critically examine the idea of a wholesale paradigm shift in criminal justice and consider the reasons why – and extent to which – risk has made inroads into criminal justice practice and thinking. It is argued that risk emerged at a time of crisis for criminal justice systems in many jurisdictions, appearing to pose solutions to problems of legitimation and of resourcing, and to offer rational means through which to recast policy and practice. The chapter concludes by considering the future trajectory of risk and asks the question: is there a future beyond the risk paradigm?

Two explanatory frameworks

Neither 'criminal justice' nor other areas of public administration exist in a vacuum. Instead, they are situated in and evolve within wider social and cultural contexts which provide (or at least suggest) the resources, and arguably set the outer limits, for change (Rose, 1999). In order to understand the rise of risk in criminal justice, therefore, we need to accept the idea that broader social and cultural forces have played a part in shaping the terrain. This takes us into the realm of macro-level theoretical analyses which have sought to explain a growing consciousness of risk at the level of 'society' or – slightly less broadly – at the level of 'governance' in the latter part of the twentieth century. Here I briefly review the two principal frameworks which have inspired analyses of risk in criminal justice (O'Malley, 2004): they are the 'risk society' thesis and the 'governmentality' perspective.

The 'risk society' thesis

The conceptualization of contemporary Western jurisdictions as *risk societies* appeared in parallel in the writing of two European sociologists in the late 1980s and early 1990s: Ulrich Beck [1986] (1992) in Germany and Anthony Giddens (1990, 1991) in Britain. Both scholars documented and sought to explain the contemporary prominence of risk as a social construct, and both proposed that it should be understood as a 'consequence of modernity' (Giddens, 1990): that is, as an unavoidable and increasingly salient side effect of twentieth-century developments, particularly in the fields of science and industry. Prominent in their analyses were large-scale, high-consequence risks, including pollution, nuclear radiation and the spread of disease made possible by mass transportation: risks that potentially affect everyone and have the potential to create a shared awareness or consciousness of risk in late modern societies. Importantly, though, neither Beck nor Giddens saw risk as a new idea; nor did they regard contemporary societies as inherently more risky than premodern ones. Rather, they posited a fundamental difference between premodern and modern societies in their sources, patterns and perceptions of risk. So, for example, Giddens argued that in premodern societies 'environments of risk' derived from natural dangers, such as the threat of human violence from warlords and robbers, as well as the possibility of falling from religious grace and malicious magical influence. In contrast, he argued, the risk profile of modernity had come to be characterized by dangers which are wholly man-made. Furthermore, distributions and perceptions of risk had also fundamentally altered. Many contemporary risks (such as those noted above) could be said to be 'global', affecting everyone, with the potential to erode traditional social divisions based on class or wealth. A corollary of this, Giddens argued, was both a growing awareness of risks and an understanding that they could not be entirely removed or converted into certainties, even by the supposed 'expert systems' on which we generally rely:

> To recognise the existence of a risk or set of risks is to accept not just the possibility that things might go wrong, but that this possibility cannot be eliminated. The phenomenology of such a situation is part of the cultural experience of modernity in general. (Giddens, 1990, p. 111)

But whilst the future might be inherently unknowable, the quest for control was not abandoned: for Giddens, living in the 'risk society' meant – for lay actors and technical specialists alike – living with a 'calculative attitude' toward the future. It is in this process, he argued, that the identification and management of risks had become structuring principles of contemporary organizational and political life:

> A significant part of expert thinking and public discourse today is made up of *risk profiling* – analysing what, in the current state of knowledge and in current conditions, is the distribution of risks, in given milieu of action. Since what is 'current' in each of these respects is constantly subject to change, such profiles have to be chronically revised and updated. (Giddens, 1991, p. 119)

The 'risk society' thesis, then, essentially suggests that the emergence of risk thinking in any number of areas of social life and administration – including criminal justice – is to be expected as part of a more generalized, heightened consciousness of risk (and a 'calculative attitude' towards it) in the social domain.

The 'governmentality' perspective

On a slightly less grand/global scale, the second framework which has had a major influence on scholars' quests to understand the rise of risk in criminal justice is grounded in Michel Foucault's 'governmentality' perspective, which pertains principally to the political field. This approach takes as its object of analysis modes and techniques of government (conceived quite generally in Foucault's work as 'the conduct of conduct'), and posits a shift from 'social welfare' to 'advanced liberal' or 'neoliberal' styles of government in the latter part of the twentieth century (e.g. Rose, 1996). This shift is associated with the relinquishing of a vision of society of universal security – dubbed by some neoliberal critics as 'no-risk society' – in which risk (whether in the guise of poverty, unemployment, crime or ill health) was regarded as a product of pathology to be corrected or eliminated (O'Malley, 1996). In its place is a vision of society in which the perception of risk is fundamentally altered: risk can be calculated, predicted and managed, but never extinguished. As Pratt has explained, the rejection of the welfarist strategy is associated with the realization that the more welfarism tried to guarantee security and minimize risks, 'the more it fostered dependency and established new risks – risks that were perceived as both the product of its own inefficiencies and its entrapment of its subjects' (1999, p. 143).

In common with the 'risk society' thesis, this approach does not regard risk as an invention of late modern societies; rather, it suggests that shifts in modes of government have been accompanied by changes in the *deployment of risk* as a technique of government. O'Malley (1992) describes this as a shift in modes of risk management away from the 'socialized' techniques characteristic of the welfare state (e.g. social insurance), in favour of more individualized, private forms, or what he terms 'prudentialism'. Under neoliberalism, O'Malley argues, the role of the state is no longer to absorb and share risks, but rather to promote autonomous risk management by individuals and private sector entities alike. Central to the neoliberal project is the idea of 'responsibilization', whereby individuals cease to depend upon the state for security and instead are 'empowered' to make 'informed choices' about risk and its management in their own lives. As Rose explains:

> The state is no longer to be required to answer all society's needs for order, security, health and productivity. Individuals, firms, organizations, localities, schools, parents, hospitals, housing estates must take on themselves – as 'partners' – a portion of the responsibility for their own well-being. (1999, p. 142)

As we shall see later, the 'governmentality' perspective, with its emphasis on the political field and modes of social control, has spawned or influenced a number of key analyses of developments in the criminal justice field with risk at their heart. In the next section my attention turns to the most influential of these analyses: the 'new penology' thesis, developed by US scholars Jonathan Simon and Malcolm Feeley in the early 1990s.

From 'crime as risk' to the 'new penology'

Despite their differences, both of the theoretical frameworks outlined above share a concern with a 'reflexive moment' – albeit an extended one – in the latter part of the twentieth century, whereby the 'dark side' of modernity was coming to light and seemed to demand different approaches to social problems of various kinds. In many Western jurisdictions, the problem of crime (and how to respond to it) was intimately bound up in this process, as old certainties about the propensity of the criminal justice apparatus to deal effectively with crime were increasingly coming to be questioned, and the legitimacy of that apparatus more generally came under attack. Garland (1990) has referred to this as a 'crisis of penal modernism', which brought with it a questioning of traditional assumptions and a quest for new ways of dealing with the problem of crime.

In the latter 1980s and early 1990s, several scholars developed analyses of what Garland (1996) has called the 'reconfiguration of crime control' that drew inspiration from the Foucauldian 'governmentality' perspective outlined in the previous section. Among these was a paper by Nancy Reichman (1986) which included the first explicit formulation of the notion of *crime as a risk*. In light of the failings of the modern correctional apparatus, the notion of 'crime as risk' seemed, to a growing number of commentators, to capture well a collective adjustment in perceptions of crime, whereby offending had come to be viewed not as a sign of pathology or abnormality but rather as a contingency or 'normal social fact' (e.g. Cohen, 1985; Reichman, 1986; Feeley and Simon, 1992; Garland, 1996). The notion of crime as risk implied a rejection, or at least a modification, of modern penality's quest to eliminate crime, in favour of more modest, 'managerial' objectives. Reichman, for example, argued that 'A risk management approach to crime does not offer any promises to eliminate crime by seeking out and correcting its underlying causes or by rehabilitating offenders' (1986, p. 164). She further argued that crime was becoming detached from the moral realm, such that assigning blame was now less important than reducing risk (see also Simon, 1988). Such an approach, it was argued, was also associated with the application of actuarial, insurance-based techniques based not on biographical knowledge of individuals but of aggregates or populations and distributions of risk among them. Several commentators noted an 'actuarial turn' in the realm of crime prevention strategies in the 1980s, aimed at surveillance, prediction and opportunity reduction (e.g. Simon, 1987).

Whilst these signs of a risk-based approach were initially documented in analyses of the crime prevention context (Shearing and Stenning, 1985), similar developments were soon being observed in respect of the treatment of offenders in the penal realm. One of the first scholars to bring the penal sphere under the umbrella of such analyses was Cohen (1985), who observed, across the whole spectrum of crime control strategies, 'an uneven move away from internal states to external behaviour, from causes to consequences, from individuals to categories or environments' (p. 154).

As part of this shift Cohen observed a retreat from Freudian-derived 'inner states' models of offender rehabilitation, in favour of a less ambitious vision of behaviour modification, content to 'settle for sullen citizens, performing their duties, functioning with social skills, and not having any insights' (1985, p. 151).

But whereas Cohen suggested a partial retreat from correctional interventions, American criminologists Feeley and Simon (1992, 1994) took the argument a stage further. Their 'new penology' thesis posited a wholesale shift from a penality characterized as clinical, individualized and treatment-oriented, in favour of a 'new' penality characterized, in contrast, as actuarial, managerial and control-oriented. In summary, Feeley and Simon argued, the new penology 'is managerial, not transformative... It seeks to *regulate* levels of deviance, not intervene or respond to individual deviants' (1992, p. 452).

In the context of an actuarial or risk management regime, Feeley and Simon continued, new justifications for 'old' practices were emerging. No longer were imprisonment or supervisory penalties anchored in aspirations to correct or rehabilitate offenders: the prison had become little more than a warehouse for the highest risk groups, whilst community-based sanctions simply offered opportunities to maintain control over lower risk offenders for whom custody was judged to be too expensive or unnecessary. Whether in the context of custody or community-based supervision, they argued that the technology of risk assessment would increasingly be relied upon to perform the task of classification; serving simply to 'sort' individuals into groups according to 'the degree of control warranted by their risk profiles' (1992, p. 459). For writers like Feeley and Simon and Cohen, the rise of a rationality of risk in the criminal justice realm, and of actuarial techniques alongside this increasingly dominant way of thinking, was explicable by virtue of their economic sense:

> Rather than seeking to change people ('normalize them', in Foucault's apt phrase), an actuarial regime seeks to manage them in place ... The movement from normalization (closing the gap between distribution and norm) to accommodation (responding to variations in distributions) increases the efficiency of power because changing people is difficult and expensive. (Simon, 1988, p. 773)

Refining the 'new penology'

The 1990s saw the publication of a number of empirical studies which sought to investigate the salience of ideas associated with the 'new penology' thesis in a variety of jurisdictions and criminal justice contexts. For example, Ericson and Haggerty's (1997) study of policing in Canada provided a convincing account of policing as a 'risk profession'. However, other studies seemed to suggest the continuing importance of punitive and/or rehabilitative goals in some settings, despite evidence (in a number of contexts) of the adoption of risk management approaches and technologies (e.g. Lynch 1998, 2000; Hannah-Moffat, 1999; Kemshall and Maguire, 2001; Robinson, 2002). These and other scholars thus began to think more carefully about the place of risk in criminal justice, and to challenge the idea of its inexorable rise and uncritical acceptance as *the* dominant, global paradigm.

In a series of influential essays in the late 1990s, Pat O'Malley took issue with the treatment of actuarialism in the new penology thesis and elsewhere, disputing its inevitable and unilinear expansion, as well as explanations based on the 'evolutionary criterion' of its superior economic and/or political efficiency. His argument was that the role and effects of actuarial practices could be understood without reference to the political context in which they were deployed. 'What influences the spread of technologies', O'Malley asserted, 'is most likely to be their appropriateness to particular ends' (1996, p. 193). In other words, actuarialism must be understood as a technology which had been – and would continue to be – utilized in different ways in relation to different political programmes. In a related argument, O'Malley and Mugford (1992) disputed the association of actuarialism with a 'de-moralization' of social regulation. Their own analysis of the actuarial technique of random drug testing led them to argue that, far from being a morally neutral and thus efficient means of reducing drug use, it was in fact part of a deeply moral crusade against drug use per se. This analysis chimes with Hannah-Moffat's finding of a 'hybrid moral/ actuarial penality' in Canadian women's prisons, whereby actuarial assessments of risk were infused with moral evaluations of women's behaviour (1999, p. 82).

O'Malley and others, then, encouraged an approach to the understanding of risk and its associated technologies capable of taking into account the political context and the relationships, articulations and alliances between actuarialism and other forms of exercising power. For O'Malley, the idea that actuarial power had rendered either punitiveness or individualized, 'rehabilitative' tendencies redundant was too simplistic: thus, 'rather than there being an implied redundancy, there comes into being a dynamic interaction' such that different forms of exercising power 'may be expected to collide as well as collude' (1992, pp. 255–6). Both Bottoms (1995) and Garland (1996, 1997a) picked up this point, observing that Feeley and Simon not only overstated the dominance of actuarial power but also ignored both punitive and rehabilitating (or 'disciplinary') impulses which continued to be parallel – albeit arguably less 'efficient' – forces in contemporary criminal justice.

Indeed, Garland argued that the neglect of the punitive dimension of recent policy and rhetoric was a serious oversight of the new penology thesis. Garland saw the resurgence of punitiveness as the 'most visible and striking phenomenon of recent penal policy in Britain and the USA' (1996, p. 445). Garland proposed that expressive and instrumental traditions or rationalities were conflicting but nevertheless *coexisting* phenomena, and described their relationship in psychoanalytic terms: that is, as 'rational' and 'hysterical' attempts to (respectively) *adapt to* and *deny* the uncomfortable reality of the state's limited ability to control crime (Garland, 1996). Meanwhile, O'Malley argued that attention to the political context showed that 'explicit political rationales link the punitive and the actuarial in viable and socially dynamic arrangements' (1996, p. 197). For O'Malley, actuarialism and punitiveness could be understood as consistent with a rationality of government ('governmentality') which he characterized as 'prudentialism', both being based on the notion of responsible and rational individuals who take command of their own lives and bear the consequences of freely made decisions. The more sophisticated positions of O'Malley and Garland thus enabled them to incorporate – albeit in different ways – what, in the accounts of Simon (1988) and Feeley and Simon (1992, 1994), appeared as a technologically irrational anomaly.

Garland also invoked the notion of modern penality's 'instrumental tradition' to show that the contrast between the 'old' (disciplinary) and 'new' (actuarial) rationalities which Feeley and Simon described had been exaggerated. He argued that, despite their well-documented differences, these rationalities were in many respects *mutually supportive* rather than in conflict:

> *Both* the 'Old' and the 'New' penologies, so described, are neutral, knowledge-based, purpose-rational approaches, sponsored by social science professionals. Although they differ in their characteristic technologies and forms of reasonings ... *both* 'penologies' offer 'rational', 'technical' solutions to the problems of punishment. To the extent that they now coexist – and there is no doubt that they do – they represent two *adjacent* positions in a common field of instrumental penality. (1997a, p. 203)

Here Garland suggested that although rehabilitation no longer claimed to be the overriding purpose of late modern penal systems (in countries like the United Kingdom and the United States), it had not disappeared: rather, its meaning and status had changed in important respects. Garland argued that rehabilitation was being 're-inscribed in a risk management regime': in other words, it was increasingly being 'represented as an instrument of risk management, inculcating self-controls, reducing danger, enhancing the security of the public' (1997b, p. 6). O'Malley (1999) similarly argued that the welfare state or 'social' disciplines had survived by translating their discourses and strategies into risk-based ones. In psychiatry, for example, he noted a discursive move away from interest in 'causality' in favour of 'risk factors'.

These analyses suggest then that the 'story' of risk in criminal justice is more complex than early analyses perhaps suggested. Whilst social theories go some way towards explaining the contemporary prominence of 'risk profiling' across a broad spectrum of institutions – including criminal justice ones – they cannot, by themselves, account for the particularities of its purchase there, or differences in its reach and grasp across different jurisdictions or criminal justice contexts. For that, we need detailed local studies capable of making sense of risk in a particular context and at a particular historical juncture. There is, then, more than one story to tell about risk in criminal justice.

Researching risk in context: An example from the UK

One such story is told in my own research on the rise of 'risk management' in the probation service in England and Wales in the late 1990s (Robinson 2002, 2003). This was a context, I argued, in which risk was not a new idea: risk had been around for decades as a way of thinking about the criminal justice fates of offenders, most notably in terms of their 'risk of custody'. However, when in the early 1990s legislative changes introduced the notion of 'public protection' as a justification for passing custodial sentences in cases of violent and sexual offences, risk was reconfigured such that a new onus was placed on the probation service to assess the risks posed to the public *by* offenders in its pre-sentence reports. In the first half of the decade, the service's ability to assess risk, to share information about risk with other agencies (such as the police) and its acceptance of 'risk management' as a key part of its role, became central to its external and internal legitimacy as part of a 'public protection' infrastructure. By the late-1990s, some commentators were arguing that the new centrality of risk in the probation service was evidence that it was part of the 'new penology' described by Feeley and Simon (e.g. Kemshall et al., 1997).

However, I argued that this was a somewhat oversimplified version of events, because whilst there was clear evidence of the rise of risk in probation policy and practice, this did not imply the obliteration of rehabilitation or transformative optimism. Far from it: whilst risk was coming to the fore in the context of probation's new 'public protection' function, it was being further promoted and embedded under the influence of an international 'What Works' movement which introduced a new body of knowledge about effective approaches to reducing reoffending (e.g. McGuire and Priestley, 1995; Andrews et al., 1990). In other words, risk and rehabilitation grew in parallel and, to a great extent, served to reinforce – rather than contradict – each other. In England and Wales, probation researchers and managers were quick to see the potential of 'What Works' research to enhance the credibility of probation interventions, and pushed hard to develop the service's approach to risk assessment in line with the 'risk principle' at the heart of the model of rehabilitation developed by Canadian correctional researchers. The risk principle dictated that, in order to maximize the rehabilitative potential of the service's work, there should be a match between the level of reoffending risk posed by the offender and the degree or intensity of intervention, such that higher risk offenders should receive more intensive services, whilst those at the lower end of the risk spectrum should receive lower levels of intervention. The service's ability to routinely assess risk of reoffending thus came to be an accepted prerequisite for effective practice and, in this context, the adoption of risk-need assessment instruments such as Level of Service Inventory Revised (LSI-R) served to bolster the service's perception of itself as an agency capable of both effectively managing risk and delivering rehabilitation (albeit to a carefully selected few) (Robinson, 2001).

In this context, we can see how in the latter 1990s and into the early part of the twentieth century, risk spoke to and helped to operationalize the twin agendas of 'public protection' and 'effective rehabilitation' that have come to dominate the probation service. It also offered the service a legitimate means to ration its resources (in line with assessments of risk of harm/reoffending). The utility of the concept of risk as a resource management or 'triage' tool has been noted by a number of researchers (e.g. Kemshall, 1998), and its role in this regard remains central to contemporary probation practice in England and Wales. For example, in a recent study of probation workers' constructions of 'quality' in their supervisory practice, *reducing risk* emerged as a taken-for-granted element of good quality probation practice among a large sample – although not at the expense of the value practitioners ascribed to the relational aspects of their work (Robinson et al., 2014). The findings of this study appear to confirm then both the continuing salience of risk for English and Welsh probation staff, but also its perceived compatibility with other practice priorities.

Challenging risk

The above example, which centres on risk in probation in one jurisdiction, provides a good illustration of O'Malley's assertion that we need to understand the rise of risk in criminal justice in particular contexts. It follows that, whilst there may well be some common drivers of risk thinking and risk technologies in different settings – among these the spread of the Risk, need and responsivity (RNR) model of rehabilitation promoted by Canadian correctional researchers – there are also likely to be some important differences which make risk a more – or less – appropriate or attractive solution to the problematics of criminal justice in different places. Thus, for example, McNeill et al. (2009) argued that in the Scottish context risk had not made the same inroads in criminal justice social work as it had in probation south of the border, because Scotland's different political, professional and organizational contexts rendered welfarism more durable there than in England and Wales, at least in policy and practice rhetoric (cf. Gelsthorpe et al., 2010).

It is also worth noting the differential impact of risk at different stages in the criminal justice process. Whilst risk has come to dominate *post-sentence* decision-making in at least some jurisdictions, it remains a more problematic idea in relation to decisions about the *allocation* of punishment: namely, sentencing decisions. It is here that we are confronted with fundamental questions about the relationship between a risk-based approach and notions of justice and fairness. Proponents of desert theory argue that punishment should be limited to offences which people have actually committed, rather than those which they might commit in the future (e.g. von Hirsch, 1986). While the principle of desert essentially looks back at and punishes the offence(s) committed, a preoccupation with risk and risk assessment indicates an approach which is essentially future-oriented, and which undermines the connection between crimes and punishment. Taken to its extreme, it dispenses with this connection altogether. Hudson (2001) offers the example of proposals to introduce preventative detention in some jurisdictions – that is, incarceration in the absence of a criminal conviction or after the expiry of a criminal sanction – on the basis that a person conforms to the 'profile' of a potentially dangerous offender (for an Australian example, see Brown, 2011). In England and Wales, the sentence of imprisonment for public protection (IPP) introduced by the Criminal Justice Act 2003 enabled courts to imprison for an indefinite period individuals convicted of violent and sexual offences and deemed to be dangerous, but whose offences were not serious enough to qualify them for a life sentence (Jacobson and Hough, 2010). The emphasis on risk in sentencing options such as this undermines the principle of *proportionality* of punishment in relation to offending, as well as the principle of *equality* (the treatment of like offences with similar punishments). These problems exist independently of additional issues around the reliability and validity of particular risk assessment tools with particular populations/in particular jurisdictions, and around the lack of certainty in risk assessment processes, whereby both *false positives* and *false negatives* can have serious implications for offenders' liberty and public safety, respectively. It is arguably for these reasons, then, that risk has not gained the same purchase in sentencing decisions as it has, in at least some jurisdictions, in decisions about the allocation of resources and the delivery of punishment post-sentence.

Seeing beyond risk?

In this introductory chapter we have sought to argue that risk is neither an inevitable nor ubiquitous paradigm in criminal justice. However, that is not to under-emphasize its foothold in certain parts of criminal justice systems and/or in particular jurisdictions. In England and Wales, for example, risk has proven to be a strong and resilient concept for the past 20 years, particularly in relation to resource allocation decisions at the post-sentencing stage.

That said, and with the benefit of 30 years of research and analysis, perhaps the techniques and practices of actuarial justice and the new penology (just like the welfarist approaches that preceded them) contain the seeds of their own demise. Thus, just as welfarism's pursuit of rehabilitation suffered its 'nothing works' crisis, so risk assessment and management inevitably fail – at least some of the time. Many commentators have pointed out that the promise of protection from risks is therefore a dangerous one for policymakers and practitioners to make (Robinson and McNeill, 2004; McNeill, 2011); though it is intended to ameliorate our anxieties, it may tend to confirm them. Similarly, just as welfarism's critics decried how its paternalism threatened the human rights of those subjected to it, so critics of the 'risk agenda' (and more broadly of the quest for security) bemoan not only how it comes to threaten the liberties of those deemed risky subjects but also how it affects the freedoms of all citizens. More broadly still, some argue that the late-modern privatization of risks (and the retreat from collective social security through welfare) is linked, through neo-liberalism, to the deregulation of markets that exposed the global economy to the consequences of the 2009 financial collapse, thereby exposing all of us to the strictures of the contemporary 'austerity' agenda. It remains to be seen how the reaction to that economic crisis will affect the wider social and cultural contexts of crime and justice.

At the more practical level, empirical studies of criminal justice, like the one reported earlier, suggest that welfarism and rehabilitation have also proved to be more durable than some scholars of risk expected. Perhaps, therefore, rather than seeing risk as the successor of welfarism, and now looking for a successor to risk, we would do better to examine the braiding of these two related discourses throughout their evolution. Welfarism, after all, was always about the protection of society as well as of the vulnerable or disadvantaged individual. While, therefore, it makes sense to debate moving 'beyond risk' as an overriding or overbearing preoccupation in criminal justice, risk has always been with us, and it isn't going away. There is nowhere 'beyond risk' in that second sense. The question is not whether we can escape risk, but rather how we can best engage with it.

References

Andrews, D. A., Zinger, I., Hoge, R. D., Bonta, J., Gendreau, P. and Cullen, F. T. (1990) 'Does correctional treatment work? A clinically relevant and psychologically informed meta-analysis', *Criminology* 28(3): 369–404.

Beck, U. (1992) *Risk Society: Towards a New Modernity*. London: Sage.

Bottoms, A. E. (1995) 'The philosophy and politics of punishment and sentencing', in C. Clarkson and R. Morgan (eds) *The Politics of Sentencing Reform*. Oxford: Clarendon Press.

Brown, M. (2011) 'Preventive detention and the control of sex crime: Receding visions of justice in Australian case law', *Alternative Law Journal* 36: 10–15.

Cohen, S. (1985) *Visions of Social Control*. Cambridge: Polity Press.

Ericson, R. V. and Haggerty, K. D. (1997) *Policing the Risk Society*. Oxford: Clarendon Press.

Feeley, M. and Simon, J. (1992) 'The new penology: Notes on the emerging strategy of corrections and its implications', *Criminology*, 30: 449–74.

———. (1994) 'Actuarial justice: The emerging new criminal law', in D. Nelken (ed.) *The Futures of Criminology*. London: Sage.

Garland, D. (1990) *Punishment and Modern Society*. Oxford: Clarendon.

———. (1996) 'The limits of the sovereign state: Strategies of crime control in contemporary society, *British Journal of Criminology*, 36(4): 445–71.

———. (1997a) "Governmentality' and the problem of crime: Foucault, criminology, sociology', *Theoretical Criminology* 1(2): 173–214.

———. (1997b) 'Probation and the reconfiguration of crime control', in R. Burnett (ed.) *The Probation Service: Responding to Change* (Proceedings of the Probation Studies Unit First Colloquium: Probation Studies Unit Report No. 3), Oxford: University of Oxford Centre for Criminological Research.

Gelsthorpe, L., Raynor, P. and Robinson, G. (2010) 'Pre-sentence reports in England and Wales: Changing discourses of need, risk and quality', in F. McNeill, P. Raynor and C. Trotter (eds) *Offender Supervision: New Directions in Theory, Research and Practice*. Cullompton: Willan.

Giddens, A. (1990) *The Consequences of Modernity*. Cambridge: Polity Press.

———. (1991) *Modernity and Self-Identity*. Cambridge: Polity Press.

Hannah-Moffatt, K. (1999) 'Moral agent or actuarial subject: Risk and Canadian women's imprisonment', *Theoretical Criminology* 3(1): 71–94.

Jacobson, J. and Hough, M. (2010) *Unjust deserts: Imprisonment for public protection*. London: Prison Reform Trust.

Kemshall, H. (1998) *Risk in Probation Practice*. Aldershot: Ashgate.

Kemshall, H. and Maguire, M. (2001) 'Public protection, partnership and risk penality: The multi-agency risk management of sexual and dangerous offenders', *Punishment and Society* 3(2): 237–64.

Kemshall, H., Parton, N., Walsh, M. and Waterson, J. (1997) 'Concepts of risk in relation to organizational structure and functioning within the personal social services and probation', *Social Policy and Administration* 31: 213–32.

Lynch, M. (1998) 'Waste managers? The new penology, crime fighting, and parole agent identity', *Law and Society Review* 32(4): 839–69.

———. (2000) 'Rehabilitation as rhetoric: The ideal of reformation in contemporary parole discourses and practices', *Punishment and Society* 2(1): 40–65.

McGuire, J. and Priestley, P. (1995) 'Reviewing 'what works': Past, present and future', in J. McGuire (ed.) *What Works: Reducing Reoffending*. Chichester: Wiley.

McNeill, F., Burns, N., Halliday, S., Hutton, N. and Tata, C. (2009) 'Risk, responsibility and reconfiguration: Penal adaptation and misadaptation', *Punishment and Society* 11(4): 419–42.

O'Malley, P. (1992) 'Risk, power and crime prevention', *Economy and Society* 21: 252–75.

———. (1996) 'Risk and responsibility', in A. Barry, T. Osborne and N. Rose (eds) *Foucault and Political Reason: Liberalism, neo-liberalism and rationalities of government*. London: University College London Press.

———. (1999) 'Reconfiguring risk: Crime control and risk societies', paper presented to the British Society of Criminology Conference, 13–16 July 1999, Britannia Adelphi Hotel, Liverpool.

———. (2004) 'The government of risks', in A. Sarat (ed.) *The Blackwell Companion to Law and Society*. Oxford: Blackwell.

O'Malley, P. and Mugford, S. (1992) 'Moral technology: The political agenda of random drug testing', *Social Justice* 18: 122–46.

Pratt, J. (1999) 'Governmentality, neo-liberalism and dangerousness', in R. Smandych (ed.) *Governable Places: Readings on Governmentality and Crime Control*. Aldershot: Ashgate.

Reichman, N. (1986) 'Managing crime risks: Toward an insurance-based model of social control', *Research in Law, Deviance and Social Control* 8: 151–72.

Robinson, G. (2001) 'Power, knowledge and what works in probation', *Howard Journal* 40: 235–54.

———. (2002) 'Exploring risk management in probation practice: Contemporary developments in England and Wales', *Punishment and Society* 4: 5–25.

———. (2003) 'Technicality and indeterminacy in probation practice: A case study', *British Journal of Social Work* 33: 593–610.

Robinson, G., Priede, C., Farrall, S., Shapland, J. and McNeill, F. (2014) 'Understanding "quality" in probation practice: Frontline perspectives in England and Wales', *Criminology and Criminal Justice* 14(2): 123–42.

Rose, N. (1996) 'The death of the social? Re-figuring the territory of government', *Economy and Society* 25(3): 327–56.

———. (1999) *Powers of Freedom: Reframing Political Thought.* Cambridge: Cambridge University Press.

Shearing, C. D. and Stenning, P. C. (1985) 'From the panopticon to Disney World: The development of discipline', in A. N. Doob and E. L. Greenspan (eds) *Perspectives in Criminal Law.* Ontario: Canada Law Book.

Simon, J. (1987) 'The emergence of a risk society: Insurance, law and the state', *Socialist Review* 95: 61–89.

———. (1988) 'The ideological effects of actuarial practices', *Law and Society Review* 22: 771–800.

von Hirsch, A. (1986) *Past or Future Crimes.* Manchester: Manchester University Press.

2

THREE NARRATIVES OF RISK: CORRECTIONS, CRITIQUE AND CONTEXT

Peter Raynor
Swansea University, UK

Abstract: Attempts to measure and control risk have become a central concern in criminal justice. Critics have pointed out how the use of risk assessments can conflict with proportionality and have also argued that it can increase the general level of punitiveness and social disadvantage. Developers and supporters of risk assessment have pointed to advantages, such as the support it offers for rehabilitative measures. This chapter discusses the development of risk assessment in British criminal justice practice and argues that its consequences, both positive and negative, have depended not simply on the use of risk-related practices but also on the policies they have been deployed to serve.

Acknowledgement: This chapter contains a revised and expanded English version of material which first appeared in the journal *Déviance et Société*, 34(4) 2010, pp. 671–87, under the title 'Usage et abus du risque dans la justice pénale britannique'.

Introduction: Risk in society and criminal justice

Many social commentators agree that the citizens of contemporary Western countries live in a 'risk society' (Beck, 1992), characterized by a preoccupation with risks, dangers and threats and constant attempts to control or reduce them. Many reasons have been advanced for this, including a loss of faith in the scientific progress which was one of the central promises of modernity; the decay of overarching social and political theories which offered grand models for the organization of society;

a loss of confidence in the capacities and sometimes the integrity of 'experts' and professionals, and perhaps most importantly a sense of exposure to social and economic changes outside our control through the globalization of finance and industry. Other changes have included the decline of manufacturing industries (which migrate to countries offering cheaper labour), increased personal mobility and changes in family structure. As individualistic consumers and units of flexible labour we are increasingly detached from traditional sources of identity and meaning such as stable communities, multigenerational extended families and long-term involvement with traditional crafts or industries. Beck argues that 'risks, as opposed to older dangers, are consequences which relate to the threatening force of modernisation and to its globalisation of doubt' (Beck, 1992, p. 21). This is not the place for a detailed discussion of these theories, but all the causes mentioned above are likely to be playing a part in the emergence of concern about risk as a major feature of our culture and everyday life. Criminologists have also commented on this: the late Jock Young wrote about the 'vertigo of late modernity' (2007), others point to ontological insecurity and lack of trust in traditional sources of authority, and Garland describes how a sense of threat helps to produce a punitive 'culture of control' (2001).

Whilst there is always a risk of overgeneralization in such theorizing, and it is still the case that offending is controlled more by valued relationships and community ties than by any formal systems (Braithwaite, 1989) and that different countries vary greatly in the extent of punitiveness in their criminal justice systems (Christie, N., 2004), it is also true that some societies, including some of the most powerful nations, show many features of a 'culture of control'. A pervasive sense of risk and insecurity offers an explanation for some of criminology's paradoxical findings, such as public beliefs that crime is getting worse at times when it is in fact falling (Roberts and Hough, 2002), and increasing use of imprisonment when community-based penalties are becoming more effective in reducing further offending (Hollis, 2007). Politicians' belief that only more severe punishment can win public support has shown itself in Britain in an unprecedented amount of criminal justice legislation and a dramatic increase in the prison population, from 60,131 at the start of the 'New Labour' governments in May 1997 to 85,902 at the time of writing.

Criminologists, then, should not be surprised at the emergence of new risk-related concerns and practices in criminal justice (Kemshall, 2003). In the criminal justice system of England and Wales, we have seen the emergence of a general concern about risk, the progressive modification of sentencing practice to reflect perceptions of risk and the development of complex evidence-based risk assessment techniques which increasingly shape and even dominate the practice of criminal justice agencies. Because of the central role played by the Probation Service in the assessment of offenders, both prior to sentence (through 'pre-sentence reports') and after imprisonment through the provision of risk assessments in relation to the discretionary release of prisoners, this chapter concentrates particularly on the risk-related practice of probation officers. Much of the discussion focuses on England and Wales, which share the same criminal justice legislation and systems, and in which both prisons and probation services are centrally managed from the Ministry of Justice in London. By way of contrast and to illustrate a different pattern of development for risk-related thinking, some data are also introduced from the small independent jurisdiction of the British Channel Island of Jersey. The chapter goes on to identify and outline two contrasting accounts or narratives of the impact of risk assessment on criminal justice and proposes a third, more realistic way of understanding the strengths and weaknesses of risk-informed practice.

Incorporating risk in British criminal justice

The sentencing of offenders in Britain traditionally seeks to combine several different aims, including retribution, deterrence, rehabilitation and public protection through incapacitation. Different elements appear to take priority at different times and in relation to different categories of offender, and occasionally there are clear shifts in policy or legislation intended to alter the emphasis and purposes of sentencing. For example, long before risk became a dominant theme of policy, there was a lively debate in Britain about how far the sentencing of young offenders should be based on the seriousness of the offence (proportionality, or the 'just deserts' model) and how far it should reflect the level of intervention needed in order to meet the young person's needs and provide rehabilitation. In England and Wales the Children and Young Person's Act of 1969 created a needs-based sentencing system with an emphasis on supervision by social workers and residential care, but in practice this resulted in much higher levels of coercive intervention and much more incarceration (Thorpe et al., 1980) and led to a demand from progressive lawyers and some social workers for a movement 'back to justice'. Similarly, in the adult jurisdiction, concerns about perceived unfairness in discretionary release and about offenders receiving longer sentences in order to facilitate 'treatment' resulted in very strong advocacy of 'just deserts' models (e.g. by Hood, 1974), using arguments very similar to those advanced by 'back to justice' campaigners in the United States (e.g. the American Friends Service Committee, 1971). It is important to recognize that these early advocates of proportionality believed that its general adoption would probably *reduce* the general level of severity in the sentencing system, because they aimed to eliminate the practice of passing more severe sentences in an attempt to provide more treatment for 'welfare' needs; they were particularly concerned about people who received longer sentences or more intervention on apparent 'welfare' grounds than would have been justified by the seriousness of the offence. There were, for example, cases in which young people committed the same offence, but the more socially disadvantaged offender would receive the longer sentence in order to give social workers an opportunity to supervise and intervene. Hood argued that a justice-based system would be 'fairer, not necessarily less effective, possibly less, not more punitive and appeal to that sense of social justice on which any acceptable system of social control must be founded' (1974, 7).

Increasingly principles of 'just deserts' were incorporated in legislation on both sides of the Atlantic Ocean, although often with disappointing results as a more punitive climate resulted in much higher levels of imprisonment than were suggested by advocates of proportionality such as Von Hirsch (1976) and Hood. Although these early controversies tended to be seen as arguments between a 'welfare' principle (based on 'needs') and a 'justice' principle (based on proportionality), many of the same arguments were later revived because of a perceived conflict between principles of proportionality and risk. To state this in its simplest form, does justice require that people should be sentenced only in relation to the crimes they have actually committed, or should sentencers also take into account possible or probable future crimes, and seek to protect the public from them through longer periods of detention? Critics of 'welfare' models were quick to see similar problems arising from sentencing on the basis of future risk (e.g. Von Hirsch, 1986), and debates about proportionality, which had been current long before the widespread use of risk assessment techniques, became part of a critique of the new methods.

In England and Wales the 1991 Criminal Justice Act marked the high point of proportionality in sentencing: the main determinant of the severity of the sentence was to be the seriousness of the current offence. The Act also intended to bring about a general reduction in the severity of sentencing and did so quite successfully for a few months until modified by politicians who did not want to appear 'soft on crime'. However, the same Act also marked the beginning of a new approach to risk in criminal justice by creating the possibility of special extended sentences for offenders judged to be dangerous (primarily violent and sexual offenders). Probation officers and others in criminal justice began to talk and write about the 'risk management approach'; the National Standards for probation officers' reports indicated that they were now expected to comment on risk, and by 1995 probation officers were required to include a specific section in their reports, entitled 'Risk to the Public of Re-offending' (Home Office, 1992, 1995). Meanwhile criminologists on both sides of the Atlantic were commenting on the emergence of risk as a central concern: Feeley and Simon (1992, 1994) in the United States produced their theory of 'actuarial justice', in which they saw measures of coercive control being applied to whole sections of society on the basis of perceived or measured risk, with little regard for traditional notions of justice or even guilt: what mattered was belonging to a risky group rather than having actually been convicted of offences. In Britain, Kemshall was beginning to work on a series of studies of the management of dangerous people by the criminal justice system (Kemshall, 1998), in which the probation officer was beginning to take over the risk assessment role formerly occupied by the psychiatrist or the psychologist.

At this early stage in England and Wales, two major problems were already evident. The first was that probation officers had no reliable methods available for assessing risk, beyond their own individual and subjective judgement. The second was that they were really being asked, under the heading of 'risk', to address two rather different problems. One was the risk of reoffending presented by the ordinary recidivist offender responsible for his or her share of the high-volume property crimes (mainly thefts and burglaries) which make up most of the crime figures. The other was what is often described as 'risk of harm' or 'dangerousness', which relates to those offenders (far fewer in number) who may commit serious violent or sexual offences resulting in major personal trauma or even death. These are relatively rare events but cause severe harm and are the focus of much public anxiety, and also of public anger at the criminal justice authorities if they are committed by people who are under supervision or have recently been released from prison. For the high-volume perpetrators of routine crime, the point of risk assessment was to match levels of intervention to risk, since Canadian research had already provided strong support for the 'risk principle' that rehabilitative measures were more useful for offenders with a high or medium risk of reoffending than for those with little risk, who might even be made worse by intervention (Andrews et al., 1990). For those who presented a significant risk of harm, assuming that they could be identified, the point of risk assessment was more to inform measures of pubic protection and risk management: the precise probability of the offence (which is difficult to estimate in the case of rare events) is perhaps less important than the development and implementation of a risk management plan to prevent it. However, in the early 1990s, probation officers in Britain (and in most other places) lacked evidence-based methods for approaching either of these problems.

Three generations of risk assessment

The Canadian criminologist and psychologist James Bonta, who has been a leading figure in the international development of risk assessment methods for criminal justice, has described 'three generations' of risk assessment (Bonta and Wormith, 2007). The 'first generation' is individual professional judgement, which tends to be subjective, non-standardized and unreliable in predicting reoffending: some individual professionals will obtain good results from using this approach to risk assessment, but others will not, and overall it is the least reliable approach. The 'second generation' refers to actuarial instruments developed by identifying correlates of reconviction in large samples of offenders' criminal records, usually using statistical techniques of logistic regression to generate lists of weighted risk factors which can be used to estimate the probability of reoffending (or, more accurately, reconviction) for individual offenders. Typically these will produce a probability score indicating the percentage risk of reconviction in a specific follow-up period such as two years. Such methods have the practical advantage that they can use criminal history data stored in central databases and do not require personal contact with the offender, so risk assessments can be carried out quickly using computer programmes. They can also achieve useful levels of reliability (around 70% correct prediction of reconviction is regarded as a fairly good performance in this field: see, for example, Raynor et al., 2000). A good example of a second-generation instrument is the Offender Group Reconviction Scale developed by the Home Office in London and widely used to assign offenders to risk categories in England and Wales (Home Office, 1996). However, because second-generation instruments are based only on 'static' risk factors (such as sex, age and previous criminal history) which cannot be changed by intervention, they do not point to social and personal circumstances which can be changed through effective offender management or supervision in order to reduce the risk. They also fail to take into account other changes which can make a substantial difference to the prospect of reconviction, such as the start of a stable relationship with a non-criminal partner, the acquisition of a rewarding job or the arrival of children.

These disadvantages led to the development of 'third generation' risk assessment methods, also known as 'risk-need' assessments, which use a range of information about the offender, including personal interviews, to identify social or personal needs which are known from research to be associated with a higher risk of offending. These are usually 'dynamic' risk factors, meaning that they can in principle be modified (examples are educational achievement, employment status, attitudes and beliefs). These dynamic factors, also known as 'criminogenic needs', are combined with static factors to produce overall risk scores, but in addition they can point to targets for change: in other words, to rehabilitative intervention which can lower the risk of reconviction by reducing dynamic risk factors. Several such instruments are now in use in various countries, including the LSI-R developed by Bonta with Don Andrews in Canada (Andrews and Bonta, 1995). A 'fourth generation' has recently emerged with various enhancements, including specific case management guidance based on the risk and need assessment (e.g. the LS/CMI [Andrews, Bonta and Wormith, 2004] currently in use in Scotland and elsewhere), but this has yet to impact on practice to the same extent as the widely used third-generation instruments.

The introduction and effects of risk management methods

Risk assessment practice in England and Wales has followed roughly this generational sequence of development. Work on the development of an actuarial reconviction predictor started in the early 1990s: a statistical analysis of the criminal records of 13,711 offenders was used to develop the first national reconviction predictor for use in probation services in England and Wales (Copas, 1992). This predictor, based on age, sex, previous convictions, sentencing history and current offence ('static' risk factors) was the immediate ancestor of OGRS, the Offender Group Reconviction Scale, which is still used and regularly updated (Home Office, 1996; Taylor, 1999). As an actuarial instrument based on centrally recorded data, it has proved reliable and practical, but as it includes no information on risk factors which correctional agencies might try to change ('dynamic' risk factors), it cannot be used to assess need or to plan or evaluate supervision.

A report from the Probation Inspectors on 'Dealing with Dangerous People' (Her Majesty's Inspectorate of Probation, 1995) identified a number of problems in probation officers' approaches to risk assessment, and the following year saw the publication of a Home Office research review (Kemshall, 1996), an assessment, case management and evaluation instrument (ACE) developed by the Oxford Probation Studies Unit (Roberts et al., 1996) and the introduction to several probation areas of the LSI-R. In the following year the Home Office published an evaluation of some simple assessment scales for probation officers which were not particularly effective (Aubrey and Hough, 1997), and in 1998, following a number of pilot studies, the Home Office responded to the widespread adoption of LSI-R and ACE by commissioning an evaluation of both, which was published two years later (Raynor et al., 2000). This study showed that both instruments, and particularly LSI-R, could provide reasonably reliable risk assessments when used by probation officers: they were slightly less accurate than the OGRS (65.4% correct prediction with LSI-R in the Home Office study compared to 67.1% with OGRS) but helped officers to identify needs which supervision could address.

Following this study, the Home Office in London started work on its own risk-need assessment system known as OASys (OASys Development Team, 2001), which became the standard system throughout England and Wales by 2006. OASys was a complex and sophisticated instrument which aimed to produce an assessment of dangerousness or risk of harm in addition to a risk score for reconviction, but its introduction was slow and difficult: probation officers initially found it difficult and very time-consuming to use (Mair et al., 2006), and the official evaluation reports concerning its accuracy and reliability remained unpublished for several years. When eventually published, they showed that OASys could achieve a level of reliability in predicting reconviction which was comparable with LSI-R or very slightly better, but not quite as accurate as OGRS (Debidin, 2009). For risk of harm, there was less evidence of accurate prediction, but this was to be expected because of the known difficulties of predicting statistically rare events. More important, perhaps, is the fact that it aims to focus the officer's mind on risk of harm in all cases, so that possible dangers should be less likely to be overlooked. However, this kind of beneficial impact on practice is harder to achieve when an assessment system is not welcomed by many probation officers, who find themselves spending more and more of their time at the computer rather than in contact with offenders. It is interesting that neighbouring jurisdictions (Scotland, Ireland, the Channel Islands) have chosen to use the simpler LSI-R or its derivative LS/CMI, in spite of energetic marketing of OASys by its developers (Raynor, 2007a). The latest embarrassment for proponents of OASys is that following the planned privatization in 2015 of 70% of the work of the Probation Service in England and Wales, the new private operators will not be required to use OASys.

In fairness, it should also be recognized that OASys was introduced at a time of major reorganization in the Probation Service of England and Wales, much of which was unpopular with practitioners. Probation services which had previously been locally organized and locally accountable were centralized under national management in 2001, and this coincided with a sharp increase in regulation and managerialism, which reduced the discretion and autonomy of individual probation officers: for example, OASys computer software was developed to tell probation officers what proposals should be made in a pre-sentence report following particular assessment scores, and software was developed which could produce actual text for the report directly from the OASys assessment (Gelsthorpe, Raynor and Robinson, 2010). The introduction of cognitive-behavioural programmes for offenders, which was in principle a positive development, was clumsily handled and failed to win the support of many practitioners (Raynorn, 2007b), and at the same time criminal justice policy was becoming more punitive and more politicized so that probation officers became an easy target for criticism when politicians wanted to look tough. All this created a climate for the introduction of risk-need assessment in which it was not easy to realize its potential benefits.

Other criticisms were also made: in addition to the concerns mentioned above about proportionality and actuarial justice, some commentators argued that risk assessment techniques derived from research on white male offenders could have limitations when uncritically applied to minority ethnic groups or to women (Hudson, 2002; Shaw and Hannah-Moffatt, 2000). One study pointed to possible over-prediction of risk among minority ethnic groups (Hudson and Bramhall, 2005), and there were also concerns that if sentencers took likely future offending into account, this could result in more severe sentencing for women who committed minor offences. Certainly the rate of imprisonment of women increased steadily in England and Wales as risk assessment came into general use, but there were also other pressures towards more punitive sentencing, and it is not clear how far risk assessment methods might have contributed to this trend. There is some evidence of possible overestimation of risk for women offenders from at least one jurisdiction outside England and Wales (Raynor, 2007a), and evidence that although the relationship between risk factors and offending is *broadly* similar for men and women (Andrews et al., 2012), there are also important differences in motivation, opportunity, onset and desistance (Gelsthorpe, Sharpe and Roberts, 2007). However, all these criticisms, although seen as arguments against risk assessment, could equally be seen as arguments for more thoroughly researched and better implemented risk assessment, as advocated by some of the key developers of the risk-need approach (Andrews, Bonta and Wormith, 2006).

In 2003, a new Criminal Justice Act reversed many of the 'just deserts' provisions of the 1991 Criminal Justice Act and introduced a wider range of options for community sentences as well as new indeterminate sentences for some violent offenders and others considered to be 'dangerous'. The 2003 Act was the result of a far-reaching official review of sentencing policy (Halliday, 2001) which was itself strongly influenced (some would say over-influenced) by the new risk assessment practices and evidence-based programmes being introduced into probation services, and although it was not the intention of the 2003 Act to increase the use and length of prison sentences, in practice the established trend towards more imprisonment of offenders simply continued in spite of general reductions in offending. So overall in England and Wales, the experience of introducing risk assessment methods into criminal justice practice has been mixed. Practitioners have been slow to accept them, and they have been introduced alongside a large number of other changes and major reorganizations which have been disruptive and often unwelcome. In particular, there is no evidence that the use of risk assessment methods has resulted in more community-based rehabilitation and less imprisonment: although there have been more community sentences supervised by the Probation Service, this has been because of a reduction in other non-custodial penalties such as fines, and the prison population has continued to rise (Raynor, 2007b).

However, it can be argued that the routine practice of risk assessment has improved the management of dangerous offenders in the community. These are now subject to regular assessment and supervision by multi-agency panels as part of Multi-Agency Public Protection Arrangements (MAPPA), and some high-risk violent or sexual offenders, including paedophiles, may be in contact with probation and/or police several times per week. They may also be subject to restrictions about where they can live and where they can go, and to such measures as electronic tagging and supervised accommodation (Kemshall, 2008). Good practice in these arrangements is based on thorough planning and careful decision-making, in which the risk assessment is only one element. While it is difficult to demonstrate conclusively that the public is safer as a result, it certainly seems likely that this is the case, in spite of some high-profile exceptions. In general it could reasonably be argued that improvement in MAPPA arrangements has been a beneficial consequence of the focus on risk in England and Wales. However, for the routine recidivist offender committing the less serious offences that make up the vast majority of the crime figures (the so-called volume crimes), it is less clear whether risk assessment has led to improvements in sentencing or more effective rehabilitation. One fairly recent study, however, suggested that the effectiveness of group programmes for offenders in England and Wales was beginning to improve (Hollis, 2007) and that they were starting to achieve reconviction rates below predicted levels. This is likely to reflect better targeting and selection for the programmes, which in turn may be a consequence of better initial assessment.

It would certainly be wrong to condemn and reject risk assessment techniques on the basis of the rather mixed experience of England and Wales. In some ways the circumstances of their introduction were unfavourable, since many other trends in criminal justice were adverse. We can also point to more favourable results in some other places: for example, in the small independent jurisdiction of Jersey in the British Channel Islands the systematic use of risk-need assessment since 1996, based on LSI-R, has been associated with reductions in short-term imprisonment and improvements in the effectiveness of rehabilitative programmes and supervision, as well as reductions in intervention with low-risk offenders who were unlikely to benefit (Raynor and Miles, 2007). Again context is important: in Jersey, developments in risk assessment have formed part of a thorough commitment to effective practice based on providing probation staff with the skills and techniques to improve their practice, rather than a managerialist attempt to control them and restrict their discretion. There is also an ongoing partnership with criminological researchers which produces regular external evaluation of performance and collaboration in several research studies. Such curiosity about results provides a good context for innovation, and although not everything has worked perfectly, the general impression of the impact of risk-need assessment is very positive. (For a recent example outside Britain, see Van Winderen, Van Wilsem and Moerings [2014], who describe how the introduction of risk-based presentence reports in the Netherlands has led to less 'controlling' and more 'diverting' sentencing, contrary to the predictions of 'actuarial justice' theorists.)

Finally in this review of current British practice, it is worth mentioning one further benefit of risk-need assessment. If carried out well, it can provide evidence about the impact of intervention by comparing initial and subsequent assessments. Repeat assessment can track the progress of individual offenders to show whether improvement has occurred, and in which risk factors. Most importantly, research has now shown that when offenders' scores improve they are likely to reconvict at lower than expected rates, whereas the reverse is true for offenders whose scores deteriorate. By way of illustration, Table 2.1 shows the one-year reconviction rates of all those offenders on probation who received repeat LSI-R assessments in the pilot studies in England and Wales, and in Jersey up to 2001. (It should be noted that increases and decreases in scoring during supervision occur across the full range of initial scores, and do not simply represent regression towards the mean: see Raynor [2007a]).

Table 2.1 Direction of change in LSI-R scores and reconviction (N = 360)

LSI-R scores:	Reconvicted in one year	Not Reconvicted
Risk increased during supervision	79 (67%)	39 (33%)
Risk decreased during supervision	102 (42%)	140 (58%)

Significance (chi-square): p < 0.001

Contrasting narratives of risk assessment: Corrections, critique and context

To sum up, it is clear from the evidence and experiences reviewed in this chapter so far that the story of risk discourse and risk assessment practices in criminal justice can be told in several different ways, all with some empirical support. This final section reviews three core narratives which each encapsulate a particular approach to understanding and using risk assessment in criminal justice, and discusses the policy contexts and management styles which tend to determine which of them is dominant at particular times and places.

First, and most influential in the initial adoption of risk-related professional practices in British criminal justice, is the positive correctional narrative which emphasizes the potential of risk-driven techniques and practices to improve criminal justice, reduce reoffending and promote the rehabilitation of offenders. As we have seen, there is evidence that the systematic use of risk assessment methods in probation services can help to determine the level and kind of supervision needed by individual offenders, and can sometimes be deployed in pre-sentence reports to avoid unnecessary over-intervention. It can also point to areas of need where supervision can make a difference, and can improve real-time evaluation of services to show how far offenders are benefiting from the supervision provided. These improvements in the rehabilitation of offenders are associated particularly with the techniques known as risk-need assessment, since these include factors in the risk calculation which are 'dynamic' or potentially able to change or improve. Such improvements in services, for the benefit both of offenders and the community, were among the central aims of the researchers who first introduced routine risk-need assessment into criminal justice practice as part of the 'Risk, need and responsivity' model of rehabilitative practice (Andrews et al., 1990). This model, strongly informed by research evidence and essentially progressive in its aims, advocated the targeting of rehabilitative efforts on offenders with a substantial risk of reoffending rather than on low risk offenders where there was less need for change; the use of forms of supervision which reduced risk by helping to meet offenders' criminogenic needs; and the provision of social learning opportunities specifically designed to increase the likelihood of a positive response.

The designers of the LSI-R (Andrews and Bonta, 1995) intended to support this way of working, and there is evidence that this has happened in some places. In Jersey, as mentioned above, risk assessment is integrated into a pattern of probation practice which still substantially retains a traditional focus on helping offenders to change: practitioners retain a considerable amount of autonomy and discretion in their work, and the probation service is trying to encourage approaches to local criminal justice which are less punitive and coercive, and more effective in reducing further offending. These developments so far tell a positive story about risk assessment in criminal justice, because it is being used in the context of a probation policy which prioritizes rehabilitation and the development of practitioners' skills. It is also demonstrably linked to improvement in services and outcomes (Raynor and Miles, 2007). However, this evidence from a small jurisdiction is yet to be matched in the larger jurisdiction of England and Wales.

Critique

The second narrative which can be read in the history of risk assessment in criminal justice is less optimistic and less progressive. It emphasizes managerialism and punitiveness rather than improvements in services, and some of the developments reviewed in England and Wales have conformed more to this model than to the more optimistic account. The OASys risk assessment instrument, although performing at least as well as others in relation to accuracy, was often regarded as cumbersome and over-elaborate by practitioners (Mair et al., 2006) and was imposed on them by managers rather than being seen by practitioners as a logical enhancement of what they were already trying to do. Generally, it seems that innovations are more acceptable to practitioners if they can see how they add value to their practice, but in the very centralized management system which has existed in the National Probation Service of England and Wales since 2001, the tendency has been to try to manage change by very directive methods, with an increase in targets, regulations, procedures and form-filling which has greatly reduced the discretion and autonomy of individual staff. Some probation officers say they are spending 70% of their time working on the computer rather than seeing offenders. At the same time, the whole criminal justice system has become more punitive, with greater use of imprisonment and stricter enforcement of community sentences so that many of them are not completed, and prison numbers are increased further by offenders who have breached their community sentences or their post-custodial supervision requirements. This is partly due to a political strategy of 'populist punitiveness' (Bottoms, 1995), in which political parties compete with each other to announce the toughest-sounding policies, and partly due to unintended consequences of poorly designed legislation.

To take just two examples, the 1991 Criminal Justice Act introduced the concept of probation as a punishment rather than an alternative to punishment, and the 2003 Criminal Justice Act required any court dealing with a breach of a community order to impose a more severe sentence or order, without the option of giving a warning or a token punishment, which would have been a frequent response in the past. Together with stricter requirements on probation officers to prosecute offenders for minor breaches of supervision requirements, this could lead to quite severe punishments which neither the probation officer nor the judge would have considered necessary if they had been free to use their own judgement. In such a context, we begin to find evidence of cultural changes which move the probation service away from its traditional concern with the welfare of offenders: for example, one recent study in which solicitors were asked about their experience of probation officers reported comments that enforcement had become over-rigorous and that probation officers 'have drifted towards an emphasis ... on punishment in the community or imprisonment' (Whitehead, 2007, p. 147). In another recent example, a small exploratory comparison of samples of pre-sentence reports from different decades (Gelsthorpe, Raynor and Robinson, 2010) finds that reports recently presented to courts are more negative in tone than in the past, concentrating on offenders' weaknesses and defects, their responsibility for harm done to victims, and the probability of future offending. There are few comments about positive aspects such as strengths, desire to change or motivation to co-operate with supervision. We speculate that some of this may be a problem of stereotyped interviewing to meet the requirements of a computerized risk assessment questionnaire, rather than a genuine conversation and dialogue with the offender. This seems particularly likely if the officer's attention is on the computer more than on the person. Good practice, of course, would be to interview the offender first and complete the assessment questionnaire afterwards, and this is the recommended approach which many probation officers try to follow; however, conversations with probation staff suggest that pressures on time will sometimes lead to the kind of shortcut which our data led us to suspect. One possible consequence of more negative reports is, of course, more severe sentencing and more custodial sentencing.

This, then, is the second, less optimistic narrative about risk: as predicted by actuarial justice theorists, the discourse of risk can contribute to the emergence of a 'new penality' in which proportionality and desert become less important, and more coercive and punitive outcomes result from the attempt to control future crimes. However, this does not appear to be an inevitable development: instead, it occurs in a context where we find a particular management style and particular penal policies. The combination of coercive managerialism, which disempowers practitioners who want to work in a flexible, individualized and rehabilitative way, with a penal policy dominated by the politics of toughness and the growth of imprisonment, creates an environment in which it is difficult for risk assessment methods to produce advantages and easy for them to produce problems. Critics need to think carefully about how far this is due to risk assessment techniques and how far it is due to the policy context of implementation. Are they in favour of abandoning risk-need assessment altogether or of returning to arbitrary and inconsistent first-generation methods? The contrasting results of research on pre-sentence reports in England and Wales and the Netherlands, reviewed above, suggests that the impact of risk assessment can be very different in different policy contexts, and we now turn to some implications of this.

Context

The third and last of these emergent narratives of risk concerns the relationship between social and individual risk factors, and consequently the balance between the responsibilities of society as a whole and the responsibilities of individuals. Here again we are invited to take a critical look at the assumptions and processes of risk assessment and to consider how risk-driven approaches might interact with the process of social policy formation. To put this in historical context, many countries (particularly but not exclusively Anglophone countries) have been through a process of trying to redefine the relative responsibilities of the State and the citizen in the field of social problems. The 'Welfare States' constructed around the middle of the twentieth century, usually by left-of-centre governments, were significantly reshaped by right-wing governments in the 1980s and subsequently. In Britain this has been particularly associated with the governments led by Margaret Thatcher and to some extent Tony Blair, and embraced with new budget-slashing enthusiasm by the current Conservative-led coalition government: welfare expenditure and levels of personal taxation have been contained; inequalities of wealth and income have increased; and people have been encouraged to take individual responsibility for their own welfare and economic situation in a process often described as 'responsibilization' (Rose, 2000). This has proceeded alongside an emphasis on the personal responsibility of offenders and increases in punitive sentences such as imprisonment.

Critics of risk assessment and risk-need assessment have pointed out that although such methods may be designed to help offenders by facilitating the use of rehabilitative programmes, they may carry different messages when applied in a context of responsibilization. Because risk assessments are carried out on individuals, risk factors are presented in a way which makes them appear as individual characteristics. Modern risk assessment measures make the very important distinction between static risk factors (which cannot be changed) and dynamic risk factors (which are in principle subject to change), but there is little attempt to distinguish between dynamic factors which are subject to change through the decisions or efforts of offenders themselves, and those which are socially imposed deprivations beyond the capacity of the individual to change, and alterable only by broader social or economic measures. For example, an impulsive personality is a risk factor for offending and is a dynamic factor which individuals can address: reductions in impulsiveness are regularly reported among individuals who undertake appropriate rehabilitative programmes (Raynor and Vanstone, 1996). Living in an area of cheap and poor housing and social disorganization is also a risk factor, dynamic in principle, but not easily alterable by the individual offender who cannot afford to move to a better area.

Such distinctions between individual and social risk factors are not absolute (e.g. individual personality characteristics may result from early childhood experiences in families stressed by poverty) and depend to some extent on context (e.g. being unemployed is a risk factor which individuals can address if there are plenty of jobs, but not so easily when unemployment is high). However, the basic point that risk assessments tend to translate social disadvantage into what look like individual risk factors is clear and can be problematic when governments have an ideological commitment to decreasing social provision and enlarging the sphere of individual responsibility. To take just one example from the field of risk factor research on young offenders: the fact that families likely to produce delinquent children can be identified with better-than-average accuracy, as a result of developmental cohort studies, has encouraged politicians to develop 'early intervention' policies directed at these particular families and to use methods such as training in parenting (Garside, 2009). At the same time, one of the most sophisticated cohort studies yet undertaken has shown that the risk of offending can be *increased* by early contact with the criminal justice system (McAra and McVie, 2007). One possible mechanism to account for this is labelling: receiving special attention of a type known to be targeted on troublesome families will mark a family as troublesome and its children as likely to offend. Even if it has some positive effects, which cannot be guaranteed, it is likely also to have this negative effect. Add to this the problem of 'false positives', or children being mistakenly treated as predelinquent when they are not, and it becomes clear how difficult it is to get early intervention right. To improve the circumstances of stressed families in a non-stigmatizing way probably requires a universalist or area-wide programme of assistance to all low-income families so that particular families are not singled out. However, one can understand why governments of the centre-right are more interested in policies that target less than 100,000 'problem' families rather than policies which aim at a broad and significant attack on inequalities affecting millions of families. Such policies are seen as too expensive, requiring too much progressive taxation, even if they would in the long term have better crime-reduction effects (Wilkinson and Pickett, 2009). We also need to remember that even individual risk factors can be socially relative: impulsive and irresponsible risk-taking among low-income youngsters is likely to get them a criminal record, but impulsive and irresponsible risk-taking among wealthy bankers appears to earn them a public subsidy to continue behaving in much the same way.

A final darkly comic illustration of the misuse of risk factor research under an authoritarian regime can be found in the account given by the Scottish anarchist Stuart Christie of his imprisonment in Franco's Spain in the early 1960s (Christie, S., 2004). He describes being taken to a special room for 'anthropometry', consisting largely of examination and measurement of his head and the shape of his skull. The anthropometrists were delighted to find that he had no ear lobes, which students of Lombroso (1876) will recognize as one of the physical characteristics which he claimed to have identified as typical of *l'uomo delinquente*. By identifying this supposed risk factor, they could attribute Christie's beliefs and behaviour to atavistic criminal tendencies, thereby reducing a social question of political differences to an individual defect.

All these three narratives about the impact of risk discourse and risk practices in criminal justice encapsulate real features of the current situation. Criminal justice organizations and personnel have some relative autonomy in relation to broad social and economic trends, but this is limited: although there is convincing evidence that risk-need assessment methods can improve the rehabilitation of offenders, this is most likely to happen when they are applied in a political context of progressive reforms in criminal justice and when they are used and supported by practitioners who understand them and believe they can be useful in their work. In a more punitive context, and against the background of social and economic policies which perpetuate disadvantage and inequality, their impact will be limited, and they may have unintended adverse effects such as increasing the severity of punishment or reducing the apparent need to address social problems in a social way. During the 1980s in Britain, it often seemed that the only way to attract resources to meet social needs was to present them as risk factors for crime, but this also risked redefining social problems as aspects of criminal conduct, contributing to a punitive attitude to the social difficulties of individuals. Risk-need assessment techniques are undoubtedly one of the major steps forward in contemporary approaches to the management of offenders, but to have their best effects they need the right kind of criminal justice policies and a commitment to addressing offending primarily through rehabilitation rather than punishment.

All this suggests that, in practice, risk assessment methods (and in particular risk-need methods which emphasize dynamic factors) can make a positive contribution to the rehabilitation of offenders and even to penal reform, provided that the context is favourable to the development and improvement of rehabilitative sentencing. Although the hybridization of risks and needs (Hannah-Mofatt, 2005) has its own dangers, it has the clear merit of maintaining at least some focus on needs within criminal justice. However, these methods can also have undesirable consequences if the context for their use is wrong. Some safeguards are necessary: for example a policy of proportionality in sentencing so that predicted risks do not add too much to the sentence or order; a policy of penal reductionism, aiming to reduce custodial punishment and to address offending through rehabilitation rather than incapacitation; and a parsimonious approach to the use of protective measures such as indefinite sentences for dangerous individuals, based on clear evidence of probable harm and permeated by a strong commitment to human rights. The reduction of antisocial behaviour is more likely to happen in prosocial communities.

In addition, experience suggests that the use of risk-need assessment methods within criminal justice is most likely to have a positive impact when properly validated in relation to a range of diverse populations and when introduced in a user-friendly fashion: for example, involving practitioners in development and implementation and emphasizing that its purpose is to support their work rather than to control and manage it. The best-developed systems allow professional override (i.e. the modification of the risk assessment through professional judgement). The most promising environment for innovations will be one where a range of effective professional practices is already in place, including appropriate organizational culture, effective programmes and services implemented with integrity, well-trained and supported staff, appropriate skills, good integration with community resources and service evaluation (Gendreau and Andrews, 2001; Bonta et al., 2013). Finally, the importance of the wider social context is well summarized in a recent British text:

'[W]hat really matters, we would argue, is not so much the technical competences which practitioners deploy, or even the benevolence of their intentions, but the ways in which their practice is linked with other tides in the collective life of a society'. (Jordan and Drakeford, 2012, p.176)

References

American Friends Service Committee (1971) *Struggle for Justice: A Report on Crime and Punishment in America*. New York: Hill and Wang.

Andrews, D. A. and Bonta, J. (1995) *The Level of Service Inventory-Revised Manual*. Toronto: Multi-Health Systems.

Andrews, D. A., Bonta, J. and Wormith, J. S. (2004) *LS/CMI Level of Service/Case Management Inventory*. Toronto: Multi-Health Systems.

Andrews, D. A., Bonta, J. and Wormith, J. S. (2006) 'The recent past and near future of risk assessment', *Crime and Delinquency* 52(1): 7–27.

Andrews, D. A., Guzzo, L., Raynor, P., Rowe, R. C., Rettinger, L. J., Brews, A. and Wormith, J. S. (2012) 'Are the major risk/need factors predictive of both female and male reoffending?', *International Journal of Offender Therapy and Comparative Criminology* 56(1): 113–33.

Andrews, D. A., Zinger, I., Hoge, R. D., Bonta, J., Gendreau, P. and Cullen, F. T. (1990) 'Does correctional treatment work? A clinically relevant and psychologically informed meta-analysis', *Criminology* 28: 369–404.

Aubrey, R. and Hough, M. (1997) *Assessing Offenders Needs: assessment scales for the Probation Service*. Research Study 166, London: Home Office.

Beck, U. (1992) *Risk Society: Towards a New Modernity*. London: Sage.

Bonta, J. and Wormith, S. (2007) 'Risk and need assessment', in McIvor, G. and Raynor, P. (eds) *Developments in Social Work with Offenders*. London: Jessica Kingsley.

Bonta, J., Bourgon, G., Rugge, T., Gress, C. and Gutierrez, L. (2013) 'Taking the leap: From pilot project to wide-scale implementation of the Strategic Training Initiative in Community Supervision (STICS)', *Justice Research and Policy* 15(1): 17–35.

Bottoms, A. E. (1995) 'The philosophy and politics of punishment and sentencing', in C. Clarkson and R. Morgan (eds) *The Politics of Sentencing Reform*. Oxford: Clarendon Press.

Braithwaite, J. (1989) *Crime, Shame and Reintegration*. Cambridge: Cambridge University Press.

Christie, N. (2004) *A Suitable Amount of Crime*. London: Routledge.

Christie, S. (2004) *Granny Made Me an Anarchist*. London: Simon and Schuster.

Copas, J. B. (1992) *Statistical Analysis for a Risk of Reconviction Predictor*. Report to the Home Office, Warwick: University of Warwick, unpublished.

Debidin, M. ed. (2009) *A Compendium of Research and Analysis on the Offender Assessment System.* London: Ministry of Justice.

Feeley, M. and Simon, J. (1992) 'The new penology: Notes on the emerging strategy of corrections and its implications', *Criminology* 30: 449–74.

Feeley, M. and Simon, J. (1994) 'Actuarial justice: The emerging new criminal law', in D. Nelken (ed.) *The Futures of Criminology.* London: Sage.

Garland, D. (2001) *The Culture of Control.* Oxford: Oxford University Press.

Garside, R. (2009) *Risky People or Risky Societies? Rethinking Interventions for Young Adults in Transition.* London: Centre for Crime and Justice Studies.

Gelsthorpe, L., Raynor, P. and Robinson, G. (2010) 'Pre-sentence reports in England and Wales: Changing discourses of need, risk and quality', in McNeill, F., Raynor, P. and Trotter, C. (eds) *Offender Supervision: New Developments in Theory, Research and Practice* (pp. 471–91) Cullompton: Willan.

Gendreau, P. and Andrews, D. (2001) *Correctional Program Assessment Inventory 2000.* St. John: University of New Brunswick.

Halliday, J. (2001) *Making Punishments Work: Report of a Review of the Sentencing Framework for England and Wales.* London: Home Office.

Hannah-Moffat, K. (2005) 'Criminogenic needs and the transformative risk subject: hybridizations of risk/need in penality', *Punishment and Society* 7(1): 29–51.

Her Majesty's Inspectorate of Probation (1995) *Dealing with Dangerous People: the Probation Service and Public Protection.* London: Home Office.

Hollis, V. (2007) *Reconviction Analysis of Programme Data Using Interim Accredited Programmes Software (IAPS).* London: National Offender Management Service.

Home Office (1992) *National Standards for the Supervision of Offenders in the Community.* London: Home Office.

———. (1995) *National Standards for the Supervision of Offenders in the Community.* London: Home Office.

———. (1996) *Guidance for the Probation Service on the Offender Group Reconviction Scale.* Probation Circular 63/1996, London: Home Office.

Hood, R. (1974) *Tolerance and the Tariff.* London: NACRO.

Hudson, B. (2002) 'Gender issues in penal policy and penal theory', in P. Carlen (ed.) *Women and Punishment.* Cullompton: Willan.

Hudson, B. and Bramhall, G. (2005) 'Assessing the "other": Constructions of "Asianness" in risk assessments by probation officers', *British Journal of Criminology* 45: 721–40.

Jordan, B. and Drakeford, M. (2012) *Social Work and Social Policy under Austerity.* Basingstoke: Palgrave Macmillan.

Kemshall, H. (1996) *Reviewing Risk: A review of research on the assessment of risk and dangerousness: Implications for policy and practice in the Probation Service.* Report to the Home Office Research and Statistics Directorate. Birmingham: University of Birmingham.

———. (1998) *Risk in Probation Practice.* Aldershot: Ashgate.

———. (2003) *Understanding Risk in Criminal Justice.* Maidenhead: Open University Press.

————. (2008) *Understanding the Community Management of High Risk Offenders*. Maidenhead: Open University Press.

Lombroso, C. (1876) *L'Uomo delinquente studiato in rapporto alla antropologia, alla medicina legale ed alle discipline carceriare*. Milan: Ulrico Hoepli.

Mair, G., Burke, L. and Taylor, S. (2006) 'The worst tax form you've ever seen? Probation officers' views about OASys', *Probation Journal* 53(1): 7–23.

McAra, L. and McVie, S. (2007) 'Youth Justice? The impact of system contact on patterns of desistance from offending', *European Journal of Criminology* 4(3): 315–45.

OASys Development Team (2001) *Offender Assessment System User Manual*. London: Home Office.

Raynor, P. (2007a) 'Risk and need assessment in British probation: The contribution of LSI-R', *Psychology, Crime and Law* 13(2): 125–38.

————. (2007b) 'Community penalties: probation, 'What Works' and offender management', in *The Oxford Handbook of Criminology*, 4th edn. M. Maguire, R. Morgan and R. Reiner (eds). Oxford University Press: 1061–99.

Raynor, P. and Miles, H. (2007) 'Evidence-based probation in a microstate: The British Channel Island of Jersey', *European Journal of Criminology* 4(3): 299–313.

Raynor, P. and Vanstone, M. (1996) 'Reasoning and Rehabilitation in Britain: The results of the Straight Thinking on Probation (STOP) programme', *International Journal of Offender Therapy and Comparative Criminology*, 40: 272–84.

Raynor, P., Kynch, J., Roberts, C. and Merrington, M. (2000) *Risk and Need Assessment in Probation Services: An Evaluation*. Research Study 211, London: Home Office.

Roberts, C., Burnett, R., Kirby, A. and Hamill, H. (1996) *A System for Evaluating Probation Practice*. Probation Studies Unit Report 1, Oxford: University of Oxford Centre for Criminological Research.

Roberts, J. and Hough, M. (eds) (2002) *Changing Attitudes to Punishment: Public Opinion, Crime and Justice*. Cullompton: Willan.

Rose, N. (2000) 'Government and control', *British Journal of Criminology* 40: 321–39.

Shaw, M. and Hannah-Moffatt, K. (2000) 'Gender, diversity and risk assessment in Canadian corrections', *Probation Journal* 47: 163–72.

Taylor, R. (1999). *Predicting reconviction for sexual and violent offenders using the revised Offender Group Reconviction Scale*. Research Findings 104, London: Home Office.

Thorpe, D. H., Smith, D., Green, C. J. and Paley, J. (1980) *Out of Care*. London: Allen & Unwin.

van Wingerden, S., van Wilsem, J. and Moerings, M. (2014) 'Pre-sentence reports and punishment: A quasi-experiment assessing the effects of risk-based pre-sentence reports on sentencing', *European Journal of Criminology* 11(6): 723–44.

von Hirsch, A. (1976) *Doing Justice: The Choice of Punishments,* report of the Committee for the Study of Incarceration. New York: Hill and Wang.

———. (1986) *Past or Future Crimes.* Manchester: Manchester University Press.

Whitehead, P. (2007) *Modernising Probation and Criminal Justice.* Crayford: Shaw and Sons.

Wilkinson, R. and Pickett, K. (2009) *The Spirit Level: Why More Equal Societies Almost Always Do Better.* London: Allen Lane.

Young, J. (2007) *The Vertigo of Late Modernity.* London: Sage.

SECTION 2

THE CONSEQUENCES OF THE RISK PARADIGM

3

RISK ASSESSMENT IN PRACTICE

Chris Trotter
Monash University, Australia

Introduction

This chapter is concerned with the one-to-one supervision of offenders on probation, parole or other community corrections orders and the extent to which working within the risk paradigm can successfully assist effective work in this area. After briefly defining the risk paradigm, the chapter considers a number of assumptions which underlie the concept: first, that medium- to high-risk offenders benefit more from supervision than medium- or low-risk offenders; second, that actuarial risk assessment profiles are successful in practice in predicting the likelihood of reoffending; and third, that focusing on criminogenic needs which are defined by a professional worker through risk assessment is more effective than working with issues or problems defined by the client. The literature relating to these assumptions is discussed, including the research which suggests that medium and low-risk offenders may benefit as much from good quality supervision as high-risk offenders, that actuarial risk profiles do not achieve high levels of prediction in practice and that when issues or problems are defined by the clients rather than the workers, clients may be more engaged in the supervision process and have better outcomes.

What is the risk paradigm?

The risk paradigm has been defined elsewhere in this volume; suffice to say at this stage that its practical applications include the use of actuarial methods of predicting risks, in other words the use of a checklist by workers which assesses a range of variables leading to a risk score and a categorization of the offender's risk level on a continuum from low risk to high risk. Some risk tools also include the identification of individual risk factors (criminogenic needs), for example pro-criminal attitudes, lack of employment or negative family relationships, which are assessed as relating to offending and as dynamic or changeable and which should therefore be targeted by workers in one-to-one supervision (or through appropriate group or individual programs).

There are many risk assessment instruments available for use by youth justice and adult corrections departments. It might be more accurate to say that there are many instruments on the market, as most of them can only be used if they are purchased from the developer of the profile. In some cases these instruments assess only risk of further offending, and in other cases they assess risk of further offending and also aim to identify criminogenic needs which may then become targets for supervision.

A review by the department of communities in Queensland in Australia (Thompson and Steward, 2005) identified six different risk assessment profiles available for use with young offenders. These included 'The Youth Level of Service/Case Management Inventory (YLS/CMI) (Canada) and the YLS/CMI-AA (NSW); The Victorian Risk/Needs Assessment (recently replaced with the VONIY); ASSET – United Kingdom; Youth Assessment Screening Instrument (YASI) New York; Washington State Juvenile Court Risk Assessment (WSJCA); Secure Care Psychosocial Screening (SECAPS) South Australia; and Santa Barbara Assets and Risks Assessment (SB ARA)' (Thompson and Steward, 2005, p. 54).

There are also numerous adaptations of instruments used to predict recidivism among specific groups, including, for example, offenders with intellectual disability, women, sex offenders, violent offenders and others (Baker, Kelly and Wilkinson, 2011; Fitzgerald et al., 2011). There are also numerous generic risk assessment tools available for use with adult offenders.

Do high-risk offenders benefit most from supervision?

The risk paradigm rests on the principle that high-risk offenders benefit most from supervision and that low-risk offenders benefit only minimally from supervision or may even be harmed by it. A number of reviews of the many studies on this issue have found that this is true – high-risk and medium-risk offenders generally benefit from correctional interventions, particularly intensive services, and low-risk offenders tend to show minimal benefits (e.g. Bonta and Andrews, 2010; Gaes and Bales, 2011; Lowenkamp et al., 2006). The reviews have argued that low-risk offenders are unlikely to reoffend, regardless of the intervention, and that minimal or even no intervention is needed (Andrews and Bonta, 2010).

These reviews have not, however, generally focused on probation or community-based supervision, and when they have, they have often not distinguished supervision by supervisors using effective practice skills from supervisors who do not use these skills. Numerous other research studies have suggested, however, that the impact of probation supervision may be positive and negative in different circumstances, and that *effective* supervision may lead to reductions in reoffending by as much as 50%, whereas *less effective* supervision may actually lead to more offending.Effective supervision is characterized by prosocial modelling and reinforcement, problem-solving, relationship and cognitive behavioural skills (see Trotter [2013] for a review of the research). While the benefits of supervision as a whole may be more evident with medium- to high-risk offenders, the research suggests, in contrast to the 'risk principle', that *most* offenders benefit from *good quality* supervision – including medium-, moderate- and low-risk offenders. Two studies actually suggest that high-risk offenders may benefit least from supervision.

A study undertaken in Victoria, Australia (Trotter, 1996), examined file notes for more than 300 adult probation and parole clients (of more than 50 officers). It found that recidivism rates were significantly lower than those of a control group when workers showed evidence in file notes of use of prosocial modelling and problem-solving. An early version of the Level of Service Inventory (Andrews and Bonta, 2010) was used to determine risk levels, and it was found that low-, medium- and high-risk offenders all had lower reoffending when their workers demonstrated good skills

Pearson et al. (2011) examined a programme in the United Kingdom known as citizenship. This was a structured probation supervision programme, based on 'what works' principles, which aimed to engage offenders in targeted interventions complying with the risk principle and included training in motivational interviewing and prosocial modelling; the offenders also worked through problem-solving modules depending on the offender's particular risk and needs. An experimental and control group was made up of about 7000 offenders. Through use of regression analysis and other statistical techniques, the authors concluded that the programme had an impact on recidivism. Pearson et al. (2010) found, however, that medium- to low- and medium- to high-risk clients benefited from skilled intervention but that high-risk offenders did not.

Robinson et al. (2011) examined tapes of more than 700 taped interviews between adult probation officers and their clients. They examined the use of active listening, role clarification, use of authority, effective disapproval, effective reinforcement and punishment, problem-solving and use of the cognitive model. They used a multivariate analysis of the data to show that those using the model had clients with significantly lower recidivism. They found that the impact on offending by supervisors trained in effective practices was greatest with moderate-risk offenders, with less impact on high-risk offenders.

Smith et al. (2012) in a United States study provided training to 21 youth and adult probation officers in effective practices including anti-criminal modelling, reinforcement, effective disapproval, structured learning, problem-solving, cognitive restructuring and relationship skills. They then analysed audiotapes from 272 clients, including those supervised by the trained officers and those in a control group. The results were somewhat mixed, with trained officers who used more skills generally doing better but with varying results across the different locations. They found most impact with high-risk offenders, although not at statistically significant levels.

Another study (Trotter, 2012) used direct observation and taping of interviews in a juvenile justice setting in Australia. One hundred and seventeen interviews were observed and then coded for use of various skills, such as relationship, role clarification, prosocial modelling, problem-solving and use of CBT techniques. The researchers used a global score as a measure of overall use of the skills as well as scoring individual skills. The global score was significantly related to client recidivism, after taking account of other factors through a regression analysis. The study found that workers who scored 5 or above on the global score had clients with significantly lower recidivism than those who scored 4 or below. The organization used the Level of Service/Case Management Inventory to assess risk levels, and it was found that low- to medium-risk offenders (below 22 on the LS/CM scale) had a further offending rate within two years of 52% when supervised by skilled officers and at 74% when supervised by less skilled officers. For higher-risk offenders the difference was less and not statistically significant, 83% compared to 93%.

It seems therefore that the view that medium- to high-risk offenders benefit most from supervision may be accurate when supervision is routine. In fact the high levels of recidivism evident for offenders supervised by workers assessed as having poor skills suggests that low- to medium-risk offenders may in fact be harmed by poor-quality supervision. The research suggests however that good-quality supervision based on evidence-based principles is good for most offenders, including low-risk offenders, but that the impact may be less with high-risk offenders.

Do actuarial risk profiles accurately predict risk in practice?

The second key assumption on which the risk paradigm is based is that actuarial risk assessment profiles can effectively predict reoffending rates of offenders and they can do this more effectively than professional or clinical judgements by corrections workers and more effectively than by briefly identifying a few items such as criminal history, age and illegal drug use. The research does support the view that risk assessment profiles generally do predict risk more accurately than assessments by corrections workers using clinical or professional judgement alone. In fact there is evidence that workers overestimate their ability to predict risk through their professional judgement (Childs et al., 2014).

There are a number of examples, however, where *in practice* the actuarial risk assessment profiles are not completed accurately by staff and as a result lose much of their predictive capacity. An Australian study (Ching, Caputi and Byrne, 2011) found that correlations between recidivism and the LSIR were often quite weak, in the range of 0.13 to 0.35, depending on the measure used. Correlations were even lower at 0.11 to 0.13 in a sample in Colorado in the USA (Dowdy, Lacy and Unnithan, 2002). In a study undertaken in Australia with an early version of the Level of Supervision Inventory, the correlation was 0.215 with any further offence and 0.312 for imprisonment. Slightly higher correlations with reoffending were found when the only measure used was the number of prior convictions. In this case the correlations were 0.279 and 0.313, respectively (Trotter, 1995). In other words the risk assessment profiles in these studies predicted no better than simply using an easily accessible measure such as prior convictions. The imprecision of risk assessment profiles was also highlighted in a study by Hart and Cook (2013, p. 81) using a violence risk assessment profile in a forensic mental health setting. They concluded that 'without major advances in our understanding of the causes of violence, ARAIs (actuarial risk assessment inventories) cannot be used to estimate the specific probability or absolute likelihood of future violence with any reasonable degree of precision or certainty'.

One factor which may limit the effectiveness of risk assessment instruments is that they are, of course, dependent on being completed accurately in practice. This seems obvious but may be problematic given the generally variable acceptance of risk assessment tools by corrections workers. Baker et al. (2011) point to a number of studies which found that while workers sometimes find that risk assessment tools allowed for greater consistency, quality and defensibility, they also often found them too time consuming, deskilling, and that they add little to the decision-making process,

One further issue relating to the practical application of risk assessment instruments is that not only are they often poorly applied, but also their results are often not used to guide interventions. In other words subsequent levels of supervision may not be in accord with the risk levels determined by the assessment, and the criminogenic needs which are identified through the risk assessment may not be specifically addressed. Viglione

et al. (2015) undertook a study of risk-need assessments in two adult probation settings in the United States, using interviews and observations,
and found that the assessments rarely informed case management and
supervisory decisions, and that POs emphasized risk rather than focusing
on criminogenic needs. The authors argue for the development of a more
client-centred model of supervision.

The benefits of working with identified criminogenic needs

As mentioned earlier, in addition to identifying risk levels, some risk
assessment instruments may also identify specific criminogenic needs
which may be addressed in supervision. The LS/CMI, for example, identifies specific criminogenic needs which are directly related to criminal
behaviour (e.g. pro-criminal attitudes, peers, family, employment, recreational activities) and provides guidance to workers regarding how to
address those criminogenic needs (Andrews and Bonta, 2010; Bourgon
et al., 2010). It is argued that workers should focus on the issues or needs
which are assessed as being related to the offending behaviour.

Risk assessment instruments have generally been developed by examining the relationships between risk factors and further offending, and there
would be little argument that changes in pro-criminal attitudes, improved
family relationships and employment, for example, are likely to be associated with low recidivism. The concept of criminogenic needs rests on the
assumption, however, that the factors associated with further offending
and the factors which have led someone *into* offending are the factors
which will lead them *out of* offending.

The factors which lead people into particular behaviours may not,
however, be the factors that lead people out of them. This has been
shown in longitudinal research (e.g. Vaillant, 2012). To illustrate this
point – marriage or a regular partner may not be identified as a criminogenic need. It is not criminogenic to be single. In many studies, however,
stable marriage and co-habitation have been found to be associated with
desistance from crime (Forrest, 2014). Supporting relationships and helping offenders develop relationship skills may not address a criminogenic
need which has been identified in the risk assessment. However, it may
be crucial in supporting desistance by helping an offender develop a more
law-abiding lifestyle.

One of the effective practice skills which has been consistently identified in the research on offender supervision is problem-solving (Trotter
2013). The first step in most problem-solving models is identifying the

problem or issue to be addressed. In the risk-driven model this would involve identifying criminogenic needs which have been identified in the risk assessment process (Bonta et al., 2010). However, problem-solving models commonly involve the client identifying the problem, rather than the worker. This is consistent with several studies which have examined effective supervision practices. Robinson et al. (2011), for example, suggest that the most important aspect is allowing the client to articulate the problem *and* the potential solution. Taxman (2007) refers to working with one criminogenic need and at the same time working with an interest of the client in order to motivate the client to commit to the change process.

The difficulties of engaging offenders in supervision when workers rather than clients identify issues were shown in our youth justice study referred to earlier (Trotter, 2012). In this study, research officers rated the use of problem-solving by the workers and the level of response or engagement by the young offenders. The researchers used a coding manual with high levels of reliability to code a range of skills used by workers (Trotter and Evans, 2012). The skill of identifying problems was scored on a 1 to 5 scale using the following guidelines for the coders:

> The worker and the young person talk about a range of problems the young person might be facing. To score 5 the problems identified must be generated from the young person's perspective. EXAMPLE: The worker may ask a general question: Tell me about issues of concern to you. If identified as a specific issue e.g. unemployment, the worker might seek to clarify with the young person how long they have been unemployed, how they feel about this, whether they have worked previously, how they fill in their days. Score this item high if the worker spends time with the young person eliciting problems from them from the young person's perspective. (Trotter and Evans, 2010, p. 16)

The immediate response from the client was then scored using the following definition:

> The scoring of 1–5 represents the degree to which the client is engaged when the worker is using a particular skill. This is captured by the client's immediate response to the skill used by the worker. A score of 1 would be given if the client was non-responsive, looking away, and offering monosyllabic responses. A score of 5 would be given if the client is 'taking notice, listening, responding to the worker, actively learning. (Trotter and Evans, p. 3)

There was a strong statistically significant correlation between rating of the worker's skill and the client's response (r 0.625 sig 0.000). In other words, the more the workers discussed problems from the young person's perspective, the more the young person responded to the discussion. The more the problems were identified by the worker without the offender's input, the less responsive or engaged was the young person. To put this another way – the coders were able to identify a clear response to problem identification in 61 of the 117 interviews. In 23 of those instances, the workers were coded as working with the client's view of the problem, and in 78% of those cases the young people were coded as engaged. The young people were engaged in only 22% of the instances when their workers identified the problem.

A further criticism of the concept of criminogenic need stems from the importance of prosocial modelling and reinforcement which has been shown to be related to reduced offending in numerous studies (Dowden and Andrews, 2004; Raynor et al., 2014; Bonta et al., 2011). This involves a process whereby the workers influence their clients through modelling and focusing on prosocial attitudes and activities of offenders (Andrews et al., 1979; Trotter, 2015; Cherry, 2005). This involves spending time in interviews talking to clients about the prosocial things they say and do. This means that discussions in interviews revolve around things that clients do well, for example going to work or going to school, mixing with non-criminal friends or developing a new relationship, or they may revolve around the offender's prosocial aspirations, for example owning a house or starting a business. If interviews are predominantly about criminogenic needs as defined by workers, this may compromise the ability to focus on the client's prosocial attitudes and activities – clearly one of the most important aspects of offender supervision.

It seems then that the concept of criminogenic needs may be problematic. This view is certainly supported by the proponents of the good lives model and desistance theory. Ward, Meltzer and Yates (2007), for example, argue that the focus on risk and risk assessment has been at the expense of opportunities for offenders to develop 'good lives' on their own terms. He and others (e.g. McNeill et al., 2005) have emphasized the importance of therapeutic alliance and the worker/client relationships which they argue may be compromised by a focus on risk factors, which may be defined by workers rather than clients.

What does this mean for the development of effective supervision?

In this chapter I have argued that some of the assumptions underlying the risk paradigm can be questioned. First, the assumption that medium- to high-risk offenders benefit most from supervision does not seem to apply if the quality of the supervision offered is taken into account. Second, the risk paradigm rests on the assumption that detailed risk assessment profiles are effective in predicting risk in practice. However, while actuarial risk assessment methods have been shown to be more accurate in predicting risk of further offending than professional judgement, the detailed risk assessment profiles on the market are sometimes poorly completed in practice and may be no more effective in predicting risk than a method involving individual items such as age and prior offending. Third, the paradigm rests on the assumption that working on criminogenic needs as determined by the worker can engage offenders in a change process and lead to lower reoffending. Some research suggests, however, that offenders are more likely to be engaged in supervision and to change their behaviour if they play a part in determining the nature of the issues addressed in supervision.

What does this mean in practice for the development of effective supervision? Given that routine supervision in probation is often not characterized by effective practice skills (Andrews and Bonta, 2010) care should certainly be taken not to provide high levels of supervision to low-risk offenders and to ensure that high levels of supervision are reserved for medium- to high-risk offenders. On the other hand, if probation services offer training and accreditation in effective practice skills (as some are beginning to do) and have confidence in the ability of staff to deliver high-quality supervision, then high levels of supervision might be confidently offered to all offenders regardless of risk. There may be an argument that in the context of scarce resources, medium-risk offenders (and perhaps high-risk) should get more supervision than low-risk offenders because they are more likely to offend, and the supervision will therefore lead to fewer offences overall. On the other hand, if resources allow, then high levels of supervision might also be given with confidence to low-risk offenders.

Probation services sometimes put a lot of energy and effort into risk assessment, often at the expense of working constructively with clients to address their issues or criminogenic needs (Viglione et al., 2015). There are brief risk assessment methods and screening tools which can, as pointed out earlier in this chapter, assess the likelihood of further offending with some accuracy. Given the poor implementation of more complex risk assessment instruments, the limited use which workers make of them in practice and the doubtful place of risk as a guide for level of intervention when quality of supervision is taken into account, there is a strong argument to use brief methods to assess risk levels. The use of screening tools with a small number of items, including criminal history, age and illegal drug use, may be sufficient to provide a guide. This would allow more time to focus on working with client issues.

Working with criminogenic needs as determined solely by workers is likely to disengage offenders. Desistance theory (McNeill, 2006) and Good

Lives (Ward, 2010) and my own work (Trotter, 2015) favour a method of working with client strengths and issues identified by offenders themselves which would not necessarily be identified as criminogenic needs in the risk paradigm. *Working with Involuntary Clients* (Trotter, 2015) outlines a supervision model which is characterized by a focus on offenders' prosocial strengths, which allows offenders to identify their own problems and which encourages clients to work on issues that may lead them into more prosocial and non-criminal behaviour. An approach such as this overcomes many of the shortcomings of the risk paradigm and has considerable support in the research as a method of reducing recidivism.

Conclusion

This chapter has considered three assumptions underlying the risk paradigm as it relates to offender supervision in probation, parole and community corrections. It has argued that while medium- to high-risk offenders may benefit more from supervision than low-risk offenders, this does not appear to be the case once the quality of supervision is taken into account; that actuarial risk assessment profiles may be successful in predicting the likelihood of reoffending under research conditions but in practice are poorly used and little better than shorter screening tools; and, third, that focusing on criminogenic needs defined by a professional worker is likely to disengage clients and may mitigate against the use of a prosocial approach to supervision which has proved successful in many settings.

Finally, I have argued that levels of supervision should be determined by the resources available rather than risk levels, that the use of short screening tools for risk assessment is sufficient and that the most effective approach to offender supervision is not one which focuses on criminogenic needs, but one which works with clients on issues of concern to them and focuses on the prosocial aspects of their lives.

References

Andrews, D. A. and Bonta, J. (2010) *The Psychology of Criminal Conduct.* Cincinnati: Anderson Publishing.

Baker, K., Kelly, G. and Wilkinson (2011) *Assessment in Youth Justice.* Bristol: The Policy Press.

Bonta, J. and Andrews, D. (2010) 'Viewing offender assessment and rehabilitation through the lens of the risk-need-responsivity model', in McNeill, F., Raynor, P. and Trotter, C. (eds) (2010) *Offender Supervision: New Directions in Theory, Research and Practice.* Cullompton: Willan.

Bonta, J., Bourgon, G., Rugge, T., Scott, T.-L., Yessine, A.K., Gutierrez, L. and Li, J. (2011). 'Community supervision: An experimental demonstration of training probation officers in evidence-based practice', *Criminal Justice and Behavior* 38(11): 1127–48.

Childs, Kristina, Frick, Paul J., Ryals, John S., Lingonblad, Annika and Villio, Matthew J. (2014). 'A comparison of empirically based and structured professional judgment estimation of risk using the structured assessment of violence risk in youth', *Youth Violence and Juvenile Justice* 12(1): 40–57.

Ching-I Hsu, Peter Caputi and Mitchell K. Byrne. 'The level of service inventory-revised (Lsi-R) and Australian offenders: Factor structure, sensitivity, and specificity', *Faculty of Health and Behavioural Sciences– Papers* 600–18. Available at http://works.bepress.com/mitchell_byrne/5. Accessed on 15.6.15.

Dowden, C. and Andrews, D. A. (2004). 'The importance of staff practice in delivering effective correctional treatment: A meta-analytic review of the literature', *International Journal of Offender Therapy and Comparative Criminology,* 48(2): 203–14.

Dowdy, Eric R., Lacy, Michael G. and Unnithan, N. Prabha. (2002) Correctional prediction and the Level of Supervision Inventory', *Journal of Criminal Justice* 30(1): 29–39.

Fitzgerald, Suzanne, Gray, Nicola S., Taylor, John and Snowden, Robert J. (2011) 'Risk factors for recidivism in offenders with intellectual disabilities', *Psychology, Crime & Law* 17(1): 43–58.

Forrest, W. (2014) 'Cohabitation, relationship quality, and desistance from crime', *Journal of Marriage and Family* 76(3): 539–56.

Gaes, G. and Bales, W. (2011) 'Deconstructing the risk principle : Addressing some remaining questions', Criminology & Public Policy 10(4): 979–85.

Hart, S. and Cooke, D. (2013) 'Another look at the (im-)precision of individual risk estimates made using actuarial risk assessment instruments', *Behavioral Sciences & the Law* 31(1): 81–102.

Lowenkamp, Christopher T., Latessa, Edward J. and Holsinger, Alexander M. (2006) 'The risk principle in action: What have we learned from 13,676 offenders and 97 correctional programs?', *Crime & Delinquency* 52(1): 77–93.

McNeill, F. (2006) 'A desistance paradigm for offender management', *Criminology and Criminal Justice* 6(1): 39–52.

Pearson, D., McDougall, C., Kanaan, M., Bowles, A. and Torgerson, D. (2011). 'Reducing criminal recidivism: Evaluation of Citizenship, an evidence-based probation supervision process', *Journal of Experimental Criminology* 7(1): 73–102.

Raynor, P., Ugwudike, P. and Vanstone, M. (forthcoming) 'The impact of skills in probation work: A reconviction study', *Criminology and Criminal Justice* 14(2): 235–49.

Robinson, C., VanBenschoten, S., Alexander, M. and Lowenkamp, C. (2011). 'A random (almost) study of Staff Training Aimed at Reducing Re-arrest: Reducing recidivism through intentional design', *Federal Probation* 75(2): 57–63.

Smith, P., Schweitzer, M., Labrecque, R. M. and Latessa, E. J. (2012). 'Improving probation officers' supervision skills: An evaluation of the EPICS model', *Journal of Crime & Justice* 35(2): 89–199.

Taxman, F. (2007, May/June). 'The role of community supervision in addressing re-entry from jails', *American Jails*.

Thompson, Carleen and Stewart, Anna. 'Review of empirically based risk/ needs assessment tools for youth justice: amended report for public release', accessed at www.griffith.edu.au/__data/assets/pdf_file/0018/208206/Review-of-empiricall-based-risk_needs-assessment-tools.pdf.

Trotter, C. (1995) *The Supervision of Offenders: What Works? First and Second Reports to the Criminology Research Council*. Department of Social Work, Monash University, and Department of Justice, Melbourne.

———. (1996) 'The impact of different supervision practices in community corrections', *Australian and New Zealand Journal of Criminology* 29(1): 29–46.

———. (2012) 'Effective supervision of young offenders', *Trends and Issues in Criminal Justice* 448: 1–8.

———. (2013) 'Reducing recidivism through probation supervision: what we know and don't know from four decades of research', *Federal Probation* 77(2): 43–48.

———. (2015) *Working with Involuntary Clients,* 3rd edn. Sydney: Allen and Unwin and UK: Routledge.

Trotter, C. and Evans, P. (2010) *Analysis of Supervision skills by juvenile justice workers - Transcript coding manual*. Unpublished document available from the authors.

———. (2012) 'Analysis of supervision skills in juvenile justice', *Australian and New Zealand Journal of Criminology* 45(2): 1–19.

Vaillant, George E. (2012) *Triumphs of Experience The Men of the Harvard Grant Study*. Harvard University Press.

Viglione, Jill, Rudes, Danielle S. and Taxman, Faye S. (2015) 'Misalignment in supervision: Implementing risk/needs assessment instruments in probation', *Criminal Justice and Behavior* 3 March 2015, 42(3): 263–85.

Ward, T. (2010) 'The good lives model of offender rehabilitation: Basic assumptions, aetiological commitments and practice implications', in McNeill, F., Raynor, P. and Trotter, C. (eds) (2010) *Offender Supervision: New Directions in Theory, Research and Practice*. Cullompton: Willan.

Ward, T., Melser, J. and Yates, P. M. (2007). 'Reconstructing the risk need responsivity model: A theoretical elaboration and evaluation', *Aggression and Violent Behavior* 12: 208–28.

4

TAKING THE RISK OUT OF YOUTH JUSTICE

Stephen Case
Loughborough University, UK

Kevin Haines
Swansea University, UK

Introduction

In the contemporary 'risk society' of rapid social change and globalization (cf. Beck, 1992), youth justice systems across the industrialized Western world have chosen to understand and respond to youth offending in terms of the 'risk' presented by young people – the risk of first-time offending, reoffending, conviction, reconviction, causing harm to self and others and so on. Risk has been explored by academics and represented by politicians and the mass media as an entirely negative phenomenon; as a harm or threat to be managed as opposed to a positive sensation or challenge for young people to pursue (cf. Katz, 1988). The reduction of risk has shaped and driven youth justice systems internationally, riding the wave of government anxieties over (alleged) growing youth crime rates and the ineffectiveness, inappropriateness and inefficiency of traditional youth justice responses such as welfare, justice and the rehabilitative ideal (see Haines and Case, in press). The perceived failures of traditional youth justice approaches and the growing influence of 'risk society' concerns have encouraged governments to utilize 'risk' as a predictor to enable the 'evidence-based' and defensible pre-emption and prevention of crime. The emergence of risk prediction has fed into a 'new penology' (Feeley and Simon, 1992) of actuarial justice based on assessing the statistical probabilities (risks) of future offending in aggregated populations in order to more effectively target resources and preventative activities. Actuarial justice has constituted a practical rather than a principled approach and provided for the accelerating, global 'Risk Factor Research' movement that provides the evidential foundation for risk-based youth justice.

However, the hegemonic risk-based paradigm in the field of youth justice is fatally flawed in methodological, philosophical and ethical terms. In this chapter, we illustrate and explore these developments by charting the emergence, rise to power, dominance decline and ultimate fall of risk-based youth justice in the Youth Justice System of England and Wales – a system underpinned by managerialist and interventionist policies that have been animated by risk assessment practice. We explore the theoretical and evidential bases for the risk-based approach that lie in developmental and artefactual 'Risk Factor Research' and the ostensible logic of the 'Risk Factor Prevention Paradigm', discussing their practical application in the 'Scaled Approach' to risk assessment and intervention. From there, we conduct a detailed methodological critique of the reductionist oversimplification, partialities, indefinities and invalidities of risk-based youth justice, moving into a philosophical and ethical critique of its negative-facing, value-laden, governmentalist and anti-child nature. The chapter concludes with critical discussion of recommendations for progressive youth justice, focused particularly on *AssetPlus* (YJB, 2014) and the *Children First, Offenders Second* approach (Haines and Case, in press).

The emergence of risk-based youth justice: Beguiled by risk factor research

The Labour Government took office in the United Kingdom in 1997 in a (risk-society) climate of escalating media and public concerns over young people's behaviour and the apparent failure of existing welfare- and justice-based approaches in successfully addressing the youth crime 'problem'. A foregoing review of the Youth Justice System (YJS) of England and Wales commissioned by the outgoing Conservative Government, entitled 'Misspent Youth' (Audit Commission, 1996), had concluded that it was ineffective, inefficient and uneconomical in dealing with youth crime and that youth justice agencies were working poorly together. The central recommendations of Misspent Youth were managerialist and interventionist – focused on the utility of multi agency partnership working (after Morgan, 1990) that is evidence based and focused on early intervention and risk management. Advocacy of the need for a managed system underpinned by evidence-based practice stemmed from concerns that welfare approaches had been over-discretionary and subjective – incongruous with the evidential, transparent and defensible requirements of modern practice in the risk society. In turn, justice-based approaches were purportedly lacking in cogent evidence of 'effectiveness' in terms of reducing reoffending and the public's fear of crime, due in large part to the collapse of faith in the rehabilitative ideal, combined with ineffective working practices within and between youth justice agencies.

At a time when the effectiveness of traditional youth justice approaches was under critical scrutiny, the early to mid-1990s witnessed the rise to prominence of an alternative model of understanding and responding to young people's offending behaviour. The 'Risk Factor Research' (RFR) movement was rapidly gaining favour within youth/developmental criminology and across youth justice systems in the industrialized Western world, particularly in the United Kingdom and the United States. RFR provided an 'evidence-based', (purportedly) objective, deterministic and developmental explanation for youth offending based on a raft of international longitudinal and cross-sectional survey studies that claimed to have identified the personal and social 'risk factors' (risk quantified into an 'artefact') experienced by young people that predicted their increased (statistical) likelihood/probability of future offending and reoffending (cf. Farrington, 2000; Thornberry and Krohn, 2003; YJB, 2003; see also Case and Haines, 2009). Thus, 'artefactual' RFR (Kemshall, 2008) provided a theoretical (positivist, developmental) and empirical (replicated, evidenced) rationale for a new risk-based approach to youth justice. This rationale was animated and applied through the 'Risk Factor Prevention Paradigm' (Hawkins and Catalano, 1992), a practical and common-sense assessment and intervention model for working with young people in the YJS:

> Identify the key risk factors for offending and implement prevention methods designed to counteract them. There is often a related attempt to identify key protective factors against offending and to implement prevention methods designed to enhance them. (Farrington, 2007, p. 606)

The Risk Factor Prevention Paradigm (RFPP) offered numerous practical advantages to politicians and policymakers seeking an evidence-based alternative to 'failing' youth justice practices; crucially an approach that 'links explanation and prevention ... is readily accepted by policy makers, practitioners, and the general public... [and is] based on empirical research' (Farrington, 2000, p. 7). In short, the RFPP was an idea whose time had come. The Misspent Youth recommendations for risk-based practice were consolidated in the 1997 Labour Government White Paper 'No More Excuses: A New Approach to Tackling Youth Crime' and legislated into existence in 1998 by the 'Crime and Disorder Act'. The managerialist intent of the new UK Government was animated by the creation of a quasi-autonomous monitoring body entitled the 'Youth Justice Board' (YJB) to oversee and guide the operation of the YJS, notably the delivery of youth justice by newly formed, multi-agency 'Youth Offending Teams' (YOTs) in every local authority area in England and Wales – consisting of representatives from each of the 'statutory' agencies (police, probation, local authority [e.g. social services] and health), along with representatives from voluntary and charitable agencies where appropriate. The primary duty of YOTs under the Crime and Disorder Act was to be the *prevention* of offending by young people – a significant step-change from previous (principled) systemic concerns with welfare, rehabilitation and justice.

The rise of risk-based youth justice: Risk assessment and intervention

The prevention goal of the YJS as set out by the Crime and Disorder Act was to be pursued in highly prescriptive, tightly managed, intervention-ist and, crucially, risk-focused ways. All YOT staff were to complete a new structured risk assessment instrument known as *Asset* in interview with every young person (aged 10–17 years) entering the YJS, in order to produce a risk rating that would inform and guide subsequent interventions to reduce risk and prevent further offending.

In focus: ***Asset* risk assessment**

YOT practitioners complete *Asset* to rate a young person's risk of reoffending (more accurately, their risk of reconviction) by measuring their (current or recent) exposure to risk factors in 12 psychosocial domains: living arrangements, family and personal relationships, education, training and employment, neighbourhood, lifestyle, substance use, physical health, emotional and mental health, perception of self and others, thinking and behaviour, attitudes to offending and motivation to change, alongside additional sections measuring positive (protective) factors, indicators of vulnerability, indicators of risk of serious harm to others and a self-assessment 'What do you think?' section (YJB, 2000). The risk domains and additional sections within *Asset* contain a series of risk-based statements rated 'yes' or 'no' by YOT practitioners to indicate the presence or absence of that risk factor in the young person's life. Practitioners then quantify the extent to which they feel that the risks in each domain are associated with 'the likelihood of further offending' by that young person: 0 = no association, 1 = slight or limited indirect association, 2 = moderate direct or indirect association, 3 = quite strong association, normally direct, 4 = very strong, clear and direct association. These quantitative judgements are supplemented with qualitative, narrative explanations provided in a small, summative 'evidence box' at the end of each section. The standardized and structured completion of *Asset*, therefore, animates, applies and builds upon the 'evidence-base' for understanding (assessing) and responding to (intervening) young people in the YJS of England and Wales.

In accordance with the RFPP, the identification and assessment of risk factors was intended to feed into and shape risk-focused interventions with young people in the YJS, with a focus on intervention at an early stage in the young person's 'criminal career' (i.e. early intervention), as a means of 'nipping crime in the bud' (Blair, 2007). Priority was given to interventions (typically pseudo-psychological programmes imported from the United States) that had been evidenced through scientific, quasi-experimental evaluation as 'what works' in the risk-based reduction of crime (see Sherman et al., 1998). Taken together, quantitative *Asset* risk assessment and risk-focused 'what works' intervention constituted the 'evidence base' for practice that the YJB privileged as 'effective'. YOT practice was underpinned by a series of 'Key Elements of Effective Practice' (KEEPs) and their associated guidance documents, the central KEEP being 'Assessment, Planning Interventions and Supervision,' or 'APIS' (YJB, 2003). The APIS guidance prescribed that youth justice assessment and intervention should be risk based and that the influence of risk factors on young people's offending should be understood in a developmental and deterministic manner (i.e. risk factors experienced in childhood and adolescence predict and influence offending behaviour in later life (cf. Farrington, 1996; Sampson and Laub, 1993; Thornberry et al., 1997), so any (early) intervention should target the prevention of exposure to risk factors (risk and crime *prevention*) and the reduction of harm caused by previous and existing exposure to risk factors (risk and crime *reduction*). Early evaluations of the *Asset* tool were considered positive by the YJB. Evaluation found that Asset was able to successfully predict outcomes for young people (i.e. reconviction or no reconviction) in 67% of cases one year after completion (Baker et al., 2002) and in 69% of cases two years after completion (Baker et al., 2005), superseding the prediction rates of equivalent assessment tools in the adult system. Criticisms that outcomes for one-third of young people were incorrectly predicted by *Asset*, and thus informed potentially disproportionate and unnecessary intervention, have been countered by arguments that the risk assessment process is not intended to be rigid and prescriptive, but more of a guide for practitioners, which can be validated and supplemented with other forms of assessment (Baker, 2005; for a critique, see Pitts, 2001; Case and Haines, 2009; see also below). Statistical evidence of the 'reliability' of *Asset* (for two of every three children at least) and qualitative practitioner feedback attesting to the user-friendly nature of the tool, consolidated the UK Government's faith in risk-based youth justice (i.e. assessment and intervention – in line with the RFPP) as a practice model that was not only 'effective' but also afforded the YJB a simple and straightforward approach to monitoring and managing the delivery of youth justice at systemic (YJS), organizational (YOTs) and individual (YOT practitioner) levels.

The domination of risk-based youth justice: All hail the scaled approach

On the strength of a promising initial evaluation of *Asset* (Baker et al., 2002) and an evidence-base from artefactual RFR that self-replicated internationally at an alarming pace, the question for the UK Government moved beyond whether the RFPP was an appropriate practice model (if indeed such a reflective and critical question had ever been asked, as opposed to the evidence following the policy) and into a consideration of how the objective, 'evidence-based' and 'effective' RFPP could be applied more widely. Beguiled by the evidential appeal of risk-based practice as a means of informing prevention practice (despite a paucity of evidence that targeting risk factors actually prevented future offending), the YJB introduced *Onset*, a condensed baby brother version of *Asset*, for use with 8- to 13-year-olds assessed as being on the cusp of offending (i.e. measuring the risk of the onset of offending) and thus likely to enter the YJS. Young people identified by *Onset* as 'at risk' of offending were to be referred to a 'Youth Inclusion and Support Panel' (YISP), which would provide early preventative intervention in the form of a risk-focused, individualized support package for the young person (see McCarthy et al., 2007). The inception of *Onset* evidenced the strength of the Government's commitment to the RFPP (i.e. risk assessment and 'what works' intervention) through its application to a broader range of (pre-offending, antisocial) behaviours demonstrated by a broader range of young people – those outside of the YJS and those below the age of criminal responsibility (10–17 years old). But the expansion of the RFPP would not end there.

In November 2009, the *Scaled Approach* assessment and intervention framework was born, heralding the zenith of the UK Government commitment to risk-based youth justice (and the RFPP) in policy and practice terms. Concerned to address conclusions from the *Asset* evaluations that YOT practitioners were not consistently or explicitly linking the outcomes of risk assessment to the interventions that followed, the YJB has provided a clear framework to manage and prescribe this link. The *Scaled Approach* prescribes that practitioners aggregate the ratings across the *Asset* domains to provide a total risk score from 0–64 (16 domains × possible 0–4 rating in each). The risk score dictates the frequency, nature and intensity of the post-assessment intervention the young person receives: standard (risk score of 0–14), enhanced (risk score of 15–32) or intensive (risk score of 33–64). Thus, the *Scaled Approach* involves 'tailoring the intensity of intervention to the assessment' (YJB, 2007, p. 4). Prior to its roll-out nationally, the implementation of the *Scaled Approach* was evaluated across four pilot YOTs (compared with four non-pilot YOTs). The evaluation concluded that the pilot YOTs were more likely both to provide comprehensive risk (assessment) information to the courts and to have their risk-related recommendations followed by those courts. Crucially, the evaluation identified 'broad and clearly defined consensus among the practitioners in the four pilot YOTs that the risk-based approach results in better outcomes for young people' (YJB, 2010, p. 15), appearing to justify the central rationale for the *Scaled Approach*. However, the short-term evaluation was unable to consider the direct impact of the *Scaled Approach* on reconviction, so claims of 'better outcomes for young people' remain unsubstantiated and vague at best. Furthermore, there were 'variations in implementation and the different elements of risk-based approaches' (YJB, 2010, p. 23) between the pilot YOTs in relation to pivotal practice elements such as risk rating and intervention planning (e.g. linking risk profile to recommended intervention). Therefore, the prescriptive, allegedly value-free *Scaled Approach* (RFPP) framework was actually mediated and adapted to suit local need, resources, practices and contexts (Sutherland, 2009). Ultimately, the evaluators were forced to concede that 'lack of information is a constraint in making objective assessments of the variety of practices that were adopted' (YJB, 2010, p. 14). Indeed, our own research, based on YJB data covering the *Scaled Approach* pilot period, showed that the YOT deemed by the YJB to have assiduously applied the *Scaled Approach* in practice evidenced a 64% increase in reoffending (Haines and Case, 2012). The YJB's promotion of the 'benefits' of the *Scaled Approach* on the basis of a partial (limited and biased) and problematic 'evidence base' exemplifies how risk-based youth justice more broadly has been oversold, misrepresented and invalidated by a body of naïve, overzealous and unreflective politicians, policymakers and academic proponents of developmental and artefactual RFR (see Haines and Case, 2012). It is to the methodological weaknesses of risk-based youth justice that we now turn.

The decline of risk-based youth justice: Methodological weaknesses

A small group of vociferous critical youth justice academics and campaigners have consistently castigated the UK Government for its risk obsession, largely due to the negative, value-laden and iatrogenic perceptions and treatment of young people in the YJS that are promulgated by RFPP and its various incarnations, notably the *Scaled Approach* (cf. Bateman, 2010; O'Mahony, 2009; Kemshall, 2008; see the following sub-section). There has also been a robust critique of the prescriptive, technical and superficial (box-ticking) nature of *Asset* risk assessment and how this has served to 'deprofessionalize' YOT practitioners, robbing them of valuable discretion-ary capacity and fostering 'automated' and 'routinized' practice akin to 'Korrectional Karaoke' (Pitts, 2001). However, few critics have examined in detail the methodological bases of RFR and the RFPP in order to evalu-ate the validity of its research designs, methods, analytical techniques and conclusions/recommendations – which serve as the evidential rationale for the implementation of risk-based youth justice.

The publication of the evidence-based polemic 'Understanding Youth Offending: Risk Factor Research, Policy and Practice' (Case and Haines, 2009) radically altered the critical landscape, offering a through-going exposition of the methodological weaknesses that pervade artefactual RFR; a research movement that dominates contemporary theoretical under-standings of youth offending and that drives practice in youth justice systems across the globe. Following a comprehensive review of the most important studies in the evolution of artefactual RFR and its application in the YJS through the RFPP, the authors offered a damning evaluation of a methodology undermined by oversimplification, partiality, indefinity and invalidity. Taking each methodological criticism in turn:

- **Oversimplification** – the majority of artefactual RFR studies (as opposed to qualitative, 'constructivist' studies that explore how young people understand, perceive, experience, resist and negotiate risk in their everyday lives – see Kemshall 2008) have measured and understood 'risk' as a quantifiable, numerical, statistical 'factor', thus dumbing down a potentially complex and multifaceted component of young people's lives that is experienced, perceived and negotiated contingent on the individual. The 'factorization' of risk (Kemshall, 2003) has been a reductionist tool to facilitate statistical analyses (e.g. associating a risk 'score' aggregated across a group with the presence/absence of offending) that produce deterministic (yet often imputed, adult-centric and invalid) conclusions regarding the nature of the risk factor–offending relationship – typically developmental conclusions that exposure to risk factors predicts later offending;

- **Partiality** – RFR has privileged the examination of risk factors situated within psychological/individual and immediate social (family, educa-tion, neighbourhood, lifestyle) domains of a young person's life whilst relatively neglecting the potential influence of broader socio-structural issues (e.g. poverty, unemployment, neighbourhood disorganization, changes in the Law and the practices of criminal justice agencies) and social interactions with significant adults within and outside of the YJS. This pervading 'psychosocial' bias has created a partial evidence base, biased towards and limited to restricted and individualized psychosocial explanations of youth offending and equivalent recommendations for responsive intervention;

- **Indefinity** – there have been divergences between the most influential RFR studies in terms of the measurement and nature of their central concepts, namely the 'risk factor' and 'offending' behaviour. Both concepts have been measured inconsistently and vaguely, using scales of varying length and nature (e.g. linear, ratings, Likert, dichotomous), differing definitions (e.g. risk factors as independent of or dichotomous to protective factors, offending classified as official, self-reported, first-time, reoffending, serious, persistent, general, antisocial behaviour), at different ages and developmental stages (e.g. childhood, early and late adolescence, adulthood) and over different time periods (e.g. lifetime, past year, past month, current). Little attention has been given to whether exposure to risk factors or offending behaviour has temporal precedence, time of onset, duration and intensity of exposure and so on. This has created indefinity and uncertainty over the precise nature and even existence of any identified statistical relationships between the two concepts – for example, is the relationship predictive, indicative or causal (if so, in which direction)? Do the two concepts interact? Are they related at all?

- **Invalidity** – RFR has been characterized by invalid measures of risk (e.g. due to their oversimplification, partiality, indefinity and inconsistency across studies) and invalid analyses (e.g. relying on statistical tests of probability that require 'samples' of young people and 'normal distributions' – neither of which is common in RFR and certainly not in the YJS). The consequence has been invalid conclusions regarding the nature and existence of the risk factor–offending relationship (based on imputation and inappropriate extrapolation of statistical results) and the purported homogeneity of RFR studies (which can actually vary greatly in design and methodology), compounded by invalid recommendations for intervention based on imputed relationships, the application of aggregated risk profiles to individual young people and the 'scaled', potentially disproportionate use of intervention based on prospective, subjective risk rather than substantive, actual need.

On these methodological grounds alone, the artefactual RFR movement appears seriously flawed, if not invalidated as a suitable empirical, evidential basis for youth justice processes. When these criticisms are considered in conjunction with the philosophical and ethical problems inherent to RFR, the case for abandoning risk-based youth justice is clear, cogent and pressing.

The decline of risk-based youth justice: Philosophical and ethical problems

Privileging 'risk' and the RFPP as the vehicle to understand and respond to young people in the YJS is negative and value laden. The psychosocial, deterministic bias within RFR has served to individualize the causes of offending and place the blame on young people, rather than considering broader and less controllable socio-structural, political, systemic and interactional influences that may be criminogenic. As such, young people (not adult practitioners, policymakers, politicians, parents) have been responsibilized to resist the negative impact of exposure to risk factors and to respond favourably to risk-focused interventions, despite the influences on, and causes of, their offending being more complex, dynamic, embedded and intractable than they are presented by oversimplified risk assessment and intervention processes. Risk-based youth justice fosters an offender and offence-focused perspective of offending behaviour by young people, using the concept of risk to label and stigmatize young people as personally deficient, feckless, troublesome and dangerous, rather than disadvantaged, deprived, in need or resourceful. The negative-facing, retrospective RFPP provides an 'evidence-based' rationale (albeit drawing on a partial and problematic evidence-base) for governmentality, exercised through increasing levels of interventionism, control and surveillance targeted on 'at risk' groups of young people and 'high risk' neighbourhoods. The premise is straightforward – without early intervention by the adult representatives of the State (Government, police, YOTs), young people facing certain individual and social problems will inevitably offend. Therefore, the practicality and evidence-base of RFR/RFPP justifies pre-emptive (preventative) targeted intervention *before* offending has taken place, on the basis of what young people *may do*, rather than what they actually have done. This is anti-rights, anti-welfare, anti–due process ... anti-child.

The fall of risk-based youth justice and the rise of progressive youth justice

The exponential critique of risk-based youth justice and the application of the RFPP in England and Wales prompted a YJB stakeholder consultation exercise and reflective review of the appropriateness of the *Scaled Approach* to assessment and intervention, less than two years after its introduction. The review was precipitated by developments in assessment practice, theoretical debates around 'risk' and the perceptions and experiences of practitioners and 'offenders' (Baker, for the YJB 2012). In June 2015, a revised assessment and intervention framework entitled *AssetPlus* will come into force (YJB 2013) – intended (and promoted) as a holistic, complex, contextualized and dynamic set of processes prioritizing young people's needs (over risks), young people's perspectives and practitioners' discretion (over prescribed assessment procedures), strengths (over deficits) and the promotion of positive behaviours (over the prevention and reduction of risks and negative behaviours). The YJB have championed *AssetPlus* as a direct challenge to extant risk-focused assessment and intervention mechanisms by providing the conceptual and practical space for assessments of positive characteristics (e.g. young people's strengths, capacities, aspirations, motivations to change) and prospective interventions orientated towards the achievement of positive behaviours and outcomes (YJB, 2014). Early working models of *AssetPlus* indicate an ongoing assessment cycle (prevention to custody) driven by practitioner completion of a three-stage, iterative Core Record consisting of 'Information Gathering and Description' to inform 'Explanations and Conclusions' to inform 'Pathways and Planning'. Crucially, *AssetPlus* purports to eschew numerical, quantitative ratings and measures, signifying a drastic departure from the oversimplification of risk within the *Asset* instrument.

The *AssetPlus* tool has the potential to affect a culture shift across the YJS away from measuring and responding to psychosocial risk factors using risk-focused intervention and towards a more explicit emphasis on young people's needs, strengths and the child-friendly pursuit of positive behaviours and outcomes. However, there remains a proposed explanatory reliance on assessing 'risk and protective factors' (expressed in the 'Self-assessment' portion of the 'Information Gathering and Description' section) and the rating of 'risk / likelihood of reoffending' ('Explanations and Conclusions' section) as a means of informing an ostensibly 'scaled' (to risk level) response to offending, which would appear to contradict or at least undermine this culture shift. The proposed changes, therefore, do not go far enough in re-orientating existing assessment and intervention and seem intent on amending and augmenting existing risk-focused procedures. Whilst *AssetPlus* could offer a promising advance from the methodological and ethical problems of the *Scaled Approach*, it does not attempt a sufficient overhaul of assessment principles, policies and practices to benefit young people in the YJS. Like its predecessor the *Scaled Approach*, *AssetPlus* presents as a technique without a guiding philosophy or purpose; posing a significant threat to its potential to refocus youth justice assessment and intervention in a more positive, risk-free direction.

Children First, Offenders Second: Child-friendly youth justice

We are conscious to avoid the common accusation levelled at critical youth justice criminologists like ourselves – that negativity and policy scepticism is privileged at the expense of providing constructive and practical alternatives for policy and practice development. We have argued here and elsewhere (cf. Case and Haines, in Goldson and Muncie, 2015) that using risk as the central concept to guide youth justice has been largely discredited in academic, policy and practice terms. We assert in the strongest possible terms that youth justice should be underpinned philosophically and practically by the principled and progressive *Children First, Offenders Second* model, which can serve as a touchstone for YOT staff to evaluate their daily practice against (Haines and Case, in press; Haines and Drakeford, 1998; see also Welsh Government, 2014). *Children First, Offenders Second (CFOS)* eschews risk-based, negative, offender- and offense-focused youth justice practice, replacing this with a primary duty to respond to the status of 'child' possessed by all individuals who enter the YJS (hence 'children first'). Youth justice should be delivered in child-friendly and child-appropriate ways that focus on children in holistic terms, examining their life, experiences, perspectives, needs and contexts with suitable complexity and sensitivity (as *AssetPlus* claims it will do, but clearly is not structured to do in its current form). This approach demands that practitioners and policymakers view children as part of the solution (to responding to offending behaviour and personal and social problems), not part of the problem, and that they seek to work in partnership with these young people and promote their interests, needs, rights and views as paramount and influential throughout the youth justice process. Adult practitioners must see themselves as working *for* the young people they engage with, rather than as (primarily) representing the YJS, their home organizations, communities or victims. Adults must take the responsibility to enable young people in the YJS to express their views on issues that affect them (in line with article 12 of the United Nations Convention on the Rights of the Child/UNCRC), to participate equitably in decision-making processes regarding their futures and to access the universal entitlements as set out in national policy statements and international conventions (e.g. the Welsh Government's 'Extending Entitlement' youth strategy – National Assembly Policy Unit, 2000; the UNCRC). Consequently, children's engagement with youth justice practice and practitioners will move beyond the fundamentals of voluntarism, trust, respect and fairness (albeit essential building blocks of engagement) and towards more progressive notions of partnership, reciprocity, investment and 'legitimate' participation in decision-making processes (see also Hawes, 2013).

Conclusion

Risk-based youth justice is anathema to child-friendly youth justice. A *CFOS* model advocates for the total abandonment of risk-based assessment and intervention, but not the abandonment of assessment and intervention per se. Child-focused assessment and principled diversionary responses are championed, particularly those that focus on promoting positive behaviour and outcomes for young people and that enable their access to universal entitlements to services, information, guidance and opportunities. Importantly, there is an accompanying developing evidence-base that *CFOS* can provide an effective alternative model of youth justice preferable to extant risk-based models (Haines and Case, in press; Haines et al., 2013; Haines and Case, 2012). To summarize the benefits of the proposed model, *CFOS*

> has a coherent *philosophy* (children first), an explicit sense of *purpose* (prevention is better than cure, children are part of the solution, not part of the problem), clear *goals* (responsibilising adults, evidence-based partnership working) and clearly articulated, desirable *outcomes* for children (positive behaviour, access to rights/entitlements). (Case and Haines, in Goldson and Muncie, in press)

Such a principled and progressive approach contrasts starkly with the negative, poorly evidenced, methodologically flawed, unethical and anti-child model of risk-based youth justice outlined in this chapter.

References

Audit Commission (1996) *Misspent Youth: Young People and Crime*. London: Audit Commission.

Baker, K. (2012) *AssetPlus Rationale*. London: YJB.

———. (2005) 'Assessment in youth justice: Professional discretion and the use of Asset', *Youth Justice* 5: 106–22.

Baker, K., Jones, S., Roberts, C. and Merrington, S. (2002) *Validity and Reliability of Asset*. London: YJB.

———. (2005) *Further Development of Asset*. London: Youth Justice Board.

Bateman, T. (2010) 'Punishing poverty: The scaled approach and youth justice practice', *The Howard Journal of Criminal Justice* 50(2): 171–83.

Beck, U. (1992) *Risk Society: Towards a New Modernity*. London: Sage.

Bottoms, A. E. and McClintock, F. H. (1973) *Criminals Coming of Age. A Study of Institutional Adaptation in the Treatment of Adolescent Offenders*. London: Heinemann.

Case, S. P. and Haines, K. R. (2009) *Understanding Youth Offending: Risk Factor Research, Policy and Practice*. Cullompton: Willan.

———. (in press) Risk Management and Early Intervention. In: B. Goldson and J. Muncie (eds) *Youth, Crime and Justice*. London: Sage.

Farrington, D. (2000) 'Developmental criminology and risk-focussed prevention', in M. Maguire, R. Morgan and R. Reiner (eds) *The Oxford Handbook of Criminology*, 3rd edn. Oxford: Oxford University Press.

———. (2007) 'Childhood risk factors and risk-focused prevention', in: M. Maguire, R. Morgan and R. Reiner (eds) *The Oxford Handbook of Criminology*. Oxford: Oxford University Press.

Farrington, D. P. (1996) *Understanding and Preventing Youth Crime*. York: Joseph Rowntree Foundation.

Feeley, M.M. and Simon, J. (1992) 'The new penology: Notes on the emerging strategy of corrections and its implications', *Criminology* 30: 449–74.

Flood-Page, C., Campbell, S., Harrington, V. and Miller, J. (2000) *Youth Crime: Findings from the 1998/99 Youth Lifestyles Survey. Home Office Research Study 209*. London: Home Office.

Glueck, S. and Glueck, E. (1930) *500 Criminal Careers*. New York: Alfred Knopf.

Graham, J. and Bowling, B. (1995). *Young People and Crime*. Home Office Research Study 145. London: Home Office.

Haines, K. R. and Case, S. P. (in press) *Positive Youth Justice: Children First, Offenders Second*. Bristol: Policy Press.

———. (in press) Risk management and early intervention. In: B. Goldson and J. Muncie (eds) *Youth Crime and Justice*. London: Sage.

———. (2012) 'Is the scaled approach a failed approach?', *Youth Justice* 12(3): 212–28.

Haines, K. R., Case, S. P., Charles, A. D. and Davies, K. (2013) 'The Swansea Bureau: A model of diversion from the youth justice system', *International Journal of Law, Crime and Justice* 41(2): 167–87.

Haines, K. and Drakeford, M. (1998) *Young People and Youth Justice*. London: Macmillan.

Hawes, M. (2013) *Legitimacy and Social Order: A Young People's Perspective*. Unpublished PhD thesis, Swansea: Swansea University.

Hine, J (2005). 'Early intervention: The view from On Track', *Children and Society* 19(2): 117–30.

Katz, J. (1988) *Seductions of Crime*. New York: Basic Book.

Kemshall, H. (2008) 'Risk, rights and justice: Understanding and responding to youth risk', *Youth Justice* 8(1): 21–38.

McCarthy, P., Laing, K. and Walker, J. (2004) Offenders of the Future: Assessing the Risk of Children and Young People Becoming Involved in Criminal or Antisocial Behaviour. London: Department for Education and Skills.

Morgan Report (1990) *Safer Communities: The Local Delivery of Crime Prevention through the Partnership Approach*. London: Home Office.

National Assembly Policy Unit (2000) *Extending Entitlement: Supporting Young People in Wales*. Cardiff: National Assembly for Wales.

O'Mahony, P. (2009) 'The risk factors paradigm and the causes of youth crime: A deceptively useful analysis?', *Youth Justice* 9(2): 99–115.

Pitts, J. (2001) 'Korrectional karaoke: New Labour and the zombification of youth justice', *Youth Justice* 1(2): 3–16.

Sampson, R. J. and Laub, J. H. (1993) *Crime in the Making: Pathways and Turning Points through Life*. Harvard: Harvard University Press.

Sherman, L., Gottfredson D., MacKenzie, D., Eck, J., Reuter, P. and Bushway, S. (1998) *Preventing Crime: What Works, What Doesn't, What's Promising*. Department of Criminology and Criminal Justice, University of Maryland: Baltimore.

Smith, D. J. and McVie, S. (2003) 'Theory and Method in the Edinburgh Study of Youth Transitions and Crime', *British Journal of Criminology* 43(1): 169–95.

Sutherland, A. (2009) 'The 'Scaled Approach' in youth justice. Fools rush in...', *Youth Justice* 9(1): 44–60.

Thornberry, T. P. and Krohn, M. D. (2003) *Taking Stock of Delinquency: An Overview of Findings from Contemporary Longitudinal Studies*. New York: Kluwer.

Welsh Government and Youth Justice Board (2014) *Children and Young People First*. Cardiff: Welsh Government/YJB.

West, D. J. and Farrington, D. P. (1973) *Who Becomes Delinquent?* London: Heinemann.

Youth Justice Board (2000) *ASSET*. London: YJB.

———. (2003) *Assessment, Planning Interventions and Supervision*. Source Document. London: YJB.

———. (2007) *The Scaled Approach*. London: YJB.

———. (2010) *Process Evaluation of the Pilot of a Risk-based Approach to Interventions*. London: YJB.

———. (2013) *Assessment and Planning Interventions Framework – AssetPlus*. Model Document. London: YJB.

———. (2014) *AssetPlus*. London: YJB.

5

JUSTICE, RISK AND DIVERSITY

Gill McIvor
University of Stirling, UK

Introduction

While there have been broad concerns voiced about the centrality of risk in criminal justice and the adequacy and relevance of risk assessment technologies, there are particular concerns in relation to how concepts of risk and risk assessments engage with and accommodate diversity and how, more specifically, the risk paradigm further disadvantages marginalized groups. Drawing principally on gender and ethnicity, this chapter considers international empirical evidence and theoretical debates to demonstrate how risk and risk assessment have resulted in the over-classification and regulation of marginalized individuals and groups through the reconceptualization of 'needs' and structural disadvantages as 'risks'. The chapter will critically discuss the limitations of the risk paradigm and its consequences in the context of diversity. It will consider the potential of alternative approaches – such as the development of gender-informed assessments – to offer a more nuanced assessment of risk but will conclude that fundamental problems associated with the concept of risk and its operational impact remain. Instead, it will be argued that by focusing on the risks faced by individuals rather than the risks posed by them, policy and practice might more effectively engage with processes of criminalization and desistance from crime.

The ascendancy of risk and risk assessment

Risk has become a central feature of western justice systems manifested most clearly in the development and use of instruments designed to assess the likelihood of particular types of behaviour occurring and the harm that these behaviours might present. A shift has occurred from relatively unstructured assessment practices underpinned by professional judgement to increasingly structured and consistent practices facilitated by the use of standardized tools. Such a shift in practice, especially in the use of actuarial methods for the assessment of risk, reflects the growing influence of managerialism and 'actuarial justice' (Feeley and Simon, 1994) in criminal justice settings. In the UK context, the locus of 'risk' has changed from a concern about risk *to* an individual – that is, the risk of receiving a custodial sentence – to the risk potentially posed *by* an individual, reflecting an increasing policy emphasis upon public protection. At the same time, risk assessment technology has evolved from tools based purely upon static historical data such as sex, age and number of previous convictions – such as OGRS in the UK (Copas, 1995) – to those which include a structured assessment of an individual's circumstances and needs which are amenable to change – such as the Level of Service Inventory-Revised (LSI-R) (Andrews and Bonta, 1995). Clinical assessment, actuarial tools based on static factors and tools which include dynamic risk factors and are capable of measuring change after intervention are also referred to, respectively, as first-, second- and third-generation forms of risk assessment.

Despite having been experienced by practitioners in some instances as 'deskilling' because of the limits they place on professional discretion (Gibbs, 1999; Robinson, 2003), structured risk-need assessment tools have been argued to have a number of advantages including improving and maintaining the quality and consistency of assessment; assisting in the allocation of resources; documenting the needs of those subject to supervision and assessing the effectiveness of supervision in addressing/reducing needs. Such assessments, it has been suggested, can facilitate problem identification, intervention planning, service development and outcome measurement (Aubrey and Hough, 1997; Robinson, 2003). They are also increasingly used to inform security classifications (Morash, 2009).

Narrative reviews and meta-analyses have indicated that statistical prediction tends to be as good as or better than clinical judgment in the majority of cases (Blanchette and Brown, 2006). Internationally, the use of structured approaches to the assessment (and management) of risk has been driven to a significant extent by the Risk Needs Responsivity (RNR) framework developed by Andrews and his colleagues in Canada. In essence, it is argued that interventions aimed at reducing the risk of recidivism are more effective if they are tailored to the level of risk presented by an offender, aim to address needs that have been demonstrated to be associated with an increased risk of reoffending and are delivered in ways that engage with offenders' learning styles, motivations and capacities (Bonta and Andrews, 2007). It has been argued that the RNR model is equally applicable to men and women (Andrews and Dowden, 2007; Lovins et al.,

2007), although the number of studies exploring the relationship between adherence to RNR principles and offending outcomes has been acknowledged to be 'regrettably low' (Andrews and Dowden, 2007, p. 451).

Others, however, have questioned the relevance of risk assessments that underpin the RNR approach and associated (mostly cognitive behavioural) interventions for women and other minority groups. It has been argued that risk and needs assessments are likely to be highly gendered because the factors that they incorporate are drawn predominantly from studies of men (Shaw and Hannah-Moffat, 2000, 2004). There is an assumption that 'the same classificatory factors are equally salient for both men and women' (Blanchette and Brown, 2006, p. 47), yet there is evidence that most risk assessment tools that have been developed on samples of men decline in predictive validity when they are used to classify women (Blanchette and Brown, 2006). Moreover, the RNR model has also attracted criticism for its focus exclusively on 'criminogenic needs' such that the social and structural context of offending is ignored and the 'problem' is located instead within the individual (Hannah-Moffat, 2009). Reducing individuals to a series of risk categories (Hannah-Moffat, 2006) renders it 'impossible to treat individuals fairly if they are treated as abstractions, unshaped by their particular contexts of social life' (Hannah-Moffat, 2009, p. 215).

Pathways to offending and criminogenic needs

The assumption underlying 'gender-neutral' assessment tools such as the LSI-R (and its subsequent incarnation in the form of the LS/CMI) is that they can be applied equally to predict the risk of recidivism across diverse groups of offenders because they have shared criminogenic needs. It has been argued that the RNR approach is underpinned by an assumption that the same theories of criminality apply to both genders and that it therefore fails to acknowledge that risk and need are both gendered and racialized (Hannah-Moffat, 2006). LSI-R is based on theories of male offending that ignore factors and experiences that are unique to criminality among women (Reisig et al., 2006). The inclusion of risk factors that are derived from samples of male offenders and driven by male-focused theories of crime means that 'a gender problem is built into them' through the imposition of male normative criteria upon women (Hannah-Moffat, 2009, p. 211).

It is now widely acknowledged that women's offending challenges traditional theoretical explanations of crime which were developed to explain offending by men, resulting in the development of theoretical explanations for women's offending that have incorporated feminist analyses to locate women's offending within patriarchal structures and wider socio-structural influences (Gelsthorpe, 2004). Qualitative studies that privilege women's understandings of their experiences suggest that their pathways into crime are different from those of men (Daly, 1998; Kendall, 2002; Simpson et al., 2008; Salisbury and Van Voorhis, 2009) leading to the conclusion that 'qualitative differences in the reasons for crime across gender must first be understood and then must be integrated into assessment and treatment efforts' (Manchak et al., 2009, p. 439). Women's own accounts of their offending suggest that is often rooted in structural inequalities such as poverty and deprivation or problems relating to substance misuse. Female offenders frequently have experiences of abuse, psychological problems (including depression and low self-esteem) and past or present involvement in abusive personal relationships (Chesney-Lind, 1997; Loucks, 2004; Rumgay, 2000). Critics arguing from a feminist perspective contend that actuarial risk assessments ignore the gendered context of female criminality by failing to consider women's economic marginalization, their involvement in drug-related offending and their histories of victimization (Reisig et al., 2006).

There are also differences in the context and nature of male and female offending such that women's involvement in law-breaking is qualitatively and quantitatively different from men's (Prime et al., 2001; Hannah-Moffat, 2009; Block et al., 2010). Compared to men, women are less likely to commit serious violent offences, and when they do commit violent offences, are more likely to assault someone they know. It has also been suggested that men and women's motivations for property crime differ in that women are more likely to commit acquisitive crime as a result of financial needs, while property offending by men is more often a mechanism to assert or maintain their status (Reisig et al., 2006). Women have shorter criminal careers, fewer women offend and they do so less frequently than men (Prime et al., 2001).

Although women's offending tends to be under-theorized and less well understood than offending by men, there is growing evidence that they have different criminogenic needs because their routes into offending and reasons for offending are often different (Hedderman, 2004). Some needs appear to be more specific to women or more closely associated with recidivism among women, including physical and sexual abuse (Hollin and Palmer, 2006; Belknapp and Holsinger, 2006), substance misuse (Andrews et al., 2012), poverty (Holtfreter et al., 2004; Heilbrun et al., 2008; Manchak et al., 2009), family factors (Blanchette and Brown, 2006), emotional well-being (Manchak et al., 2009; Knaap et al., 2012) and propensity to self-harm or attempt suicide (Blanchette and Brown, 2006; Belknapp and Holsinger, 2006). Even where men and women appear to share similar needs, how these needs relate to offending – and hence to the risk of recidivism – may well differ, reflecting gendered experiences, motivations and opportunities, with the result that assigning a risk score on a particular factor will fail to capture gendered experiential differences (Shaw and Hannah-Moffat, 2004; Holtfreter and Cupp, 2007; Hannah-Moffat, 2009). For example, drug misuse has been shown to play a different role in relation to male and female offending, more often preceding the onset of offending by women (Makkai and Payne, 2003; Johnston, 2004), while there is some evidence that companions may have a differential impact on risk among male and female offenders (Heilbrun et al., 2008).

How well do gender-neutral tools predict female offending?

Proponents of actuarial risk tools – and the implications for intervention that flow from them – argue that 'gender-neutral' assessment tools are equally predictive of the risk of recidivism for men and for women. It has been claimed that they tap a range of factors relevant to women's offending through domains that apply to all categories of offenders. However, as we have seen, there is now a growing body of evidence to support the conclusion that women and men have different needs (or similar needs that reflect differing underlying experiences) and to question the assumption that risk assessment tools that have been developed using data derived from (mostly white) young men can be applied unproblematically to assess risk among women. When risk assessment tools are developed using samples of male offenders, the needs included in them may not be those most relevant for predicting recidivism among women (Van der Knaap et al., 2012).

There is mixed evidence on how well the LSI-R and other 'gender-neutral' risk assessment tools predict female recidivism. Manchak et al. (2009) compared the predictive capacity of the LSI-R for men and women who had been imprisoned for serious violent offences. They found that it was reasonably good at predicting recidivism (conviction for a new offence) for women, though the factors that best predicted recidivism for men and women differed. Others have reached more optimistic conclusions, with Schwalbe (2008), for example, suggesting that gender differences in predictive validity identified in individual studies are likely to reflect gender biases in juvenile justice decision-making rather than the ineffectiveness of risk assessments with female offenders, while Smith et al. (2009) concluded that the LSI-R was equally predictive for male and female offenders. However, the quality of the studies included in Smith et al.'s meta-analysis has been questioned on the grounds that many were unpublished and many were conducted by a small number of researchers, raising the possibility of a large amount of data overlap (Taylor and Blanchette, 2009).

Several studies, by contrast, have highlighted limitations in the use of risk assessment tools with female offenders. In their study of female prison misconduct, for instance, Wright et al. (2007) found that gender-neutral needs were unable to predict women's misconduct after 6 or 12 months, suggesting that risk factors that are pertinent to men may not be applicable to women. Emeka and Sorensen (2009) found that a generic risk assessment instrument constructed from a sample of male and female juveniles worked reasonably well in predicting male recidivism but provided little predictive improvement over chance for female offenders, while Holtfreter and Cupp (2007) found little evidence from a review of 11 studies for the predictive validity of the LSI-R for female offenders, with some evidence that women were not being classified accurately.

Reisig et al.'s (2006) study examined the ability of the LSI-R to predict recidivism among women on community supervision in the United States who had been classified according to Daly's (1994, 1998) typology of women's pathways into crime, which included 'street women', drug connected women', 'harmed and harming women', battered women and a final 'other' category which Reisig et al. designated as 'economically motivated women' who offended not out of economic necessity, but to finance lifestyles that they could not afford or to support other deviant activities. The LSI-R was found to be a valid predictor of recidivism for this latter group of women whose offending appropriated more closely to offending by men, but there was no association between LSI-R scores and recidivism for the other gendered pathways, with 'harmed and harming women' tending to be over-classified and 'drug-connected women' to be under-classified with respect to their level of risk.

A factor limiting the conclusions that can be drawn from this literature, however, is the relatively limited number of studies of women with sufficiently large sample sizes to enable the reliability and validity of risk assessment instruments with women to be determined. More research with larger samples of women – and with other minatory groups – is required (Shepherd et al., 2012). As it stands, it is possible to concur with Holtfreter and Cupp (2007), who conclude that '[t]he limited number of studies on female offending suggests that it is simply too early to come to any definitive statement mirroring the optimistic conclusions reached in research on male offenders' (p. 375).

Other limitations of risk assessment

There is some evidence to suggest that gender-neutral risk assessment tools may be ineffective (or less effective) in predicting recidivism – however defined – among women. Concerns have also been articulated that women are over-classified when they are assessed using tools that have been developed for men. It has been suggested that because women are typically less violent than men and are more likely to be violent towards a family member or partner, male-based risk assessments may overestimate women's risk of violence and result in their over-classification. Some evidence in support of such a claim comes from Hardyman's (2001, cited in Blanchette and Brown, 2006) finding that the rate of institutional misconduct by *medium* security female prisoners was similar to that of *minimum* security male prisoners, Harer and Langan's (2001) finding that, while a risk classification scheme to predict prisoner violence was equally able to predict violence among male and female prisoners, women were less likely to commit serious violence misconduct than men and Andrews et al.'s (2012) finding that recidivism rates for low and moderate risk women were lower than those of lower risk men.

Van Voorhis and Presser (2001) found that prison staff believed that over-classification of female prisoners often occurred. Over-classifying women who tend to have high levels of needs can result in women receiving custodial sentences that would not be justified on the basis of proportionality alone, unnecessarily intensive (and possibly intrusive) supervision, higher security classifications than are necessary and the misallocation of services and resources. Under-classifying, on the other hand, can result in women being inadequately supervised and being denied access to services that they require (Reisig et al., 2006).

At a technical level, the usefulness of risk assessment instruments is hampered by unnecessarily large numbers of variables, unhelpful definition of factors as 'protective' when they are the reverse of 'criminogenic' and a lack of evidence regarding validity and reliability (Baird, 2009). There is limited information as to how to identify differing risk categories, with the result that determining cut-off points is 'inherently arbitrary' (Reisig et al., 2006, p. 394).

Risk and ethnicity

Thus far, this chapter has focused principally on practical issues associated with assessing risk among women. Before continuing to consider some of the theoretical critiques of risk and risk assessment and practical efforts to make risk assessments more relevant to women, it is worth briefly reviewing the (much more limited) available evidence regarding how well these tools are able to reflect the experiences and predict recidivism among minority ethnic groups, particularly since similar theoretical critiques have been advanced in relation to ethnicity as to gender. According to Rugge

(2006), research suggests that most risk factors for non-aboriginal offenders are also relevant to aboriginal offenders with the exception of family/
marital and school/employment, which may reflect cultural differences in
how the importance of these factors is perceived. Studies tend to show,
however, that minority and indigenous offenders receive higher risk scores
than white offenders (Rugge, 2006). Holsinger et al. (2003) examined the
use of the LSI-R with male and female Native American and non-Native
Americans who were imprisoned or in community settings and found that
it identified higher levels of risk among Native Americans on seven of ten
domains – education/employment, financial, family/marital, accommodation, leisure/recreation, companions and alcohol/drugs.

This, of course, has implications for security classifications and levels
of intervention and control. Indeed concerns about over-classification
resulting from structured risk assessments have been raised in relation to
ethnicity as they have in relation to gender. It has been argued that risk
assessment tools impact disproportionately upon ethnic minorities (and
the poor more generally) because the items that are commonly included
in them – such as educational achievement and (un)employment – share a
common variance with race (Gottfredson and Moriarty, 2006). It has also
been suggested that structured risk assessments can disadvantage black
offenders because they often incorporate data (such as police data) that
reflect discriminatory processes in wider society (Bhui, 1999).

Bramhall and Hudson (2007) conclude on the basis of an analysis
of risk assessments conducted on, and reports prepared in respect of,
white and Asian offenders in the United Kingdom that risk assessment
is part of a process of construction of risky identities based on popular
stereotypes. However, the identities that are thus constructed are treated
as 'real' and have tangible consequences such as exposure to the risk of
imprisonment – because community penalties are less likely to be recommended – where the 'pains of imprisonment' for 'risky' south Asian men
are aggravated by racial and religious intolerance.

Monture-Angus (1999) argues that the concept of risk management is
incompatible with aboriginal cultures, law and tradition in which people
are intended to be respected rather than managed. She argues that '[t]he
individualizing of risk absolutely fails to take into account the impact of
colonial oppression on the lives of Aboriginal men and women' (p. 27).
It has been suggested that unless assessment tools are responsive to culture
specific risk factors they may direct indigenous offenders into programmes
that are either too intensive or not intensive enough (Jones et al., 2002).
Jones et al. argue that there is a need for culturally informed versions of
standard risk tools to be developed which focus on wider needs and which
aim to promote social justice, recognizing the influences of structural
oppression.

The development of gender-responsive risk assessment tools

It has been argued that, as a consequence of the limitations of purportedly gender-neutral tools to accurately predict women's risk of offending, gender-responsive risk assessment tools are required that are better able to reflect circumstances and experience that are related to female recidivism (Taylor and Blanchette, 2009). A key question then arises as to whether existing gender-neutral tools can be amended to make them more suited to women or whether it is necessary for gender specific tools to be developed from the ground up? While Hannah-Moffat (2009) argues that assessment tools for women should not only be gender-informed but should be built from the ground up for the specific populations to which they will be applied, a significant sample would be required from which to develop and validate gender-informed risk assessment and management tools for women and girls (Blanchette and Brown, 2006).

Alternatively, it has been suggested that existing tools should have risk factors tailored to better reflect women's risks and needs by adding or deleting specific items, re-weighting existing items and/or amending the cut-off scores. Davidson (2011) argues that risk assessment tools need to take account of women's experiences of victimization, but in such a way that they are not penalized as a result. It has also been suggested that actuarial risk assessment tools should incorporate strengths or protective factors in recognition of women's lower levels of risk (Blanchette and Brown, 2006).

An example of the former approach has been described by Van Voorhis and her colleagues (Van Voorhis et al., 2008; Van Voorhis et al., 2010; Buell et al., 2011), who developed a gender-responsive risk-need assessment tool for women which incorporated domains that had been identified as being related to women's risk: trauma, victimization and abuse; mental health, especially depression, anxiety and self-injury; dysfunctional intimate relationships; self-esteem; self-efficacy; and parental stress. Items were also added to identify strengths, or protective factors, such as support from others and educational achievement. Two types of assessment were developed: a supplement to existing risk-need assessment such as LSI-R and a stand-alone assessment, both of which were tested on prison samples, probation samples and pre-release samples.

There is evidence that gender-informed risk assessments outperform 'gender-neutral' assessments. For instance, Blanchette (2005) found that a risk assessment tool that included gender-responsive variables and had been developed on a sample of women performed better at predicting women's behaviour than an ostensibly gender-neutral, male-based tool.

Wright et al. (2007) found that gender-responsive needs were better predictors of prison disciplinary misconduct, and Van Voorhis et al. (2008) reached a similar conclusion on the basis of a study of women on probation and parole. Van Voorhis et al. (2010) found that while for most of their samples gender-neutral variables predicted outcomes for women – including prison misconduct, re-arrest, technical violations and return to prison – the addition of gender-responsive factors resulted in improved predictions. However, different factors were related to recidivism across the different samples of women, suggesting that that different assessment tools may be required for different populations of women because some variables may be relevant to women in some settings (e.g. prison) but not in others (e.g. probation).

Beyond risk?

The more recent developments in risk assessment tools to incorporate gender-relevant factors appear to increase their relevance for and effectiveness with women and go some way towards addressing concerns such as those expressed by Shaw and Hannah-Moffat (2004) that 'the literature and subsequent practices ignore and dismiss the effect of gender and diversity, or the social and economic constraints on offenders' lives' (p .91). However, they do not address more fundamental concerns that risk assessment tools 'decontextualise, individualise and pathologise offending in accordance with gendered and racialised norms' (Shaw and Hannah-Moffat, 2004, p. 91). It has also been argued that by failing to draw attention to the structural barriers that contribute to women's involvement in crime (Kendall, 2002) through the redefinition of 'welfare needs' as 'psychological needs' related to risk of recidivism (Hudson, 2001), women are placed at an increased risk of imprisonment because they tend to have many and complex needs which render them apparently 'riskier' than they actually are.

Indeed, Hannah-Moffat (2005) argues that the welfare/risk distinction is overly simplistic and that needs are defined in relation to their capacity for risk reduction and intervention, with the resulting interventions 'predicated on middle-class normative assumptions that are highly gendered and racialized' (p. 37). Risk-based decision-making reframes women's histories, needs and experiences as problematic (Hannah-Moffat, 2006), requiring individualized and responsiblizing forms of intervention and risk management while the state is also exonerated for its failure to address wider social problems, so that 'systemic problems' are reconceptualized as 'individuals' inadequacies' (Hannah-Moffat, 2006, p. 187).

Hannah-Moffat (2007) further argues that correctional practices have gendered risk in ways that govern and regulate women and that make them responsible for their own behaviour, that of their children and, in the case of aboriginal women, that of their communities. She contends that risk is also racialized because it makes assumptions about dysfunctional families and relationships which are used to justify intervention by a range of agencies in the context of 'holistic' interventions. Similar arguments can also be extended to the assessment of women's risk of victimization, which is inherently gendered (Chan and Rigakos, 2002). In relation to 'at-risk' victims, it has been suggested that risk and risk assessments are 'constructed within a logic of norms and values' and serve to protect criminal justice professionals by enabling them to convey a degree of accountability despite the shortcomings of the process (Walklate and Mythen, 2011, p. 108). A similar point is made by Barry (2007), who argues that risk-focused practice encourages defensible decision-making to contain risk, but not to address the underlying problems that contribute to it, and by Silver and Miller (2002), who observe how actuarial assessment tools tend to facilitate resource management rather than targeting individual or structural need, with the result that assessments become resource led rather than needs led. They suggest that group-based methods of assessment and predication can further discriminate against already marginalized and stigmatized groups because 'actuarial risk assessment is more useful in labelling individuals than it is in understanding and resolving their problems' (p. 147)

There is a danger, too, that the increasing preoccupation with risk can result in responses by the criminal justice system that are disproportionately severe. For example, it has been suggested that by having attention drawn to risk assessments in pre-sentence reports, considerations of risk may outweigh concerns about due process and proportionality (Hudson, 2001; Cole, 2007). As Hudson (2001, p. 109) notes, 'sentencing according to risk means sentencing differently'. By focusing on risk, those who are most disadvantaged and who therefore exhibit the greatest needs are likely to be subjected to more punitive and restrictive outcomes, and often the factors associated with risk are correlated with dimensions of diversity such as gender or ethnicity. Maurutto and Hannah-Moffat (2007) propose that risk assessments undermine proportionality because people with different social circumstances who commit the same offence are likely to have very different risk assessment scores, underlining the fact that 'risk tools are not as *objective* or as *apolitical* as some postulate' (p. 481, original emphasis) but, rather involve moral and subjective judgments about an individual's character and lifestyle. Such tools have the potential to classify particular groups as higher risk because they have high levels of criminogenic needs which are often linked to social and economic disadvantage. Moreover, female offenders are often considered high risk because of the risk they present to themselves. The problem is compounded because risk tools do not differentiate between different types of recidivism, and high risk tends to be associated with notions of dangerousness and harm (Blanchette and Brown, 2006; Maurutto and Hannah-Moffat, 2007).

Conclusion

In this chapter it has been shown how contemporary risk assessment practices – and the strategies for managing risk that flow from them – can have discriminatory consequences, resulting in the over-classification and over-management of women and other disadvantaged groups. Although the potential shortcomings of 'gender-neutral' risk assessments have begun to be recognized and steps have been taken to recognize strengths as a counterbalance to the over-classificatory consequences of assessments focused solely on needs and risk, fundamental problems with the concept of risk as an increasingly dominant discourse in criminal justice remain. Elsewhere in this volume, contributors have highlighted the potential of strengths-based approaches as an alternative to risk-focused practices, especially since the former appear more compatible with the theoretical and empirical literature on desistance. I am more persuaded by the arguments put forward by Garside (2009), who draws upon a public health model in which the risks that are faced by individuals cannot be separated from the broader social context of their lives. Thus, rather than responsibilizing individuals for making poor decisions, this approach recognizes that the decisions that individuals make are 'partly determined and conditioned by the circumstances they find themselves in' (p. 13). The policy implications – which are more consistent with a commitment to social justice – are that instead of focusing on the risks posed by individuals, attention would shift to the risks experienced by them, and intervention would aim to ameliorate the socio-structural factors that constitute individual riskiness rather than on the decisions made by the individuals themselves. Such an approach is compatible with what we know about the circumstances of diverse disadvantaged groups and their pathways into crime. It is also compatible with what we understand about the structural factors associated with desistance and as such offers some promise as a more nuanced and potentially more effective approach to the concept of risk.

References

Andrews, D. A. and Bonta, J. (1995) *The Level of Service Inventory – Revised Manual.* Toronto: Multi-Health Systems Inc.

Andrews, D. A. and Dowden, C. (2007) 'The Risk-Need-Responsivity model of assessment and human service in prevention and corrections: Crime prevention jurisprudence', *Canadian Journal of Criminology and Criminal Justice* 49(4): 439–64.

Andrews, D. A., Guzzo, L., Raynor, P. Rowe, R. C., Rettinger, L. J., Brews, A. and Wormith, J. S. (2012) 'Are the major risk/need factors predictive of both female and male reoffending? A test within the eight domains of the Level of Service/Case Management Inventory', *International Journal of Offender Therapy and Comparative Criminology* 56(1): 113–33.

Aubrey, R. and Hough, M. (1997) *Assessing Offenders' Needs: Assessment Scales for the Probation Service, Home Office Research Study 166.* London: Home Office.

Baird, C. (2009) *A Question of Evidence: A Critique of Risk Assessment Models Used in the Justice System.* Madison, WI: National Council on Crime and Delinquency.

Barry, M. (2007) *Effective Approaches to Risk Assessment in Social Work: An International Literature Review.* Edinburgh: Scottish Executive Social Research.

Belknapp, J. and Holsinger, K. (2006) 'The gendered nature of risk factors for delinquency', *Feminist Criminology* 1(1): 48–71.

Bhui, H. S. (1999) 'Racism and risk assessment: Linking theory to practice with black mentally disordered offenders', *Probation Journal* 46(3): 171–81.

Blanchette, K. and Brown, S. L. (2006) *The Assessment and Treatment of Women Offenders: An Integrative Perspective.* Chichester: John Wiley & Sons.

Block. C. R., Blokland, A. A., van der Weff, C., van Os, R. and Nieuwbeerta, P. (2010) 'Long-term patterns of offending in women', *Feminist Criminology* 5(1): 73–107.

Bonta, J. and Andrews, D. A. (2007) *Risk-Need-Responsivity Model for Offender Assessment and Rehabilitation.* Ottawa: Public Safety Canada.

Bramhall, G. and Hudson, B. (2007) 'Criminal justice and 'risky' masculinities', in K. Hannah-Moffat and P. O'Malley (eds) *Gendered Risks*, Abingdon: Routledge.

Buell, M., Modley, P. and Van Voorhis, P. (2011) 'Policy developments in the U.S.', in R. Sheehan, G. McIvor and C. Trotter (eds) *Working with Women Offenders in the Community.* Cullompton: Willan.

Chan, W. and Rigakos, G. S. (2002) 'Risk, crime and gender', *British Journal of Criminology* 42: 743–61.

Chesney-Lind, M. (1997) *The Female Offender: Girls, Women and Crime.* Thousand Oaks, CA: Sage.

Cole, D. P. (2007) 'The umpire strikes back: Canadian judicial experience with risk-assessment instruments', *Canadian Journal of Criminology and Criminal Justice* 49(4): 493–517.

Copas, J. (1995) 'On using crime statistics for prediction', in M. Walker (ed.) *Interpreting Crime Statistics.* Oxford: Clarendon Press.

Daly, K. (1994) *Gender, Crime and Punishment, New Haven*. CT: Yale University Press.

———. (1998) 'Women's pathways to felony court: Feminist theories of lawbreaking and problems of representation', in K. Daly and L. Maher (eds) *Criminology at the Crossroads: Feminist Readings in Crime and Justice*. New York, NY: Oxford University Press.

Davidson, J. T. (2011) 'Managing risk in the community: How gender matters', in R. Sheehan, G. McIvor and C. Trotter (eds) *Working with Women Offenders in the Community: What Works*. Cullompton: Willan.

Emeka, T. Q. and Sorenson, J. R. (2009) 'Female juvenile risk: Is there a need for gendered assessment instruments?', *Youth Violence and Juvenile Justice* 7(4): 313–30.

Feeley, M. and Simon, J. (1994) 'Actuarial justice: The emerging new criminal law', in D. Nelken (ed.) *The Futures of Criminology*. London: Sage

Garside, R. (2009) *Risky People or Risky Societies? Rethinking Interventions for Young People in Transition*. London: Centre for Crime and Justice Studies.

Gelsthorpe, L. (2004) 'Female offending: A theoretical overview', in G. McIvor (ed.) *Women Who Offend*. London: Jessica Kingsley.

Gibbs, A. (1999) 'The Assessment, Case Management and Evaluation System', *Probation Journal* 46(3): 182–86.

Gottfredson, S. D. and Moriarty, L. J. (2006) 'Statistical risk assessment: Old problems and new applications', *Crime and Delinquency* 52(1): 178–200.

Hannah-Moffat, K. (2005) 'Criminogenic needs and the transformative risk subject: Hybridizations of risk/need in penality', *Punishment and Society* 7(1): 29–51.

———. (2006) 'Pandora's Box: Risk/need and gender-responsive corrections', *Criminology and Public Policy* 5(1): 183–92.

———. (2007) 'Gendering dynamic risk: Assessing and managing the maternal identities of women prisoners', in K. Hannah-Moffat and P. O'Malley (eds) *Gendered Risks*. Abingdon: Routledge.

———. (2009) 'Gridlock or mutability: Reconsidering "gender" and risk assessment', *Criminology and Public Policy* 8(1): 209–19.

Harer, M. D. and Langan, N. P. (2001)'Gender differences in predictors of prison violence: Assessing the predictive validity of a risk classification system', *Crime and Delinquency* 47(4): 513–36.

Hedderman, C. (2004) 'The 'criminogenic' needs of women offenders', in G. McIvor (ed.) *Women Who Offend: Research Highlights in Social Work 44*. London: Jessica Kingsley.

Heilbrun, K., DeMatteo, D., Fretz, R., Erickson, J., Yashuara, K. and Anumba, N. (2008) 'How "specific" are gender-specific rehabilitation needs?: An empirical analysis', *Criminal Justice and Behavior* 35(11): 1382–97.

Hollin, C. and Palmer, E. (2006) 'Criminogenic need and women offenders: A critique of the literature', *Legal and Criminological Psychology* 11(2): 179–95.

Holsinger, A. M., Lowenkamp, C. T. and Latessa, E. J. (2003) 'Ethnicity, gender and the Level of Service Inventory – Revised', *Journal of Criminal Justice* 31(4): 309–20.

Holtfreter, K. and Cupp, R. (2007) 'Gender and risk assessment: The empirical status of the LSI-R for women', *Journal of Contemporary Criminal Justice* 23(4): 363–82.

Holtfreter, K., Reisig, M. D. and Morash, M. (2004) 'Poverty, state capital, and recidivism among women offenders', *Criminology and Public Policy* 3(2): 185–208.

Hudson, B. (2001) 'Human rights, public safety and the probation service: Defending justice in the risk society', *The Howard Journal* 40(2): 103–13.

Johnson, H. (2004) *Key Findings from the Drug Use Careers of Female Offenders Study*. Canberra, ACT: Australian Institute of Criminology.

Jones, R., Masters, M., Griffiths, A. and Moulday, N. (2002) 'Culturally relevant assessment of indigenous offenders: A literature review', *Australian Psychologist* 37(3): 187–97.

Kendall, K. (2002) 'Time to think again about cognitive behavioural programmes', in P. Carlen (ed.) *Women and Punishment: The Struggle for Justice*. Cullompton: Willan.

Loucks, N. (2004) 'Women in prison', in G. McIvor (ed.) *Women Who Offend*. London: Jessica Kingsley.

Lovins, L. B., Lowenkamp, C. T., Latessa, E. J. and Smith, P. (2007) 'Application of the risk principle to female offenders', *Journal of Contemporary Criminal Justice* 23(4): 383–98.

Makkai, T. and Payne, J. (2003) Key Findings from the Drug Use Careers of Offenders (DUCO) Study, *Trends & Issues in Crime and Criminal Justice No. 237*. Canberra, ACT: Australian Institute of Criminology.

Manchak, S. M., Skeem, J. L., Douglas, K. S. and Siranosian, M. (2009) 'Does gender moderate the predictive utility of the Level of Service Inventory – Revised (LSI-R) for serious violent offenders?', *Criminal Justice and Behavior* 36(5): 425–42.

Maurutto, P. and Hannah-Moffat, K. (2007) 'Understanding risk in the context of the Youth Criminal Justice Act', *Canadian Journal of Criminology and Criminal Justice* 49(4): 465–91.

Monture-Angus, P. (1999) 'Women and risk: Aboriginal women, colonialism and correctional practice', *Canadian Woman Studies* 19(1 & 2): 24–29.

Morash, M. (2009) 'A great debate over using the Level of Service Inventory-Revised (LSI-R) with women offenders', *Criminology and Public Policy* 8(1): 173–81.

Prime, J., White, S., Liriano, S. and Patel, K. (2001) *Criminal Careers of those Born Between 1953 and 1978, England and Wales*. London: Home Office.

Reisig, M. D., Holtfreter, K. and Morash, M. (2006) 'Assessing recidivism across female pathways to crime', *Justice Quarterly* 23(3): 384–405.

Robinson, G. (2003) 'Implementing OASys: Lessons from research into LSI-R and ACE', *Probation Journal* 50(1): 30–40.

Rugge, T. (2006) *Risk Assessment of Male Aboriginal Offenders: A 2006 Perspective*. Ottawa: Public Safety and Emergency preparedness Canada.

Rumgay, J. (2000) 'Policies of neglect :Female offenders and the Probation Service', in H. Kemshall and R. Littlechild (eds) *Improving Participation and Involvement in Social Care Delivery*. London: Jessica Kingsley.

Salisbury, E. J. and Van Voorhis, P. (2009) 'Gendered pathways: A quantitative investigation of women probationers' paths to incarceration', *Criminal Justice and Behavior* 36(6): 541–66.

Schwalbe, C. S. (2008) 'A meta-analysis of juvenile justice risk assessment instruments: Predictive validity by gender', *Criminal Justice and Behavior* 35(11): 1367–81.

Shaw, M. and Hannah-Moffat, K. (2000) 'Gender, diversity and risk assessment in Canadian Corrections', *Probation Journal* 47(3): 163–72.

———. (2004) 'How cognitive skills forgot about gender and diversity', in G. Mair (ed.) *What Matters in Probation*. Cullompton: Willan.

Shepherd, S. M., Luebbers, S. and Dolan, M. (2013) 'Gender and ethnicity in juvenile risk assessment', *Criminal Justice and Behavior* 40(4): 388–408.

Silver, E. and Miller, L. L. (2002) 'A cautionary note on the use of actuarial risk assessment tools for social control', *Crime and Delinquency* 48(1): 138–61.

Simpson, S. S., Yahner, J. L. and Dugan, L. (2008) 'Understanding women's pathways to jail: Analysing the lives of incarcerated women', *Australian and New Zealand Journal of Criminology* 41(1): 84–108.

Smith, P., Cullen, F. T. and Latessa, E. J. (2009) 'Can 14,737 women be wrong? A meta-analysis of the LSI-R and recidivism for female offenders', *Criminology and Public Policy* 8(1): 183–208.

Taylor, K. N. and Blanchette, K. (2009) 'The women are not wrong: It is the approach that is debatable', *Criminology and Public Policy* 8(1): 221–29.

Van der Knaap, L. M., Albreda, D. L., Oosterveld, P. and Born, M. Ph. (2011) 'The predictive validity of criminogenic needs for male and female offenders: Comparing the relative impact of needs in predicting recidivism', *Law and Human Behavior* 36(5): 413–22.

Van Voorhis, P. and Presser. L. (2001) *Classification of Women Offenders: A National Assessment of Current Practices*. Washington, DC: US Department of Justice, National Institute of Corrections.

Van Voorhis, P., Salisbury, E., Wright, E. M. and Bauman, A. (2008) *Achieving Accurate Pictures of Risk and Identifying Gender Responsive Needs: Two New Assessments for Women Offenders*.www.cjresources.com/CJ_Female %20Offenders_pdfs/Accurate%20pictures%20of%20risk%20two%20 new%20assesments%20for%20women%20offenders%20-%20Van%20 Voorhis%20et%20al%202008.pdf. Accessed on 15.8.2012.

Van Voorhis, P., Wright, E.M., Salisbury, E. and Bauman, A. (2010) 'Women's risk factors and their contributions to existing risk-needs assessment: The current state of a gender responsive supplement', *Criminal Justice and Behavior* 37(3): 261–88.

Walklate, S. and Mythen, G. (2011) 'Beyond risk theory: Experiential knowledge and 'knowing otherwise', *Criminology and Criminal Justice* 11(2): 99–113.

Wright, E. M., Salisbury, E. J. and Van Voorhis, P. (2007) 'Predicting the prison misconducts of women offenders: The importance of gender-responsive needs', *Journal of Contemporary Criminal Justice* 23(4): 310–40.

6

DRUGS, MENTAL DISORDER AND RISK

David Rose

The University of Melbourne, Australia

Introduction

Many individuals who enter and move through the criminal justice system have substance misuse issues and/or mental disorders and are often portrayed as being high risk. It could be argued that substance misuse and mental disorder are in fact the norm for people who offend due to the high prevalence of both these conditions in prisoner populations. However, individuals who experience serious substance misuse and mental disorders present particular challenges for criminal justice systems and broader societal level responses to minimizing the risk of offending. In terms of community response and service delivery, these people can be framed as existing at the intersection of the criminal justice system and the health system, which in practice can mean challenges for effective service delivery across multiple policy, legislative and organizational arenas. Furthermore, people involved in the criminal justice system who have substance misuse and other mental disorders have multiple and complex needs and frequently have histories of homelessness, unemployment, breakdown of family or other supportive relationships, and poor physical health within an overall background of disadvantage.

In a situation of people experiencing multiple and complex needs within a multi-jurisdictional service response, risk also has multiple dimensions. A central focus of the criminal justice system is naturally to reduce the risk of further offending and the resultant impact on the people who offend their families, victims and the broader community. Within the mental health context, risk can be framed as risk to self or others due to mental health issues, and this is often a feature of mental health legislation and justification for mandatory treatment. In the substance use context, risk can be framed around risk of relapse and resultant harms to users, their families and the community, as well as immediate issues such as the risk of death from overdose.

This chapter examines the risk paradigm as it relates to substance misuse and mental disorder within the criminal justice system, recognizing the multifaceted nature of risk for people who experience substance use and mental disorders. First, the chapter provides an overview of the prevalence of drug use and mental disorders within prisoner populations, primarily within Australia but also internationally. It next examines the resultant conceptualizations of risk for this group, especially within the context of an increasing focus on identification and classification of risk, and associated risk reduction interventions within contemporary criminal justice systems. Some practice observations from work in offender support services, primarily in post–release/aftercare contexts, are made and developed through a practice example. The chapter concludes by linking these practice observations to developments in offender rehabilitation such as strengths-based approaches as well as separate but complementary developments in the drug treatment and mental health treatment fields around strengths-based recovery approaches.

The challenge of substance misuse and mental disorder for the criminal justice system

Substance use and misuse is a major challenge for criminal justice systems around the world. A substantial proportion of the estimated 10.2 million people currently incarcerated globally in prisons are there for drug-related offences such as use, possession or supply of drugs (UNODC, 2014). Regardless of the type of offence, people in prison frequently have higher rates of substance misuse than the general population prior, during and post imprisonment (EMCDDA, 2012). A systematic review of international studies of prisoner entry characteristics found estimated prevalence rates for alcohol dependence and abuse of between 18 to 30% for males and 10% to 24% for females and the estimated prevalence rates for abuse and dependence of other drugs of 10% to 48% for males and 30% to 60% for females. In general, these prevalence rates for substance use were many times higher than the general population prevalence rates across the different jurisdictions examined (Fazel, Bains and Doll, 2006). In Australia, the most recent Prisoner Health Data Collection (NPHCD) conducted in 2012 with samples drawn from all Australian prisons found similarly high prevalence rates of substance use issues. At the point of prison entry, 70% of the sample reported that they had used illicit drugs in the previous

12 months, and 46% reported consuming alcohol at levels likely to cause harm during the previous 12 months. Histories of injecting drug use were also common, with 46% of prison entrants reporting injecting drug use previously at some point in their lifetime. At the point of release from prison, 13% reported having continued to use illicit drugs and 7% to have injected drugs during their imprisonment (AIHW, 2013).

While problematic substance use can be seen as almost normative for people involved in the criminal justice system, other mental health disorders are also highly prevalent. Despite limitations due to differences in definitions and practices across jurisdictions, a systematic review of 62 international studies from 12 countries into mental disorder prevalence rates in prison populations found 3.7% to 4.0% had psychotic disorders, 10% to 12% had major depressive disorders and 42% to 65% had personality disorders, all at substantially higher rates than would be expected in the general population (Fazel & Danesh, 2002). Furthermore, given that a high proportion of people in prison report histories of trauma and abuse, it is estimated that around 20% experience post-traumatic stress disorder (Fazel and Baillargeon, 2011). An Australian study found a substantial overrepresentation of mental health issues for a sample of people in prison compared to a matched community sample. The 12-month prevalence of mental disorders (including substance use disorders) was 80% in the prison group compared to 31% in the community sample (Butler et al., 2006). The overrepresentation of mental disorders in prison compared to the general population continues to be a matter of concern in the Australian context, as it does in other countries. The most recent Australian National Report Card on Mental Health and Suicide Prevention notes that 38% of people entering prison in 2012 had been told by a professional that they had a mental illness and that approximately 33% of the people currently in prison who had a mental illness had previously been in prison five times or more (NMHC, 2013).

Overall, it can be concluded that substance misuse issues and mental disorders are highly prevalent amongst people who have offended and that individuals with these conditions are overrepresented within prisons and the criminal justice system more generally. There are also high rates of co-occurring substance misuse and other mental disorders (dual diagnosis or co-morbidity) within prison populations, although exact prevalence rates are difficult to establish (EMCDDA, 2012). A study of dual diagnosis prevalence in an Australian sample of 1208 prisoners found that, while 17.8% had a substance use disorder alone and 17.1% had a mental health disorder alone, 41.2% had co-morbid substance use and mental health disorders. Co-morbidity was associated with higher rates of reoffending, with 67% of the co-morbid group reoffending within two years of release compared to 55% of those with substance use disorder alone and 49% of those with a mental disorder alone (Smith & Trimboli, 2010). A study into dual diagnosis rates in a secure forensic hospital in Australia found similar high rates, with 74% of patients having a lifetime diagnosis of substance abuse or dependence in addition to a primary mental disorder (Ogloff, Lemphers and Dwyer, 2004).Involvement in the criminal justice system in combination with substance misuse and mental health problems, either alone or concurrently, results in a complex and interconnected array of health and criminal justice-related needs. As a group these people experience substantial social disadvantage. Upon release from prison they frequently face many barriers related not only to their criminal justice issues but also to poor health, lack of housing, limited employment opportunities and social isolation (Baldry, McDonnell, Maplestone and Peeters, 2003; Treloar and Holt, 2008).

Substance misuse, mental disorder and risk

The high prevalence rates of substance misuse and mental disorder amongst people in prisons is likely to be due to a number of factors. These include the individual situations and context of people who enter prisons with these issues as well as aspects of the health and community service system and the criminal justice system that struggle to meet the needs of individuals with multiple and complex needs. For example, the high rates of these disorders in prisoners could be related to associations between some substance misuse and violent crime (Fazel and Baillargeon, 2011). Furthermore, people who have serious mental disorders and substance misuse issues frequently experience high levels of social exclusion. Social exclusion can be seen as both a cause and consequence of these conditions (Buchanan, 2004; Tew, 2011) and ultimately may be a significant factor in people entering or re-entering the criminal justice system. Conversely, the overrepresentation of mental disorder and substance misuse in prisons may be due to a range of system factors such as failure to divert individuals with these conditions from the criminal justice system to the health system, or poor systems of identification and intervention for these conditions once people enter prisons. Similarly, it may be due to the general limitations of the mental health and drug treatment systems in the community that fail to prevent people with these issues becoming involved in the criminal justice system in the first place (Fazel and Baillargeon, 2011). Whether mental and substance misuse disorders are perceived as causal factors for offending, or the high prevalence of these disorders in prisoner populations is attributed to inadequate treatment and support systems in the community, these disorders are logically significant risk factors linked to offending.

Any discussion about the criminal justice system, mental disorder, substance misuse and risk needs to be framed within the context of broader conceptualizations of risk and the increasing focus on risk and risk management in society more generally (see Robinson and McNeill, this volume). Modern society has been framed as the 'risk society' (Beck, 1992) with its preoccupation on identifying and managing risks in all facets of life. This is opposed to the pre-Industrial Revolution, where risk-related events were viewed more as the result of fate rather than manageable and predictable events. Explanations for the rise in the prominence of risk in modern societies vary, as do perceptions of the consequences of this focus on risk. A whole new industry has developed around risk management as evidenced by risk management processes, accreditation systems, risk identification systems and associated insurance against the impacts of risk-related events that do occur. Broadly, these developments can be conceptualized as efforts to overcome the inherent uncertainty of modern society (Jennings and Pycroft, 2012).

The 'risk society' thesis stresses the changes that have taken place in late-modern societies. These include scientific and industrial changes and other factors such as globalization and rapid social and economic change that have presented a range of new risks and challenged the protections afforded individuals through traditional family and community structures. A second major perspective on the rise of the risk focus is linked to Foucault's 'governmentality' and the range of neoliberal-influenced reforms made by governments in the post–welfare state era. These reforms have tended to shift responsibility for managing risks away from government to individuals and families, such as the move from social protectionist government programmes to programmes focused on individual responsibility and mutual obligation (Green, 2007). Regardless of the explanation for the rise in prominence of risk generally, in the human services and statutory service provision such as corrections and mental health treatment it is argued that there have been significant, often undesirable, consequences of this change. These include a focus on risks at the expense of addressing needs, a preoccupation with predicting risky events and the associated need to apportion 'blame' when things go wrong (Green, 2007; Kemshall, 2010; Sawyer, 2008).

Within this broader context, the prediction and management of risk has become a major focus of the criminal justice system. This has been a particularly important development in relation to those people who have mental disorders and substance misuse issues, who are routinely portrayed as high risk. Consistent with the rise in risk prediction and attempts to manage and control risk in the criminal justice system, it has been suggested that there is a similar rise in fear and anxiety about the potential consequences of crime in the broader community (Clift, 2012). In the case of people with a mental illness who offend, community perceptions about the risk of reoffending are also shaped by broader perceptions about mental health and illness and the linking of risk to notions of dangerousness. The link between mental disorder and violence is much debated, although recent research suggests there is an increased likelihood of violent offending for some sub-groups of people who experience mental illness. This includes individuals who have some forms of schizophrenia, particularly where there is co-morbid substance misuse (Bennett et al., 2011; Short, Thomas, Mullen and Ogloff, 2013). However, this association is not consistent for all people who experience schizophrenia or mental illness generally, or in fact all mentally disordered offenders. Nevertheless, media portrayals of these people who have offended often strongly represent them as being high risk and potentially, or actually, dangerous, which subsequently drives community and political perceptions and subsequent policy and practice decisions (Prins, 2010).

In terms of the criminal justice system, while the primary focus of concern about risk in relation to people who experience mental disorders or substance misuse is about dangerousness and likelihood of reoffending, it is also important to recognize the risks to the self that these disorders present. For example, suicide and self-harm incidents linked to mental health and substance use are highly prevalent in prison populations (AIHW, 2013; Hawton, Linsell, Adeniji, Sariaslan, and Fazel, 2014), and there are high rates of communicable diseases such as HIV and Hepatitis B and C linked to injecting drug use prior to or during imprisonment (Fazel and Baillargeon, 2011). While for many people in prison the period of incarceration presents the opportunity for stabilization of mental health issues and a reduction in substance use, upon release their health status often rapidly deteriorates, especially when in addition to these health issues many ex-prisoners generally experience difficulties with accessing accommodation, employment and other social supports (AIHW, 2013). Consequently, release from prison, while involving potential risks of reoffending, is also a particularly crucial period of risk for the health and well-being of all people who have been in prison, but particularly those with mental health and substance misuse issues. People who have been recently released from prison experience much higher mortality related to suicide and drug overdose compared to the general community in the first 12 months following release, and particularly in the first four weeks post release. They also experience high rates of hospitalization due to physical and mental health issues (Kinner et al., 2013). The risks for these individuals related to mental and substance misuse disorders are substantial. Effectively addressing these issues can be important, not only for reducing the risk of further offending, but also on public health and human rights grounds (Kinner and Wang, 2014).

The preceding discussion has outlined the centrality of risk to conceptualizations of, and criminal justice practice with, people experiencing mental and substance misuse disorders. This can be framed in relation to the increased risk this group presents to community safety through potential dangerous behaviour and the inherent uncertainty of their actions, or the very real risks of self-harm these people experience due to the nature of their mental health and substance use issues. Furthermore, this focus on risk is taking place within a broader sociopolitical climate of 'penal populism' and being 'tough on crime' (Pratt, 2007). Political parties compete on the hardness of their law and order platforms and governments know the electoral benefits of being perceived as 'tough on crime'. The result of this is frequently policies of more severe sentencing, a focus on punishment at the expense of rehabilitation and reintegration efforts, and an ever-increasing prison population, as is currently evidenced in many developed countries.

Within this context the effective assessment and prediction of risk and associated rehabilitation efforts has been considered crucial. In the last two decades the predominant rehabilitation approach within most criminal justice systems in developed countries has been the risk-need-responsivity (RNR) model (Bonta and Andrews, 2010). A key element of this approach is assessing and targeting of dynamic risk factors/criminogenic needs (e.g. substance use or pro-criminal attitudes) that are causally related to offending primarily through psychological interventions matched to assessed level of risk. The RNR approach has a growing evidence base for its effectiveness as a risk assessment and rehabilitation approach (Bonta and Andrews, 2010), and it has been influential in work with mentally disordered and substance-misusing people in the criminal justice system.

However, there has been a growing critique of the RNR model's narrower focus on risk aspects and on personal traits and deficits at the expense of examining the influence of broader contextual factors that might have influenced offending. Linked to this are concerns about the model's capacity to address all of the issues likely to influence a person's desistance from offending, particularly in the context of reintegration endeavours following release from prison (Fox, 2014; Ward and Maruna, 2007). Various emerging approaches which can be broadly categorized as strengths-based models are gaining increasing influence. These approaches appear to have particular relevance for people in the criminal justice system who experience mental health and substance misuse disorders given the strong influence of the broader social context and social consequences for this group. In the next part of this chapter, a practice example will be used to examine the potential of this growing emphasis on strengths-based approaches from both the criminal justice perspective and from the mental health and substance misuse treatment perspectives.

Practice example – Tom

Tom had spent a considerable proportion of his teenage and adult years in either youth justice centres, prisons or psychiatric hospitals. He had been diagnosed with paranoid schizophrenia in his early twenties, had a long history of using amphetamines and periods of heavy alcohol consumption as well as frequent instances of self-harm. He had been convicted of more than 60 previous offences (mostly thefts and assaults and an attempted murder) and had a history of aggressive behaviour towards his family members and workers in support and treatment services. He originally came from a rural area where his extended family still lived, and he strongly expressed a preference to return there, even though he recognized he was 'known' and had often been ostracized in the community due to his past high-profile history in that area. The family had repeatedly attempted to gain appropriate assistance for their son, but despite many attempts – for example, in just one year 23 visits to a GP and frequent visits to the local hospital emergency department following suicide attempts – an appropriate service response had been difficult to achieve. The only way the family ultimately received a response was when a family member agreed to contact police and Tom was charged for seriously assaulting the family member.

Tom subsequently spent many years revolving between periods of incarceration in prison, periods in a forensic mental health secure hospital and short periods living in the community. The periods living in the community were characterized by a release/discharge into short-term, low-standard crisis and rooming house accommodation and a quite rapid spiralling of Tom's situation into chaotic behaviour, poor mental and physical health, increasing substance abuse and ultimately further offending and fear-inducing behaviour.

When he was 45 years old, Tom was referred to a transitional support service during a term of imprisonment. He was linked to an outreach support worker while in prison, who continued to work with him over the longer term following his release. He was also connected with community treatment services for his mental health and drug use issues. Unlike other times when he had been released from prison, rather than being accommodated in a crisis rooming house, he was able to live in his own rented unit through the transitional support service. This provided a new experience for him – a place to look after and call his 'own' – but most importantly, a secure base from which to start making connections in the community. Through a recovery-focused community mental health organization, he developed some friendships with other people in his local area and after some time was able to start working in a part-time job and to have some limited contacts with his broader family. Given his history, the risk of reoffending continued to be on the minds of both Tom and people connected with him, although as time went on his confidence in being able to manage his mental health and substance use issues grew. In his own words, he now had 'something to lose' by going back to prison.

Tom's example is typical of individuals who experience significant mental and substance misuse disorders as well as involvement in the criminal justice system. On the one hand, the nature of his mental disorder and substance misuse issues along with his history of offending meant he was assessed as being at high risk for further offending. On the other hand, he was able to make substantial progress towards desisting from crime, progress in his mental health recovery and a reduction in harmful drug use when given opportunities at a stage of his life when he was able to capitalize on them. Whether due to a process of natural maturation and desistance, or as a result of the recovery-focused services he received, he was able to make changes in his life which might not have been possible if his situation was framed only from the perspective of the risks he presented to himself and others.

From the author's experience developing, managing and evaluating transitional reintegration programmes for high-risk/high-need offenders with mental and substance misuse disorders (see for example, Rose, 1999; Rose and James, 1996; Ross, 2003), Tom's example highlights some of the challenges and possibilities in this work. People who experience these issues are released from prison and move through the transition process to living in the community while facing many complex challenges. They frequently have long histories of involvement in the criminal justice system and the perception of being both at high risk of reoffending and likely to fail, given their history of reoffending on past releases from prison. They experience difficulties managing both their mental health and substance use, which are often associated with reoffending, and they frequently return to live in difficult conditions in the community with poor accommodation, limited supportive relationships with family or friends and limited scope for employment or other activities. While they have often undertaken psychological-based programmes and interventions during their imprisonment designed, for example, to reduce the risk of drug-related offending, it can be difficult to maintain the progress made in these programmes through the transition process. It is not surprising that individuals living in poor accommodation with few or no significant supports or relationships, and possibly little hope for the future, might then struggle with their mental health or problematic drug use and subsequently reoffend. Conversely, practice experience indicates that even individuals with the most difficult and complex circumstances, when given the necessary supports, resources and opportunities can build relationships and connections in the community that build resilience and ultimately enhance their capacity to desist from offending and their recovery process. Risk-focused assessments and associated interventions such as psychological-based programmes to reduce the risk of drug-related offending are important, but only one part of the process.

Future developments

Tom's practice example highlights some of the dilemmas in working with and responding to individuals who have offended and who have mental and substance misuse disorders. Assessment of risk and the potential for further offending and/or harm to others is obviously a critical aspect to be considered. However, the complex and disadvantaged backgrounds of this group of people call for approaches that can help individuals recognize and develop personal assets, strengths and the capacity to live a meaningful and fulfilling life. This can in turn potentially provide resilience against further offending or relapse. Over the last decade, there has been an increasing interest in strengths-based approaches within the criminal justice system that offer the hope of building this resilience while also managing risk. Interestingly, parallel developments have been taking place in the mental health and drug treatment fields, with the increasing adoption of strength-based recovery approaches.

In the criminal justice context, the Good Lives Model (GLM) is a strength-based approach that aims to '(a) promote offenders' aspirations and plans for better lives, as well as (b) manage/reduce their risk to the community' (Ward, 2010, p. 50). As an approach, the GLM contends that people who have offended, similar to other people in the community, have needs and aspirations and seek 'primary human goods' such as inner peace, relatedness with others, happiness, creativity and so on, although offenders' life histories often mean they have had less than ideal circumstances to achieve these 'goods'. Although the GLM model has sometimes been framed as a critique and alternative to the predominant RNR approach, it has been argued that there are common elements across both approaches. While the RNR model focusses on deficits and risk factors, the GLM focusses on the conditions necessary to achieve a state that would reduce the risk (Ward and Maruna, 2007). Another complementary body of work in the criminal justice area that has sought to move beyond a deficits focus has been the desistance paradigm, which aims to understand 'how and why' people stop offending (McNeill, Farrall, Lightowler and Maruna, 2012). Originally drawing on observations about natural desistance, including the fact that most individuals desist from offending as they get older, approaches within the desistance paradigm concentrate on elements such as the natural and assisted development of social capital, prosocial bonds and self-identity and how these encourage desistance from further offending (Maruna and LeBel, 2010).

In largely separate but complementary developments, the mental health treatment field has seen an increasing prominence of a strengths-based orientation, primarily through the adoption of the recovery approach. The recovery approach in mental health has its foundations in the mental health consumer movements of the 1970s and 1980s, and a widely used definition of the process of recovery is '... a deeply personal, unique process of changing one's attitudes, values, feelings, goals, skills, and/or roles. It is a way of living a satisfying, hopeful, and contributing life even with limitations caused by illness. Recovery involves the development of new meaning and purpose in one's life as one grows beyond the catastrophic effects of mental illness' (Anthony, 1993, p. 17). Many mental health services in Australia, the United Kingdom and the United States are adopting a recovery approach, although there is considerable variation in how the approach is operationalized. Within the more widespread adoption of recovery approaches, a useful distinction is made between clinical recovery and personal recovery. Clinical recovery can be seen as the traditional goals of mental health treatment and includes a reduction in symptoms and return of social functioning, while personal recovery is an individual's ongoing process of recovery including developing hope for the future, self-identity, personal responsibility and meaning in life (Slade, 2013). Recovery-oriented practice provides an approach by which services can move from a clinical recovery focus to one in which individuals are supported and facilitated in their own personal recovery process. Gradually, recovery-oriented practice approaches are also being adopted in forensic mental health services, including highly secure services for serious offenders, although it is recognized that the necessarily risk-focused environment of these services presents particular challenges for the adoption of a recovery approach. However, it is argued, and is increasingly being demonstrated in practice, that it is possible to develop a forensic mental health service that appropriately identifies and manages risk while also providing an environment with a culture of hope that recognizes people as individuals with strengths and limitations, not just as the sum of their risk profiles (Ayres, Fegan and Noak, 2014; Dorkins and Adshead, 2011; Hillbrand, Young and Griffith, 2010; Simpson and Penney, 2011).

Recovery in substance misuse treatment has typically been associated with 12-step approaches such as Alcoholics Anonymous but more recently has seen a trend towards more widespread adoption of recovery principles in treatment, drawing on the developments around recovery in mental health (Best and Lubman, 2012). The language of recovery has increasingly been incorporated in drug policy frameworks in the United Kingdom and Australia and is demonstrated by the definition adopted by the Scottish Government of recovery being '... a process through which an individual is enabled to move on from their problem drug use, towards a drug-free life as an active and contributing member of society. Furthermore, it incorporates the principle that recovery is most effective when service users' needs and aspirations are placed at the centre of their care and treatment. In short, an aspirational, person-centred process' (Scottish Government, 2008). Problematic substance use is often characterized as a chronic relapsing condition that for many people can involve years of repeated relapses before abstinence or a reduction in harmful drug use is achieved, whether as part of formal treatment or by the person's own accord. Within the recovery perspective, recovery is seen as more than just ceasing the drug use. The ongoing recovery journey is likely to be influenced by the development and growth of an individual's 'recovery capital' such as social networks, supportive relationships, meaningful and reciprocal community relationships and overall quality of life (Best et al., 2012; Laudet and White, 2008; Lyons and Lurigio, 2010).

There are many commonalities between these emerging strengths-based approaches in the criminal justice, mental health and substance misuse contexts. In terms of people who have offended and who experience mental disorder and substance misuse, the development of strength-based approaches provides the opportunity for more consistent and integrated service responses between criminal justice, mental health treatment and drug treatment, whereas historically, service delivery has been quite fragmented. All the approaches recognize that individuals have strengths and abilities as well as deficits with associated needs, the centrality of hope, the inherent potential people have for growth and change, and the importance of having meaning in life. Just as it is important for individuals to reach the point of initially desisting from offending, stabilizing their mental health or ceasing problematic substance misuse, it is also important for people and the service system to be oriented towards the necessary elements that will enable ongoing desistance from crime and personal recovery.

Conclusion

This chapter discusses the potential of moving beyond the risk paradigm and associated approaches to offender assessment and rehabilitation that focus primarily on risk, to approaches that incorporate broader aspects of strengths, desistance and personal recovery. These approaches recognize individual strengths and the capacity for growth and change, and seem particularly applicable to the complex and frequently disadvantaged circumstances of most people who have offended and who have mental health and/or substance misuse issues. It is a given that the identification and management of risk will always be a critical element of working with this group of people. These individuals present with complex histories and unpredictability related to their mental and substance misuse disorders, and experience marginalization both within the service system and within the broader community. The potential risk of dangerousness and further offending should be an ever-present concern. However, the emerging strengths-based approaches provide the opportunity to take a broader focus beyond just the narrow risk presentation. These approaches have the potential to facilitate ways of working with people who have offended that build on an individual's own strengths and abilities, while also resulting in less risk of offending and enabling personal recovery and well-being.

References

AIHW. (2013). *The Health of Australia's Prisoners 2012*. Canberra: Australian Institute of Health and Welfare (AIHW).

Anthony, W. (1993). 'Recovery from mental illness: The guiding vision of the mental health service system in the 1990's', *Psychosocial Rehabilitation Journal* 16(4): 11–23.

Ayres, J., Fegan, T. and Noak, J. (2014). 'The recovery orientation of patients and staff in a high secure hospital', *Mental Health Practice* 17(7): 20–24.

Baldry, E., McDonnell, D., Maplestone, P. and Peeters, M. (2003). *Ex-Prisoners and Accommodation: What Bearing Do Different Forms of Housing Have on Social Reintegration?* Melbourne: Australian Housing and Urban Research Institute.

Beck, U. (1992). *Risk Society: Towards a New Modernity*. London: Sage.

Bennett, D. J., Ogloff, J. R. P., Mullen, P. E., Thomas, S. D. M., Wallace, C. and Short, T. (2011). 'Schizophrenia disorders, substance abuse and prior offending in a sequential series of 435 homicides', *Acta Psychiatrica Scandinavica* 124(3): 226–33. doi: 10.1111/j.1600-0447.2011.01731.x.

Best, D., Gow, J., Knox, T., Taylor, A., Groshkova, T. and White, W. (2012). 'Mapping the recovery stories of drinkers and drug users in Glasgow: Quality of life and its associations with measures of recovery capital', *Drug and Alcohol Review* 31(3): 334–41. doi: 10.1111/j.1465-3362.2011.00321.x.

Best, D. and Lubman, D. (2012). 'The recovery paradigm: A model of hope and change for alcohol and drug addiction', *Australian Family Physician* 41(8): 593–97.

Bonta, J. and Andrews, D. (2010). 'Viewing offender assessment and rehabilitation through the lens of the risk-need-responsivity model', in F. McNeill, P. Raynor and C. Trotter (eds) *Offender Supervision: New Directions in Theory, Research and Practice*. Oxon: Willan Publishing.

Buchanan, J. (2004). 'Tackling problem drug use: A new conceptual framework', *Social Work in Mental Health* 2(2&3): 117–38.

Butler, T., Andrews, G., Allnutt, S., Sakashita, C., Smith, N. E. and Basson, J. (2006). 'Mental disorders in Australian prisoners: a comparison with a community sample', *Australian and New Zealand Journal of Psychiatry* 40(3): 272–76. doi: doi:10.1080/j.1440-1614.2006.01785.x.

Clift, S. (2012). 'Chapter 2: Risk, assessment and the practice of actuarial criminal justice', in A. Pycroft and S. Clift (eds) *Risk and Rehabilitation: Management and Treatment of Substance Misuse and Mental Health Problems in the Criminal Justice System*. Bristol: The Policy Press.

Dorkins, E. and Adshead, G. (2011). 'Working with offenders: challenges to the recovery agenda', *Advances in Psychiatric Treatment* 17: 178–87.

EMCDDA. (2012). *Prisons and Drugs in Europe: The Problem and Responses* Lisbon: European Monitoring Centre for Drugs and Drug Addiction (EMCDDA).

Fazel, S. and Baillargeon, J. (2011). 'The health of prisoners', *The Lancet* 377(9769), 956–65. doi: http://dx.doi.org/10.1016/S0140-6736(10)61053-7. DOI: 10.1016/S0140-6736(10)61053-7. Accessed on 21/1/15.

Fazel, S., Bains, P. and Doll, H. (2006). 'Substance abuse and dependence in prisoners: a systematic review', *Addiction* 101(2): 181–91. doi: 10.1111/j.1360-0443.2006.01316.x.

Fazel, S. and Danesh, J. (2002). 'Serious mental disorder in 23 000 prisoners: a systematic review of 62 surveys', *The Lancet* 359(9306), 545–50. doi: http://dx.doi.org/10.1016/S0140-6736(02)07740-1. Accessed on 21/1/15.

Fox, K. (2014). 'Restoring the social: Offender reintegration in a risky world', *International Journal of Comparative and Applied Criminal Justice* 38 (3) 235–56.

Green, D. (2007). 'Risk and social work practice', *Australian Social Work* 60 (4) 395–409.

Hawton, K., Linsell, L., Adeniji, T., Sariaslan, A. and Fazel, S. (2014). 'Self-harm in prisons in England and Wales: an epidemiological study of prevalence, risk factors, clustering, and subsequent suicide', *The Lancet* 383 (9923) 1147–54. doi: http://dx.doi.org/10.1016/S0140-6736(13)62118-2.

Hillbrand, M., Young, J. L. and Griffith, E. E. H. (2010). 'Managing risk and recovery: Redefining miscibility of oil and water', *Journal of the American Academy of Psychiatry and the Law Online* 38 (4) 452–56.

Jennings, P. and Pycroft, A. (2012). 'The numbers game: a systems perspective on risk', in A. Pycroft and S. Clift (eds) *Risk and Rehabilitation: Management and treatment of Substance Misuse and Mental Health Problems in the Criminl Justice System*. Bristol: The Policy Press.

Kemshall, H. (2010) 'Risk rationalities in contemporary social work policy and practice', *British Journal of Social Work* 40 (4) 1247–62. doi: 10.1093/bjsw/bcp157.

Kinner, S., Lennox, N., Williams, G., Carroll, M., Quinn, B., Boyle, F. and Alati, R. (2013). 'Randomised controlled trial of a service brokerage intervention for ex-prisoners in Australia', *Contemporary Clinical Trials* 36: 198–206.

Kinner, S. and Wang, E. (2014). 'The case for improving the health of ex-prisoners', *American Journal of Public Health* 104(8): 1352–55.

Laudet, A. B. and White, W. L. (2008). 'Recovery capital as prospective predictor of sustained recovery, life satisfaction, and stress among former poly-substance users', *Substance Use & Misuse* 43(1): 27–54. doi: doi:10.1080/10826080701681473.

Lyons, T. and Lurigio, A. J. (2010). 'The role of recovery capital in the community reentry of prisoners with substance use disorders', [Article]. *Journal of Offender Rehabilitation* 49 (7) 445–55. doi: 10.1080/10509674.2010.510769.

Maruna, S. and LeBel, T. (2010). 'The desistance paradigm in correctional practice: from programmes to lives', in F. McNeill, P. Raynor and C. Trotter (eds) *Offender Supervision: New Directions in Theory, Research and Practice*. Oxon: Willan Publishing.

McNeill, F., Farrall, S., Lightowler, C. and Maruna, S. (2012). *How and Why People Stop Offending: Discovering Desistance*. Glasgow: Institute for Research and Innovation in Social Services (IRISS).

NMHC. (2013). *A Contributing Life: The 2013 National Report Card on Mental Health and Suicide Prevention*. Sydney: National Mental Health Commission (NMHC).

Ogloff, J. R. P., Lemphers, A. and Dwyer, C. (2004). 'Dual diagnosis in an Australian forensic psychiatric hospital: prevalence and implications for services', [Article]. *Behavioral Sciences & the Law* 22(4): 543–62.

Pratt, J. (2007). *Penal Populism*. New York: Routledge.

Prins, H. (2010). 'Dangers by being despised grow great', in M. Nash and A. Williams (eds) *The Handbook of Public Protection*. Oxon: Willan.

Rose, D. (1999). *Evaluation of a Community Forensic Psychiatric Support Program*. Thesis (M S W), University of Melbourne, Dept. of Social Work, 1999. Retrieved from http://repository.unimelb.edu.au/10187/9725. Accessed on 3/12/14.

Rose, D. and James, L. (1996). *The assertive Outreach to Forensic Psychiatric Clients and their Families Project : Report*. Melbourne: Epistle Post Release Service.

Ross, S. (2003). *Bridging the Gap: A Release Transition Support Program for Victorian Prisoners. Final Evaluation Report*. Melbourne: Victorian Department of Justice/ Criminology Research and Evaluation Unit, University of Melbourne.

Sawyer, A. (2008). 'Risk and new exclusions in community mental health practice. [Article]', *Australian Social Work* 61(4): 327–41. doi: 10.1080/03124070802428183.

Scottish Government. (2008). *The Road to Recovery: A New Approach to Tackling Scotland's Drug Problem*. Edinburgh: Scottish Government.

Short, T., Thomas, S., Mullen, P. and Ogloff, J.R.P. (2013). 'Comparing violence in schizophrenia patients with and without comorbid substance-use disorders to community controls', *Acta Psychiatrica Scandinavica* 128(4): 306–13. doi: 10.1111/acps.12066.

Simpson, A. I. F. and Penney, S. R. (2011). 'The recovery paradigm in forensic mental health services. [Article]', *Criminal Behaviour & Mental Health* 21(5): 299–306. doi: 10.1002/cbm.823.

Slade, M. (2013). *100 Ways to Support Recovery* (2nd. edn.). London: Rethink Mental Illness.

Smith, N. E. and Trimboli, L. (2010). *Comorbid Substance and Non-Substance Mental Health Disorders and Re-Offending among NSW Prisoners.* Sydney: NSW Bureau of Crime Statistics and Research.

Tew, J. (2011). *Social Approaches to Mental Distress.* Houndsmill: Palgrave Macmillan.

Treloar, C. and Holt, M. (2008). 'Complex vulnerabilities as barriers to treatment for illicit drug users with high prevalence mental health co-morbidities', *Mental Health and Substance Use* 1(1): 84–95. doi: 10.1080/17523280701759755.

UNODC. (2014). *World Drug Report 2014.* Vienna: The United Nations Office on Drugs and Crime (UNODC).

Ward, T. (2010). 'The Good Lives Model of offender rehabilitation: basic assumptions, aetiological commitments, and practice implications', in F. McNeill, P. Raynor and C. Trotter (eds) *Offender Supervision: New Directions in Theory, Research and Practice.* Oxon: Willan Publishing.

Ward, T. and Maruna, S. (2007). *Rehabilitation: Beyond the Risk Paradigm.* Oxon: Routledge.

7

PROGRAMMES FOR DOMESTIC VIOLENCE PERPETRATORS

Dave Morran
University of Stirling, UK

Introduction

Group-work programmes for domestic violence perpetrators emerged in the UK in the early 1990s (Scourfield, 1995; Gadd, 2004). As in the United States, their development encountered considerable resistance from feminist activists committed to supporting female victims/survivors who suffered at the hands of such men. Early, somewhat equivocal evaluations of North American programmes (e.g. Eisikovits and Edleson, 1989; Edleson and Grusznski, 1989) fuelled their anxieties. Concerns were expressed that they held out an (unrealistic) hope for women that men would change as a consequence of attending them, and that, whereas organizations like Women's Aid had struggled to raise awareness of this problem (and the resources to address it), the dubious 'promise' of perpetrator programmes would overturn the nature of service provision, with refuge funding becoming subordinated to unproven interventions with violent, abusive men (Horley, 1990; Scourfield, 1995; Hague and Malos, 2005).

Despite these concerns perpetrator programmes evolved considerably from their origins in the non-statutory sector. They established an early foothold within Criminal Justice Social Work services in Scotland and have developed substantially over the last 15 years within the Probation Service in England and Wales. Throughout this period there have been a number of significant theoretical, pragmatic and policy influences which have shaped their trajectories and priorities in both statutory and non-statutory sectors. This chapter examines some of these influences. In doing so it explores why there has been a gradual shift from a systemically focused, risk-driven paradigm of practice to one that acknowledges the heterogeneity of men on programmes, the various factors which may underpin or sustain their abusive behaviour and what may need to be in place to support men's desistance from abuse. Some examples of how practice has been re-appraised in order to engage more positively and achieve more sustainable outcomes for men on programmes, and consequently for those intimate others directly affected by their behaviour, is also considered.

Programmes for perpetrators: Early beginnings

Programmes for men who are violent and abusive in relationships (hereafter perpetrator programmes) originated in the United States in the 1980s. They varied considerably in their analyses of the causes of men's violence and abuse and their consequential practices with men (Pirog-Good and Stets Kealey, 1985). Situated in a 'therapeutic society' which perceived complex, cultural and political issues as psychological syndromes (Dobash and Dobash, 1992), many practitioners interpreted men's violence to partners as an individualized, often pathological problem. Its origins were said to lie in the childhood experiences of the men (for which they could not be held fully accountable), or otherwise explained as a problem of dysfunctional family systems which required that 'treatment' be focused on men and women alike, regardless of any power differential between the two. Explanations such as these set their protagonists, many of them participants in a factional and often disparate men's movement (Clatterbaugh, 1990), at odds with women activists who saw the problem of men's violence to women as profoundly social and indeed political.

Gradually, however, feminist perspectives on men's violence gained momentum and leverage, a consequence of social and political activism (Hague and Malos, 2005) and of research (e.g. Martin, 1976; Dobash and Dobash, 1979), which sought to illustrate the functional intent behind men's abuse in relationships. Psychotherapeutically influenced interventions were increasingly challenged by the alternative perspectives of interpretative and feminist researchers and practitioners working with this abuse (Dobash and Dobash, 1992). These perspectives underpinned the emergence of so-called pro-feminist programmes for abusive men which allied themselves with the women's movement, interpreted men's violence as functional – a consequence of patriarchal power and control – and as behaviour requiring criminal sanction. The most significant of these pro-feminist programmes was the model pioneered in Duluth, Minnesota, by Ellen Pence and Michael Paymar (Pence and Paymar, 1993).

The Duluth Model

This 'Duluth Model' has been hugely influential over the last 30 years in the way that interventions with men who are violent and abusive have been developed in the United States, Canada and the United Kingdom, (Bilby and Hatcher, 2004; Bowen, 2011; Gadd, 2004; Morran, 2011). Sometimes misinterpreted as a prescribed curriculum for engaging with violent and abusive men's behaviour, in fact the primary stipulation of the Duluth Model is that the 'men's programme' must be nested within a 'co-ordinated community response' to domestic violence; that is, it should not be a stand-alone intervention, merely one link in a chain of social and legal service provisions whose primary aim is the safety of women/survivors and children (Pence and Paymar, 1993). The second is that engagement with men should ideally form part of a criminal-justice response to men's violence, that is, where the man has been arrested, charged, brought before the court and required to attend the programme, with sanctions enacted if he fails to comply.

The content of the Duluth Men's Programme itself was firmly based on a feminist analysis, the essence of which was that men employed violence and abuse against women in order to establish and maintain power and control over them. They did so largely because their experience of growing up in a patriarchal society had reinforced their sense of entitlement to treat women as being there to do men's bidding. The Power and Control Wheel (App. 1) vividly illustrates this analysis and is a major learning tool used in the programme. While power and control is reinforced overtly through physical and sexual violence, even where the man does not routinely employ these behaviours, he can and will draw on a range of 'tactics of abuse' which allow him to control, intimidate and punish his partner (Pence and Paymar, 1993).

This emphasis on men being socially conditioned to believe they are entitled to behave in abusive ways is significant; it implies that violence is behaviour which is both *learned* and purposeful, (as opposed to 'essential' or pathological forces inside the man). Consequently, as men are capable of learning new skills, attitudes and behaviour, via the didactic educational approach of the programme, they can therefore choose to practise alternative behaviours premised on ideas of equality and partnership. The programme is less concerned with men's own interpretations or 'reasons' for their violence (often redefined as *excuses*) (see, e.g. also Bancroft, 2002), and more inclined to see issues such as men's personal and interpersonal insecurities, or exposure to violence as a child, as tangential factors underpinning their *choice* to be violent.

Will 'What Works?' work for perpetrator programmes?

For the Probation Service in England and Wales, interest in perpetrator programmes coincided with growing discussions on the role 'masculinity' played in offending behaviour (Senior and Woodhill, 1992; Jenkins, 1994; Newburn and Mair, 1996; Potts, 1996; Scourfield, 1998), and significantly, with renewed attention to 'evidence-based practice' and in particular the question of 'what works?' with offending behaviour.

The fallout from Martinson's 'Nothing Works' Report in 1974, and the readiness of politicians to seize on its apparent conclusions to criticize the Probation Service, has been extensively documented elsewhere (e.g. Raynor, 1985; Hollin, 1999; Mair, 2004), as has its impact upon the confidence of the Probation Service (at least at the level of management if less so in actual practice, see e.g. Robinson, 1999). Some resurgence of professional confidence was subsequently propelled, however, by Canadian research (e.g. Gendreau and Ross, 1987; Andrews 1995) and a series of academic and professional studies in the United Kingdom (e.g. McIvor, 1990; Hollin, 1995; McGuire, 1995). This body of work averred that 'effective' practice with offenders was most likely when interventions recognized the levels of risk presented by different types of offender, with intensity of provision allocated accordingly (usually in structured programme format), and offenders' (almost all of them incidentally, male offenders) cognitive skills and attitudes addressed. Successive 'What Works?' conferences throughout the 1990s examined the evidence base and explored lessons from pilot programmes (e.g. Knott, 1995; Roberts, 1995; Raynor and Vanstone, 1997). Frameworks to promote effective practice with offending populations were also proposed, most notably the Risk, Needs and Responsivity Model (Andrews, Bonta and Hoge, 1990).

Within this wider climate of academic and professional scrutiny, domestic violence perpetrator programmes such as that represented by the Duluth Model, with its structured group-work approach, utilization of cognitive-behavioural methods and, significantly, its stipulation that offenders accept personal responsibility for their behaviour, seemed broadly at least to sit alongside other programmes being concurrently developed and piloted in the United Kingdom for various types of offending populations (Mair, 2004; Gadd, 2004).

Official interest in their development was bolstered by the fact that two Scottish prototype programmes operating within a criminal justice context had been evaluated by a jointly funded Home and Scottish Office study, whose findings were broadly favourable, its authors concluding that, 'criminal justice based programmes, in contrast to men sanctioned in other ways, significantly reduced the prevalence and frequency of their violence and significantly suppressed the range and frequency of their controlling and coercive behaviours' (Dobash et al., 1996, p. vii).

While reservations were expressed about methodological limitations of this comparatively small study (Mullender, 2001), this evaluation nevertheless provided encouragement for those whose experiences of engaging directly with male clients on this serious issue had been problematic (Scourfield, 1998), and several practitioners in both probation and voluntary sectors set up similar projects (Scourfield and Dobash, 1999; Gadd 2004). A number of domestic violence programmes flourished during the early 1990s (Scourfield, 1995), which, while influenced by a general set of pro-feminist principles and practices (Eadie and Knight, 2002), varied in the methods, procedures and practices adopted with abusive men (Scourfield and Dobash, 1999).

Standardizing practice: IDAP

Within Probation the initial enthusiasm of practitioners to work innovatively, however, was subsequently restricted by pressures upon management to develop programmes which were standardized and 'replicable' (see, e.g. Singh Bhui and Buchanan, 2004). Consequently, a centrally driven approach to practice with perpetrators (which management could regulate and routinely monitor) was developed. The more autonomous early probation programmes were superseded by two prototype models; the Community Domestic Violence Programme (CDVP), already partially implemented by a minority of Probation Trusts, and the Integrated Domestic Abuse Programme (IDAP), based substantially on the Duluth Model Programme and subsequently adopted by the majority of the Probation sector (Bowen, 2011). IDAP was duly assessed by the Joint Prison/Probation Accreditation Panel in 2003 and rolled out in England and Wales in 2006. By 2008, IDAP programmes were embedded in almost all of the 35 Probation Trusts.

As with the Probation Service's investment in cognitive-behaviourally influenced programmes more generally (see e.g. Mair, 2004), IDAP soon met with criticism, not least from practitioners with experience of programme delivery (Wolf-Light, 2006; Morran, 2008), that it imposed an inflexible, simplistic approach on how practice with perpetrators should be carried out, overlooking the complexities, characteristics and other prevailing problems in these individuals' lives. Additionally, the managerial practices favoured by New Labour imposed pressures on the Probation Service which resulted in a preoccupation with programme procedures, technicalities and completion targets, and less attention to how the project of encouraging and facilitating personal change, the processes by which people desist from offending, might actually be achieved.

An important critique of IDAP's evidence base (and by implication that of Duluth) began increasingly to be voiced, namely that its analysis of men's violence being attributed to patriarchy was simplistic, not to say ideological (e.g. Dixon et al., 2011) and failed to take into account other potential contributory factors underpinning men's violence. David Gadd (2004) has argued, for example, that the reasons why the 'pro-feminist cognitive behavioural model' such as Duluth became the standard in the UK had little to do with being 'evidence-based', but instead conveniently met various needs and interests; the feminist critique of male abuse, the wider priorities and practices of criminal justice and probation systems, and the public's desire to see men punished.

Such a conflation of social policy, managerial and theoretical/ideological interests also overlooked such fundamental issues as the diversity of men on programmes (Gilchrist et al., 2003; Sartin et al., 2006), of what their own needs (criminogenic and otherwise) might be and of what personal change as men, the process of becoming non-abusive, might actually entail, and consequently of how practitioners ought to engage with them. As McNeill has observed elsewhere, a major problem of the 'what works?' paradigm is that it focuses on how practice ought to be constructed, instead of thinking about how the processes of personal change should be understood – 'the absence of a well-developed theory of how rehabilitation occurs is ... problematic.' (2006, p. 45).

Practitioners involved in the delivery of programmes readily observed, of course, that perpetrators' lives frequently involved entrenched difficulties and problems, and that while programmes might furnish them with some skills by which they could 'control' their use of abusive behaviour at home, they minimally equipped men to deal with other challenges and stresses in their lives (Bilby and Hatcher, 2004; Morran, 2006). Indeed, Gondolf (2002) in his significant (and cautiously positive) four-year evaluation of perpetrator programme outcomes had concluded that 'interruptive techniques', that is, 'Time Outs', were often the most that men (and successful completers of programmes at that) had learned; useful only if men chose to use them!

Criticisms were also levelled at the Probation Service (Eadie and Knight, 2002; Bilby and Hatcher, 2004) that practice often overlooked the interests of women or women's services and was therefore unsafe. Men seemed resistant to engage with programme staff, attrition rates were problematic (NOMS, 2008–9) and an anticipated evaluation of outcomes remained elusive (Gadd, 2007; Bowen, 2011). Probation-based practice with perpetrators was increasingly recognized as somewhat static and in need of a substantial re-appraisal of how perpetrators were engaged with, of how possibilities for 'rehabilitation' (if such were possible!) envisaged and workers re-equipped for such a task.

Programmes in the non-statutory sector

Before this re-appraisal of probation practice is addressed, though, it is necessary to examine how interventions with perpetrators had evolved in the non-statutory sector, the other significant provider of programmes in the United Kingdom. While their number continues to fluctuate, not least due to the often problematic short-term nature of funding (Kelly and Westmarland, 2015), Respect, the 'UK association for domestic violence perpetrator programmes and associated women's services', recently recorded 38 programmes operating throughout the country (Respect, 2015).

With origins lying in what Gadd, (2004, p. 174) has described as 'the idiosyncratic preserve of ... psychotherapists and anti-sexist activists', the importance of the non-statutory sector to the development of practice with perpetrators in the United Kingdom has been substantial. The term 'non-statutory' may be misleading, however. Indeed from Gadd's allegedly 'idiosyncratic' beginnings, many such programmes currently engage with men not only on a voluntary basis; increasingly programmes include various combinations of men required to attend or referred by agencies such as Children's Social Work Services or (in England) the Children and Family Court Advisory Service (CAFCASS). The responsibilities and expectations imposed upon programme providers as these partnerships have been pursued, especially concerns in relation to monitoring perpetrators' risk and maximizing children's safety, have been considerable.

The National Practitioners' Network and the Respect Standard

Significant also to the development of programmes was the formation in the early 1990s of the so-called National Practitioners' Network. The NPN (which also included many probation officers) met twice-yearly for almost 20 years with the aim of supporting and developing work with abusive men, enabling discussion and debate and, importantly, forging partnerships and alliances with organizations involved in providing services to victims/survivors of violence. Committed to providing a 'ground-up' experience, its meetings were characterized by an ad-hoc, egalitarian atmosphere. Gradually, working groups of programme practitioners, influenced by and closely associated with victim/survivor advocates and interests, began developing successive 'Statements of Principles and Minimum Standards of Practice for Perpetrator Programmes and Associated Women's Services', that is, victim/partner services (e.g. 1995, 2000, 2004). Following discussions that the membership should form a representative organization, 'Respect' was officially launched in London in March 2001.

As Respect strove to promote practice whose primary stated aim was to increase the safety of women and children, the *Guidelines* which constituted the Statement of Principles were superseded by the more formal (and therefore binding) Respect Accreditation Standard (Respect, 2006; subsequent versions, 2008, 2011, 2012). The development of the Standard caused considerable discussion and some tension among some of the Respect membership, arousing concern, for example that the Standard might become overly prescriptive, thereby influencing, that is, *restricting*, the ownership or development of innovative practice in programmes.

It is important to note that Respect has consistently refuted such concerns (see e.g. Debbonaire, 2012) and sequential versions of the Respect Standard (2006, 2008, 2012) stipulate that the system of accreditation is not aimed at prescribing one specific model of provision, but is instead concerned with providing a strong framework where many different approaches and models can be effectively used. The priority of the Standard significantly has been, and remains, concerned with establishing *systems of delivery* 'so that members of the public, funders, commissioning agencies and other professionals can be assured of a high quality and safety-focused service from organisations that achieve accreditation', (Respect, 2006). Most important among the 'other professionals' are those providing services for victim/survivors and their children. In 2007, Respect (after membership consultation) began the process of 'accrediting' those of its member organizations which satisfied the requirements of the Standard, stating unequivocally that the minimum unit considered for accreditation would consist of a programme working with perpetrators of domestic violence (DVPP) and an Integrated Support Service for partners. 'Organisations running a DVPP without an ISS cannot be considered for accreditation as they are unsafe and will automatically fail' (Respect, 2008, p. 2).

Respect's aims were in this respect therefore laudable. Its prioritization of the safety-focused interests of partners and children, and the need to develop strategic alliances with feminist organizations such as Women's Aid and other agencies providing support to victim/survivors and children are entirely appropriate. However, these important pragmatic priorities arguably had the side effect of subordinating discussions around the evolving theory and practice base of work with abusive and violent men, particularly those applying to various strengths-based and desistance-oriented approaches which increasingly questioned the Duluth Model.

Before examining these approaches, however, it is worthwhile noting in passing that Respect's attention to the importance of systems was also influenced by the findings of the most substantial evaluation (thus far) of perpetrator programmes, conducted by Ed Gondolf and colleagues in the United States (2002). Gondolf, the keynote speaker at Respect's First Annual Conference in London (2004), had produced a generally positive evaluation of four US 'batterer' programmes. Significantly, however, he concluded it was 'the system which matters':

> Our findings … suggest the need for more system development. … The empha-
> sis on system development contrasts with the heightened attention on new
> counselling approaches and innovations. (Gondolf, 2002, p. 199)

In this environment it is perhaps not difficult to see how some of the more independently minded practitioners (particularly those whose motivations were primarily driven by their interest in working with *men*; see Morran, 2008) who had helped pioneer work in this innovative area became subdued by these other cautious, systemic priorities.

As with probation practice, therefore, though for different tactical and strategic interests, the non-statutory sector formally privileged procedural, risk-driven approaches in which the possibilities for alternative, reflective and (dare one say) optimistic practice with perpetrators was (at least formally and publicly) somewhat circumscribed.

Risk assessment and risk management

This is not to suggest that practitioners (even, perhaps especially, optimistic practitioners) ought to overlook the very real risks which perpetrators present to others. For several reasons, including the fact that our understanding of risk around domestic violence and abuse is yet in need of substantial development (Kropp, 2004; Bowen, 2011) and that many programmes work with mixed populations of perpetrators, whose needs and risks vary considerably (see Gilchrist et al., 2003) the Risk, Needs, Responsivity model is not immediately transferable to practice with domestic violence offenders/perpetrators. However, instruments to conduct risk assessments with such perpetrators are widely used and include the Spousal Assault Risk Assessment Guide (SARA) (Kropp et al., 1995) – (subsequently updated) within the Probation sector – and the adapted CAADA DASH RIC Scale (2012) adapted by Respect (2012). Both are best described as checklists of risk factors, which, as Kropp (1995, p. 3) notes in relation to SARA, ensure 'that pertinent information is considered and weighed by evaluators'.

It is not intended to discuss the technicalities of either tool here other than to note that neither requires assessments of inordinate complexity, and both have been devised for use by a wide range of practitioners. Their importance lies in how they impact on practice once risk has been initially – and continuously – assessed. What is consistent concerning both instruments is the emphasis placed on detailed information-gathering, including, crucially and where possible, information provided by the victim/survivor, and significantly the nature and processes of information-sharing in order to comprehensively assess, address and manage ongoing issues of risk. Of relevance here is the fact that it has also been noted that an equally essential element of risk management and reduction is the necessity of working with perpetrators from the outset in such a way that actively engages, motivates and retains them (see e.g. Newman, 2010; Kerr, 2015, personal communication).

Beyond systems: '"New counselling approaches and innovations?"'

Having stated unequivocally that processes for risk assessment and management are requisite components of good practice, it is now appropriate to give further consideration to what might be needed as far as practice with perpetrators is concerned; attention focuses beyond risk to envisage what a more holistic and meaningful engagement with men might entail.

Here it might be worth noting that Gondolf's privileging of systems over what might be taken as a less than enthusiastic reference to 'heightened attention on new counselling approaches and innovations' actually positions him on one side of an occasionally rancorous and somewhat polarizing debate in the United States between those, like himself, who broadly favour the 'traditional', that is, feminist-inspired Duluth Model (which allegedly adheres to a somewhat homogenous view of abusive men as controlling patriarchs) and others who interpret the reasons underlying men's abuse as being multifactorial and who advocate engaging with men through more nuanced, therapeutic and significantly 'evidence-based', as opposed to didactic and apparently ideological, approaches.

In a somewhat polemical text published in the United States in 2009, editors Peter Lehmann and Catherine Simmons strongly argue the need for a paradigm shift as far as the state of perpetrator programmes is concerned (Lehmann and Simmons, 2009; Simmons and Lehmann, 2009). They consider that the Duluth model and its 'associated feminist philosophy' have had a 'stranglehold' on programmes. Despite evidence that they have been largely ineffective, they argue, the political and philosophical dogmas associated with the Duluth Model have ridden roughshod over alternative theories, approaches and empirical findings concerning the causes of intimate partner violence, and consequently of alternative, more positive approaches to working with perpetrators.

Various contributors to this volume, practitioners and academics thereafter describe several strengths-based approaches, some drawn from practice with other offending or 'problematic' service user groups and some piloted with domestic violence perpetrators. The principles of these approaches can be summed up as follows. Interventions should adopt a helping, therapeutic rather than didactic approach, be characterized by empathy, recognize individuality and resist a one-size-fits-all perspective. The client should be met where he is and have his own emotions and strengths recognized rather than his weaknesses and past mistakes constantly revisited, thus fostering shame and disengagement. Lehman and Simmons note that all of the approaches described are drawn from empirically supported therapeutic principles and techniques of behaviour change in other fields. Although they concede that the various approaches outlined, while promising, have still to provide significant evaluations of their applications to this particular field, they argue that the Duluth model is itself 'largely ineffective' (2009, p. xiii) in large measure because it ignores these very principles they describe.

Old lessons for new practice: Beyond the risk paradigm

Meanwhile, in the United Kingdom, where there is less evidence of a turf war and a somewhat more moderate tone, those interested in 'new ... approaches and innovations' have paid attention to the wider criminal-justice and criminological interest in concepts of desistance and 'desistance-focused' practice. Such practice pays particular attention to the dynamics and processes of personal change, to the significance of the therapeutic relationship (Burnett and McNeill, 2005; McNeill, 2006; Rex, 1999; Trotter, 2000, 2007), to how individual life factors and characteristics are acknowledged by practitioners and to the internal and external resources which have to be available in order to commence and sustain a desisting process or journey (Farrall, 2002).

Here, as in the United States, it has been suggested that the Duluth-influenced IDAP model has adopted a somewhat simplistic one-size-fits-all approach to practice with perpetrators that has overlooked their diversity (Gadd, 2004; Bowen, 2011) and the complexities of how personal change among perpetrators might better be conceived and enabled (Morran, 2011).

Research concerned more with questions of 'what matters?' rather than the technically-focused 'what works?' has reminded us of the importance of the professional relationship in engaging and motivating service users. In this context, it is suggested that earlier approaches in perpetrator programmes, influenced partly by research which found men's accounts of change to be spurious or evasive (see e.g. Cavanagh et al., 2001), often failed to acknowledge the confusing complexities of men's lives. Such approaches engaged with men almost entirely in terms of their abusive behaviour (behaviour, to be sure, which requires addressing) but in the process focused on men's negative, deficit characteristics and qualities (Langlands et al., 2009; Morran, 2011), significantly ignoring the various competencies and strengths which many men possess and which might be harnessed more actively to encourage changes in behaviour.

No surprise perhaps that men have often been resistant to co-operating in a process of self-examination where recognition of other more positive parts of their lives seemed of relatively little interest to the practitioner, concerned (appropriately) with the issue of the safety of the men's partners or children. Such concern, however, should not allow practitioners to forget that to engage meaningfully with the man is to begin the very process of risk reduction from the initial point of contact.

This then leads to the question of how, given the ineffectiveness of existing models, practice which takes account of risk but is also mindful of men's own strengths and goals has been reflected upon and developed in the UK context.

Shifting perceptions of working with perpetrators as men

It is useful to remember that what actually occurs in practice is often quite different from that which policymakers prescribe, managers oversee and academics endeavour to critique or evaluate. In this respect the demise of the Practitioners Network due to cost factors has constituted a lost opportunity for practitioners to reflect on how they actually practice and how this compares with prevailing public narratives, that is, the systemic preoccupation with IDAP for Probation and the Accreditation Standard for Respect.

Several practitioners, however, have (like their academic counterparts) written reflectively about practice, not least in Respect's own newsletter.

Thus in 2006, Wolf-Light discusses how one organization 'examined and amended' their original Duluth template, stressing the need for an emotional engagement with its participants so as to understand their 'world' and provide a re-analysis of the defences which men so often put forward, seeing them not just as techniques of denial (in which 'these' men excel, and moreover employ as yet a further technique of abuse – see e.g. Cavanagh et al., 2001) but instead as patterns of behaviour, beliefs and attitudes which individuals develop in order to avoid experiencing certain types of emotional discomfort (Wolf-Light, 2006, p. 10) – the type of discomfort created by an overtly 'challenging' facilitator perhaps? (See e.g. Morran, 2008.)

Macrae and Andrew (2000), working with men referred to their programme by the courts, discuss reconciling some of the polarity which they observed between the 'criminal-justice versus therapy dichotomy', emphasizing the challenge of developing practice which, while not collusive with men's violence and which holds men accountable for their behaviour, is nevertheless committed to engaging with men effectively in a process of change. Adhering to a pro-feminist approach 'does not remove the need to *listen* to each man or to ask "why is *this* man abusive?"' (2000, p. 31; italics in original). They then describe the process of engaging with the man's 'personal constructs' to explore how he conceives of his world now, but significantly of how he conceives of a future, alternative world, one in which he is non-violent and in which he feels positive, valued and of value in himself.

Similarly, the present author on the basis of numerous conversations with practitioners has commented (Morran, 2011) on how they have increasingly seen the value in providing space to hear not just the man's account of his behaviour (which may be evasive and shameful) but to allow him also to envision how life might be. These practitioners have noted that men's resistance to engagement is much reduced when they are *heard* and that men's own perceptions of why and how they act are essential to any process of their meaningful engagement with programmes.

Approaches that overlook these essential practices limit interventions to the teaching of skills at best. Their reductionist approach means that they neither connect with men on the core issues of how and in what ways their abusive behaviour has previously met their needs (and crucially how will they meet them or otherwise address them from now on) nor on establishing much motivation to change. In a recently published study (Morran, 2013), which involved interviewing 'successful completers' of two perpetrator programmes, the importance of being *listened to* (and challenged) and of being seen as someone with positive qualities comes across forcefully in men's accounts of desistance.

Looking into the future ...?

In the United Kingdom, strengths-based, solution-focused, future-oriented models have featured in those informal discussions in the NPN but have also shaped official, strategic interest in their implementation. By 2009, for example, the NOMS Lead for Prison and Probation Domestic Abuse Programmes was arguing the need for a new domestic violence programme incorporating more contemporary ideas 'including ... a ... multifactorial explanation for domestic violence'... a 'strengths-based approach using "Good Lives" principles, the use of principles/approaches associated with Narrative Therapy... and optional ... modules to address specific, individual areas of concern, e.g. alcohol abuse' (Weatherstone, 2010). These principles were substantially incorporated into the 'Building Better Relationships Model', which since 2012 has replaced the earlier IDAP Model. The BBR is at the time of writing being implemented widely throughout England and Wales, and although its effectiveness is yet to be determined, anecdotal evidence suggests that the level of resistance by men previously encountered in the delivery of IDAP is much less in evidence and that it seems to 'make more sense' to perpetrator and practitioner alike (personal communication, Nesbit, 2015).

In Scotland the Caledonian System, an 'integrated approach to address men's domestic violence and to improve the lives of women, children and men' (formally accredited by the Scottish Accreditation Panel for Offending Programmes in 2009), stresses the need for a systemic approach in which direct work done with the men who perpetrate violence is only one aspect of an overall, integrated service. Discussing the processes underlying the thinking of its various authors (all of them experienced practitioners in perpetrator, partner or children's work), one of them (Macrae, 2014) makes a number of salient points about how the principles influencing the philosophy of practice with men had evolved out of their experience. He realizes that simply to describe the purpose of the System as 'increasing women and children's safety' was in itself inadequate, recognizing from the many men they had worked with the essential *unhappiness* (italics added) of the men concerned and the need to acknowledge this as being key to engaging with them. He and his colleagues increasingly had come to see their practice being explicitly concerned with improving the quality of men's own lives as well as those of the partners and children who had been damaged by the men's behaviour. Acknowledging a history of being 'steeped in pro-feminist programmes', he recognizes the shortcomings of practice in which men's strengths had often been overlooked. Approaches to practice which were more focused on positive, strengths-based principles had therefore been embedded within the Caledonian System. At the time of writing, the Caledonian is currently running in approximately one-third of Scotland's local authority areas and will shortly undergo the process of evaluation.

More recently still, other experienced practitioners in this field who have been afforded opportunities to re-envision or redesign their approaches, such as the HELP Programme in Merseyside and the Positive Pathways motivational programme in Tyneside, have spoken to this author during the course of the writing of this chapter. They have commented positively on early evidence noting men's increased engagement with programmes; men have appreciated not being judged and having someone believe in them as individuals. Practitioners have also reflected on the need to start from where the men are, not from a predetermined explanation into which men are expected to fit, (personal communications, Cook, 2015; Nesbit, 2015).

As with the strengths-based approaches advocated by Lehmann and Simmons (2009) in the United States, these person-centred, individualized, desistance-focused approaches need to be vindicated by demonstrating that they are effective. What is significant, however, is that they have all resulted from sustained discussions and reflections on the part of practitioners, academics and researchers who have addressed the questions of *how* change works as well as for whom, in what circumstances and what needs to exist beyond the individual to support that change. What is also known, however, from the evidence from those who desist is that the processes involved take time and rely on the internal motivations, strengths and skills which individuals bring to the process, and the environments, supportive and otherwise, in which they live. Of the various other factors that may be necessary to this process, the importance of the practitioner in conveying a sense of respect, of hopefulness and a sense that change is achievable is paramount.

The following observations from a small study looking at how men negotiate the processes of desistance from violence and abuse illustrate these points succinctly and poignantly (see Morran, 2013).

Mark speaks of how his fears about how he would be regarded when he came onto a programme were proven wrong.

> I can remember ... very well ... what kept me there, there was a gain for me. And also, you know, the sensitivity in which the work was carried out in the fact of not demonising me and not making me feel toxic shame, so where I'm rotten to the core, you know? It enabled me to look at what I was doing ... and say, 'Yeah this needs to change, this isn't right and clearly it's not working for you or anybody else', but actually there are other areas in your life which are clearly functioning okay ... as a basis for giving me some self-esteem ... something that I felt I never had.

Sean speaks of how the programme taught him not only how to 'defuse' everyday situations but also about how he had gone from being

> a coward, a bully ... a little man with a chip on his shoulder

to what he is now:

> I think what it (the programme) has made me is a man, but a proper man, which may sound a bit dramatic, you know, a man with feelings and concerned for other people's feelings ... I'm a man now with a heart–that's what it's made me.

Both of these men, incidentally, still frequented the programmes which they had ostensibly completed several years previously. Their commitment to desisting from their past use of violence was in considerable part a testament to the importance of the faith of others that these men were capable of change, had the skills, strengths and courage to do so, as well as of a growing awareness and recognition within the men themselves that they were worthy of such investment.

Conclusion

This chapter has suggested that perpetrator programmes have, since their emergence both in the United States and the United Kingdom, been contested projects, shaped by a number of ideological or theoretical, pragmatic and other constraints. The first of those was how the problem should be named: transformed from one of 'abused wives' to that of 'violent men' (Dobash and Dobash, 1992). This in turn gave rise to debates around how work with perpetrators should be envisaged and practised, and to the public 'outing' of the 'batterer'. It is, at least from a UK perspective, perhaps rather startling that Lehmann and Simmons' (2009) critique of Duluth should nevertheless be entitled 'Strengths-Based Batterer Intervention'. While naming both the term and the behaviour 'battering' reflects the political struggle by various elements of the women's movement over three decades, the continual references in almost all the US academic literature to 'the batterer' indicates the tentative path which has to be trod by those who would engage with such an individual by paying him heed (for it is invariably 'him') and seeking out his qualities and strengths.

Various other constraints upon the articulation of practice have been mentioned in this chapter, including the subjection of flexible practice experienced within the Probation Service by the demands of 'accountability' from successive governments and the need for 'replicability' by management in order to achieve 'respectability' by researchers and inspectors. A combination of similar systemic priorities has also been at the forefront of the accreditation agenda pursued in the United Kingdom by Respect. This has been important to sustain alliances with women's organizations, affirming that it is a serious organization which is mindful of the risk inherent in all practice with violent and abusive men.

Vital to the emergence of our current knowledge concerning interpersonal violence (which is constantly changing) have been the voices of women. Those voices need to be heard and heeded. It is also the case, though, that the voices and experiences of others have sought to articulate complicated challenging arguments and viewpoints. In this chapter, it has been suggested that practice with men's abusive behaviour has been shaped by structural discourses which have discouraged the optimistic, even naïve, voice of the practitioner who looks for strengths and qualities in difficult places. Here, the voices of some of these practitioners seem consistently and persistently to say that if we do not listen in turn to where our 'batterer' or 'perpetrator' begins to tell us his difficult, blaming, self-justifying, confused, frightening and fear-filled story, we all fail to move forward from the risk-filled present to a difficult, challenging, but ultimately more worthwhile and safer future.

References

ACOP (1992) *Domestic Violence, Position Statement*. London: Association of Chief officers of probation.

Andrews, D. (1995) 'The psychology of criminal conduct and effective treatment', in J. McGuire (ed.) *What Works: Reducing Reoffending, Guidelines from Research and Practice*. Chichester: Wiley.

Andrews, D. A., Bonta, J. and Hoge, R. D. (1990) 'Classification for effective rehabilitation: Rediscovering psychology', *Criminal Justice and Behavior* 17: 19–52.

Bancroft, L. (2002) *Why Does He Do That? Inside the minds of angry and controlling men*. New York: Berkley Books.

Bilby, C. and Hatcher, R. (2004). 'Early stages in the development of the Integrated Domestic Abuse Programme: Implementing the Duluth domestic violence pathfinder', *Home Office Online Report 29/04*. London: Home Office.

Bowen, E. (2011) *The Rehabilitation of Partner-Violent Men*. Chichester, Wiley-Blackwell.

CAADA-DASH (2012) *Risk Identification (RIC) for MARAC Agencies*. CAADA.

Cavanagh, K, Dobash, R. E., Dobash, R. P. and Lewis, R. (2001) '"Remedial Work": Men's Strategic Response to Their Violence Against Intimate Female Partners', *Sociology* 35(3): 695–714.

CHANGE (May 1996) *Network Directory: A Directory of Organisations and Agencies Working with Men who are Violent to Women*. Grangemouth, compiled by CHANGE.

Clatterbaugh, K. (1990) *Contemporary Perspectives on Masculinity*. Colorado: Westview Press.

Cook, R. (2015) Personal communication. *Launch of the Help Programme*: Merseyside Community Rehabilitation Company, Liverpool March, 2015.

Dixon, L., Archer, J. and Graham-Kevan, N. (2011) 'Perpetrator programmes for partner violence: Are they based on ideology or evidence?', *Legal and Criminological Psychology* 2011, online, 1–20.

Dobash, R. E. and Dobash, R. P. (1979) *Violence against Wives*. New York: Free Press.

———. (1992) *Women, Violence and Social Change*. London: Routledge and Kegan Paul.

Dobash, R. E., Dobash, R. P., Cavanagh K. and Lewis, R. (1996) *Research Evaluation of Programmes for Violent Men*. Edinburgh: The Scottish Office Central Research Unit.

Eadie, T. and Knight, C. (2002) 'Domestic Violence Programmes: Reflections on the Shift from Independent to Statutory Provision', *The Howard Journal of Criminal Justice* 41(2): 167–81.

Edleson, J. L. and Grusznki (1989) 'Treating men who batter: Four Years of Outcome Data from the Domestic Abuse Project', *Journal of Social Service Research* 12(1): 2–22.

Eisikovits, Z. C. and Edleson, J. L. (1989) 'Intervening with Men Who Batter: A Critical Review of the Literature', *Social Services Review* 63(3): 384–414.

Farrall, S. (2002) *Rethinking What Works with Offenders: Probation, Social Context and Desistance from Crime*. Cullompton: Willan.

Gadd, D. (2002) 'Masculinities and Violence against Female Partners', *Social and Legal Studies* 11(1): 61–80.

———. (2004) 'Evidence-led policy or policy-led evidence? Cognitive behavioural programmes for men who are violent towards women', *Criminal Justice* 4(2): 173–97.

———. (2007) *Psychosocial Criminology: An Introduction*. London: Sage.

Gendrea, P. and Ross, R. R. (1987) 'Revivication of Rehabilitation: Evidence from the 80's', *Justice Quarterly* 2: 18–23.

Gilchrist E., Johnson, R., Takriti, R., Weston S., Beech, A. and Kebbell, M. (2003) *Domestic Violence Offenders: Characteristics and Offending Related Needs Findings, 217*. London: Home Office.

Gondolf, E. (2002) *Batterer Intervention Systems*. London: Sage.

Gorman, K. (2001) 'Cognitive behaviouralism and the Holy Grail: The quest for a universal means of managing offender risk', *Probation Journal* 48(1): 3–9.

Hague, G. and Malos, E. (2005) *Domestic Violence: Action for Change* (3rd edition). Cheltenham: New Clarion Press.

Hollin, C. R. (1995) 'The meaning and implications of "programme integrity"', In J. McGuire (ed.) *What Works: Reducing Reoffending – Guidelines from Research and Practice*. Chichester: Wiley.

Horley, S. (1990) 'Responding to male violence against women', *Probation Journal* 37(4): 166–70.

Integrated Domestic Abuse Programme (IDAP) *Annual Review 2008–9*. Ministry of Justice National Offender Management Service (NOMS).

Jenkins, J. (1994) *Men, Masculinity and Offending: Groupwork Initiatives in Probation*. London: London Acton Trust.

Kelly, L. and Westmarland, N. (2015) *Domestic Violence Perpetrator programmes: Steps towards Change*. Project Mirabal Final Report. London and Durham: London Metropolitan University and Durham University.

Kerr, V. (2014–15) Series of personal communications Lothian Criminal Justice Services Edinburgh.

Knott, C. (1995) 'The STOP Programme: Reasoning and Rehabilitation in a British Setting', in J. McGuire (ed.) *What Works: Reducing Reoffending, Guidelines from Research and Practice*. Chichester: Wiley.

Kropp, P. R., Hart, S. D., Webster, C. D. and Eaves, D. (1995) *Manual for the Spousal Assault Risk Assessment Guide,* 2nd edn. Vancouver: The British Columbia Institute Against Family Violence.

Kropp, P. R. (2004) 'Some questions regarding spousal assault risk assessment', *Violence Against Women* 10: 676–97.

Langlands, R. L., Ward, T., and Gilchrist, E. (2009) 'Applying the Good Lives Model to perpetrators of domestic violence', *Behaviour Change* 26: 113–29.

Lehmann, P. and Simmons, C. A. (eds) (2009) *Strengths-based Batterer Intervention: A New paradigm in Ending Family Violence*. New York: Springer Publishing Company.

———. (2009) 'The state of batterer intervention programs: An analytical discussion', in P. Lehmann and C. A. Simmons (eds) *Strengths-based Batterer Intervention: A New paradigm in Ending Family Violence*. New York: Springer Publishing Company.

Macrae, R (2014) 'The Caledonian System: An Integrated Approach to Address Men's Domestic Violence and Improve the Lives of Women, Children and Men' in *Ending Men's Violence Against Women and Children*. (The No To Violence Journal, Victoria Australia), Autumn 2014.

Macrae, R. and Andrew, M. (2000) 'The use of personal construct theory in work with men who abuse women partners', *Probation Journal* 47(1): 30–38.

Mair, G. (ed.) (2004) *What Matters in Probation*. Cullompton: Willan.

Martin, D. (1976) *Battered Wives*. San Francisco: Glide.

Martinson, R. (1974) 'What works? Questions and answers about prison reform', *The Public Interest* 35: 22–54.

Maruna, S. (2001) *Making Good: How Ex-Convicts reform and rebuild their lives*. Ann Arbor: Michigan.

McIvor, G. (1990) *Sanctions for Serious or Persistent Offenders: A Review of the Literature*. Social Work Research Centre: University of Stirling.

McNeill, F. (2002) 'Beyond "What Works": How and why people stop offending' Briefing Paper 5: August 2002 *Criminal Justice Social Work Development Centre for Scotland*.

———. (2006) 'A desistance paradigm for offender management', *Criminology and Criminal Justice* 6(1): 39–62.

Morran, D. (1996) 'Working in the Change Programme: probation based groupwork with male domestic violence offenders', in T. Newburn and G. Mair, (eds) *Working with Men*. Lyme Regis: Russell House.

———. (2006) 'Thinking Outside the Box: Looking Beyond Programme Integrity', *British Journal of Community Justice* 4(1): 7–18.

———. (2008) 'Firing up and burning out: The personal and professional impact of working in domestic violence programmes', *The Probation Journal* 55(2): 139–52.

———. (2011) 'Re-education or recovery? Re-thinking some aspects of domestic violence perpetrator programmes', *The Probation Journal* 58(1): 23–36.

———. (2013) 'Desisting from domestic abuse: Influences, patterns and processes in the lives of formerly abusive men', *The Howard Journal of Criminal Justice* 52(3): 306–20.

Mullender, A. (2001) 'Dealing with Perpetrators', in J. Taylor-Browne (ed.) *What Works in Reducing Domestic Violence?* (pp. 59–94). London: Whiting and Birch.

Nesbit, D. (2015) (Personal communication) Launch of Positive Pathways Plus Northumbria Community Rehabilitation Company Gateshead, Tyneside, April, 2015.

Newburn, T. and Mair, G. (1996) *Working with Men*. Lyme Regis: Russell House.

Newman, C. (2010) *Expert Domestic Violence Risk Assessments in the Family Courts*. London: Respect.

Pence, E. and Paymar, M. (1993) *Education Groups for Men Who Batter: The Duluth Model*. New York: Springer.

Pirog-Good, M. and Stets-Kealey, J. (1985) 'Male batterers and battering prevention programs: A national survey', *Response* 8: 8–12.

Potts, D (1996) *Why do Men Commit Most Crime? Focusing on Masculinity in a Prison Group*. Wakefield: West Yorkshire Probation Service.

Senior, P. and Woodhill, D. (eds) (1992) *Gender, Crime and Probation Practice*. Sheffield Hallam University: PAVIC publications.

Simmons, C. A. and Lehmann, P. (2009) 'Strengths-Based Batterer Intervention: A New Direction with a Different Paradigm', in P. Lehmann and C. A. Simmons (eds) *Strengths-based Batterer Intervention: A New paradigm in Ending Family Violence*. New York: Springer Publishing Company.

Raynor, P. (1985; 1993) *Social Work, Justice and Control*. London: Whiting and Birch.

The Respect Accreditation Standard (2008). Respect is the National Association of Domestic Violence Perpetrator Programmes and Associated Women's Services. www.respect.uk.net/.

Respect (2004) *Domestic Violence Perpetrator Programmes and Associated Women's Services & Trainers and Consultants, UK Directory*. London.

Rex, S. (1999) 'Desistance from Offending: Experiences of Probation', *Howard Journal of Criminal Justice* 38(4): 366–83.

Roberts, C. (1995) 'Effective practice and service delivery', in J. McGuire (ed.) *What Works: Reducing Reoffending, Guidelines from Research and Practice*. Chichester: Wiley.

Sartin, R. M., Hansen, D. J. and Huss, M. T. (2006) 'Domestic violence treatment response and recidivism: A review and implications of the study of family violence', *Aggression and Violent Behaviour* 11: 452–40.

Scourfield, J. B. (1995) *Changing Men: UK Agencies Working with Men who are Violent towards Their Women Partners.* Norwich: University of East Anglia, Probation Monographs, no.141.

———. (1998) 'Probation officers working with men', *British Journal of Social Work* 28: 581–99.

Scourfield, J. B and Dobash, R. P. (1999) 'Programmes for violent men: Recent developments in the UK', *The Howard Journal of Criminal Justice* 38(2): 128–43.

Singh-Bhui, H. and Buchanan, J (2004) 'What Works and Complex Individuality', *Probation Journal* 51(3): 195–96.

Trotter, C. (1999) *Working with Involuntary Clients: A guide to practice.* London: Sage (updated 2007).

———. (2000) 'Social Work Education, Pro-Social Orientation and Effective Probation Practice', *Probation Journal* 47(4): 256–61.

Weatherstone, P. (2010) *Presentation: Introducing the Building Better Relationships Programme.* NOMS London.

Wolf-Light, P. (2006) 'Duluth Perpetrator Programme – Examined and Amended', *Respect Newsletter,* Spring, 2006.

8

RISK, REGULATION AND THE REINTEGRATION OF SEXUAL OFFENDERS

Anne-Marie McAlinden

Queen's University Belfast, UK

Introduction

Media reporting of and public concern about sexual offending, particularly relating to children, affects and reflects political, policy and organizational responses to those convicted of such crimes. The development of regulatory policies on sexual offending has taken place within a highly emotive and overtly politicized public and policy discourse. This chapter charts the various ways in which the risks imagined or posed by sexual offenders have been conceptualized within public discourses and regulated and managed under the legislative and organizational 'risk paradigm'. Ultimately, it argues that risk-based responses to sexual offending are at best uncertain in their effects and at worst counterproductive in that they often reduce the potential for successful reintegration. In seeking to look 'beyond risk', the chapter also explores the usefulness of restorative and related practices in supporting sex offender reintegration aimed at the primary and secondary levels of harm prevention.

The structure of the chapter is as follows: the first part will explore the central tenets of media and public concerns about sexual offending, which are heavily premised on the risk posed by predatory 'strangers'. The second part will critically examine a range of measures which have been put in place to manage the risk posed by sex offenders in the community, including offender notification and pre-employment vetting, which are fuelled by 'precautionary logic' (Ericson, 2007) and pre-emptive approaches to 'risk' (Zedner, 2009). Within the broader theoretical context of 'strength' and 'needs-based' approaches to sex offending, the third and final part of the chapter considers alternative practical routes to countering the risk paradigm.

'Imagined risk': Media and public discourses on sexual offending

The media's portrayal of sex offenders as the ultimate 'demon' or 'monster' (Simon, 1998; Wardle, 2007) has been readily absorbed by the public (Berry et al., 2012) helping to foster public panic and fear about the risk posed by sex offenders living in the community (McAlinden, 2007a). In such a context, the conceptualization of 'risk' within public consciousness is characterized by at least three core themes: first, through the public abhorrence of sexual crime, particularly where children are victims, the sex offender becomes a 'double outsider' – literally excluded from the community and also not seen as of the community (Spencer, 2009, p. 225). This 'othering' (Garland, 2001) of sex offenders as physical and moral 'outsiders' (Becker, 1963) also helps to locate 'risk' firmly in the public sphere and 'as coming from somewhere beyond the boundaries' (Lynch, 2002, p. 560). This preservation of the sanctity of the home as the realm of safety and protection helps to create a minimalist version of risks to women and children (Cowburn and Dominelli, 2001; see also Newburn and Stanko, 1994). Indeed, such generalized constructions of gendered and sexualized forms of risk ignore in particular the family as a site of danger (Saraga, 2001), where women and children are known to be much more vulnerable to abuse at the hands of men well known to them. Research, for example, has established that approximately four-fifths of children and women are abused by intimates rather than predatory strangers (see, e.g. Grubin, 1998; Coleman et al., 2007).

Second, there is marked conflation of 'risk' into a narrow band of activity, whereby generalized risks posed by sex offenders are deemed to be synonymous with the risks posed by sex offenders against children who are considered to pose a very high level of risk (McAlinden, 2007a, pp. 10–11). Sex offending, however, is not a homogeneous category of activity, but rather encompasses a wide variety of harms from non-contact offences, including voyeurism, indecent exposure and grooming, to those at the more serious end of the spectrum such as child sexual abuse and exploitation, rape and sexual murder. Further, not all sex offenders pose the same degree of 'risk.' The popular conceptualization of the adult male predatory 'paedophile' as being symptomatic of the threat posed by sex offenders as a whole also helps to mask other forms of risk concerning, for example, adult victims or offending by women or children (McAlinden, 2014a). Indeed, as discussed in the concluding section, new and emerging forms of sexual offending such as 'sexting' or 'cyberbullying' or 'peer-to-peer grooming' present new challenges for popular and official discourses on sex offending and the contemporary risk paradigm.

Third, popular discourses on 'risk' are also reflective of and shaped by highly polarized cultural assumptions about victims and offenders of sexual crime – who poses a risk and those susceptible to such risks. In this respect, 'the real child abuse stereotype' is composed of binary assumptions about 'at-risk' victims who are deemed to be vulnerable due to their age, gender and assumed innocence as children. This social construction of risk concerning victims is juxtaposed with that of 'risky' individuals who are conversely deemed threatening because of their distal proximity to victims in terms of age, gender and relationship – the older adult predatory male who was previously unknown to his unsuspecting young victim (McAlinden, 2014a). This has also resulted in oppositional 'victim' and 'offender hierarchies' (Carrabine et al., 2004; McAlinden, 2014a) which cannot accommodate, for example, 'deviant' victims or 'vulnerable' offenders who lie outside of dominant risk paradigms. By way of example, in relation to sexually harmful behaviour by children and young people, there is a fundamental tension between 'perceptions of children as "at risk" and as potentially threatening' (Scott et al., 1998, p. 689).

Archetypal notions of the risks to children concerning sexual offending have in large part stemmed from a number of high-profile cases of sexual abuse and murder of children. These have included the murder of eight-year-old Sarah Payne by known paedophile Roy Whiting in Sussex in the summer of 2000 and the 2002 murders in Soham of two 10-year-old school girls, Holly Wells and Jessica Chapman, by school caretaker Ian Huntley. Such cases 'crystallized fears over the image of the predatory child sex offender' (Greer, 2007, p. 28) and have become 'signal crimes' (Innes, 2004) in underlying the need for further regulatory measures to control the risk posed by potential sex offenders in the community. The 'Soham murders' led to the Bichard Inquiry (2004) and reform of the law on pre-employment vetting and barring via the Safeguarding Vulnerable Groups Act 2006. Similarly, in the aftermath of the Sarah Payne case, the former *News of the World* newspaper established its 'Name and Shame' campaign, which called for authorities to publicly identify all known sex offenders. This ultimately came to fruition with the introduction of 'Sarah's Law', allowing parents or carers to check the background of those with unsupervised access to their children (see the Criminal Justice Act 2003, s 327A).

The existence of similar case examples throughout the United States and elsewhere (e.g. 'Megan's Law' in the United States and 'Natalie's

Law' in Germany) is indicative of a populist approach to policymaking (Bottoms, 1995; Johnstone, 2000) which has tended to characterize penal policy responses to this particular category of offender. In essence, in response to public concerns about the dangers posed by sex offenders and media-led calls for further punitive responses, the state has enacted a burgeoning range of risk-averse policies. However, this approach to law making has tended to result in a self-fulfilling prophecy, or what Brownlee (1998) terms 'a vicious policy cycle' – legislating against risk helps to legitimize imagined risks on the part of society, which in turn fuel the demand and reinforce the need for further regulatory responses to managing risk. As discussed further below, the result is a range of risk-based policies which are at best uncertain and unpredictable in their intended effects and outcomes. Moreover, at worst, they may also be counterproductive in increasing rather than reducing the risk of reoffending and in undermining sex offender management and reintegration.

Regulating 'risk': Legislative and policy frameworks on sex offender risk assessment and management

In the contemporary era of the 'regulatory state' (Braithwaite, 2000), or 'post-regulatory state' (Scott, 2004), risk-based logic has emerged as a key feature of debates on crime and justice (Ericson and Haggerty, 1997; Shearing, 2000). Scholars have noted a shift in the theoretical underpinnings of criminal justice policy 'from dangerousness to risk' (Castel, 1991) and towards a defining contemporary framework based on 'precautionary logic' (Ericson, 2007). Pre-emptive approaches to risk seek to govern 'worst-case scenarios' and prevent all possible manifestations of future harm before they occur (Zedner, 2009). Reactionary risk-averse policies to policing or security in general (Crawford, 2003; Loader and Walker, 2007) have formed the basis of targeted intervention with selected 'at-risk' groups such as sexual offenders. By way of example, 'Megan's Law', named after seven-year old Megan Kanka, who was raped and murdered by a neighbour with two previous convictions for sexual abuse, requires sex offenders to register with local law enforcement and permits various forms of community notification of information about sex offenders (Bedarf, 1995). Sex offenders against children have been singled out as warranting 'extra-legal' punishment because of the emotive nature of the crime and the ubiquitous risk they are seen as presenting (Pratt, 2000). This 'differential justice' (Weaver and McNeill, 2010, p. 274) has manifested itself in a policy of 'radical prevention' (Hebenton and Seddon, 2009, p. 2) with sexual offenders via preventive detention and controls placed on dangerous or 'risky' individuals in the community.

Within this broader policy context, risk has reshaped the use of punishment as a regulatory tool. A distinguishing feature of contemporary trends in social regulation is 'hyper-innovation' (Moran, 2003; Crawford, 2006), or what Lacey (2004) terms 'criminalisation as regulation', where the state attempts to assert its authority via the imposition of a burgeoning amount of criminal sanctions. Since the late 1990s, a plethora of broadly exclusionary measures have been introduced as situational attempts to control the whereabouts and behaviour of sex offenders in the community (Kemshall and Wood, 2007). Key policy developments within the United Kingdom, for example, include sex offender notification, which requires various categories of sex offenders to notify their personal details to the police, and pre-employment vetting and barring (McAlinden, 2010a). In addition, Part 2 of the Sexual Offences Act 2003 also introduced further regulatory measures in the form of risk of sexual harm orders and sexual offences prevention orders. The latter can be used to prohibit the offender from frequenting places where there are children, such as parks and school playgrounds, while the former seek to criminalize the preparatory acts involved in abuse and can be used whether or not the individual has a prior record of offending. Most notably, perhaps, the enactment of the offence of 'meeting a child following sexual grooming etc.', via section 15 of the Sexual Offences Act 2003, seeks to encapsulate potential 'risk' by criminalizing the preparatory behaviour before actual abuse or harm occurs (McAlinden, 2012).

In the United Kingdom, the legislative and policy framework has been enhanced by the development of a cohesive inter-agency infrastructure as part of 'joined-up' working (Cowan, Pantazis and Gilroy, 2001, p. 439) and 'the end-to-end risk management of the offender'. The introduction of Multi-Agency Public Protection Arrangements (MAPPA) across the United Kingdom, with some localized variations (see Stafford et al., 2011), has formalized arrangements for assessing and managing the risks posed by sexual and violent offenders. The core task of MAPPA is to facilitate the exchange of relevant information between key statutory and voluntary agencies and classify sex offenders into risk categories based on a high, medium or low risk of reoffending (Kemshall and Maguire, 2001). The logic of this risk assessment model, which has generally been endorsed as a model of best practice, is that it targets those offenders who pose the greatest risk to public safety. Via forms of community notification such as 'Sarah's Law', referred to above, or the inclusion of lay members as part of MAPPA, as happens in England and Wales and Northern Ireland, the public have also been admitted to the process of risk management, albeit on a limited and tightly controlled basis.

Criminologists have noted that expansive forms of state regulation are leading to increasingly volatile, contradictory and incoherent penal policies (Garland, 1999; O'Malley, 1999). Consistent with these broader arguments, I have previously contended that regulatory activity in the field of sex offender risk management has resulted in particularly uncertain and unsafe policies (McAlinden, 2010a). In the main, there are clear limitations to official knowledge about risks posed by largely unknown individuals who may have never come to the attention of the authorities and who remain beyond the reach of regulatory frameworks. Research shows, for example, that fewer than 5% of sex offenders are apprehended (Salter, 2003) and that only 12% of rapes involving children (Smith et al., 2000) are reported to the police. The focus on known and identifiable risks, and not the hidden and therefore most dangerous ones, may also divert resources and focus from the real risks and problems, including those which reside in the private sphere. This is indicative of what Hebenton and Seddon (2009, p. 12, quoting Sunstein, 2002) term the 'risk–risk' problem of the precautionary approach, whereby enhanced focus on managing or reducing one set of risks can create increased or displaced risks elsewhere. At the same time, the state's enactment of regulatory measures as a demonstration of its strength and commitment to controlling the problem (Garland, 2001) may create a 'punishment deficit' (Brownlee, 1998) in terms of creating unrealistic public expectations about the capacity of the state to control risk.

The ethos of regulatory mechanisms such as sex offender notification is 'knowledge-risk-security' (Ericson and Haggerty, 1997) – the aim is to garner knowledge about sex offenders and their whereabouts in order to control risk and increase public protection (Hebenton and Thomas, 1996). In practice, however, the implementation of risk-based regulatory schemes may actually be counterproductive in undermining rather than securing effective risk management. On one hand, making the community part of the risk management process and admitting the public as consumers of such knowledge about sex offenders may help to reduce risks and make communities feel safer and better protected. On the other hand, however, visible public punishments which identify individuals as potential sex offenders, such as notification or tagging, may have a negative and detrimental impact on how sex offenders are perceived and accepted by wider society and ultimately their community reintegration. The public shaming of a person as a sex offender may result in 'disintegrative shaming' (Braithwaite, 1989) which shames the offender rather than the offending behaviour, resulting in the symbolic and literal exile of sex offenders from the community. This may perpetuate a cycle of stigmatization, ostracism and ultimately a return to offending behaviour (Edwards and Hensley, 2001; McAlinden, 2005, 2007a). The underlying and unintended policy effects of precautionary approaches to criminal justice, therefore, may generate 'fear and with it intolerance,' (Ericson, 2007, p. 155), suspicion and exclusion of deviants from the local community.

'Beyond risk': From regulation to the reintegration of sexual offenders

Given the deficits of 'risk-based' approaches to the reintegration of sexual offenders which have been outlined above, this section of the chapter moves to consider the alternative 'strengths-based' model of rehabilitation (Maruna and LeBel, 2002; Burnett and Maruna, 2006). The core idea behind the strengths model, which is linked to the restorative justice tradition, is that genuine offender re-integration involves 'more than physical re-entry into the community' (Burnett and Maruna, 2006, p. 84). It should involve 'earned redemption' (Bazemore, 1999) in the sense of '"earning" one's place back in the moral community' (Burnett and Maruna, 2006, p. 84). Opportunities are provided for offenders to develop prosocial concepts of self, usually in the form of socially useful activities such as rewarding work (Burnett and Maruna, 2006, p. 84). It also considers the other main and closely related 'deficit' model outlined by Maruna and LeBel (2002) – 'needs-based' strategies which focus on helping ex-offenders to overcome addictions or learn basic skills in order to reduce the risk of reoffending.

Core to this approach is the notion of 'reintegrative shaming' (Braithwaite, 1989), which is the converse of 'disintegrative shaming' and formal regulatory approaches to risk management outlined above. Shaming of the reintegrative variety is comprised of two core elements: (1) the overt disapproval of the delinquent act by socially significant others; and (2) the on-going inclusion of the offender within an interdependent relationship (Zhang, 1995, p. 251). Reintegrative shaming focuses on shaming the offending behaviour rather than the offenders themselves and thus reinforces an offender's membership in civil society. There is a 'cognitive restructuring towards responsibility' (Toch, 2000) as the offender is actively encouraged to develop community-orientated concepts of self (Bazemore, 1999) and innate motivations for personal change. Such approaches offer a more constructive, viable and proactive means of addressing the myriad of problems which relate to offender reintegration, affecting not only the offender but also the community in which the offender is placed (McAlinden, 2005, 2007a). Measures which reflect the hallmarks of reintegrative shame culture are circles of support and accountability:

> Circles of support originated in Canada as a means of reintegrating high risk sex offenders on release from prison. They are based on the twin aims of safety and support – addressing public concerns surrounding the risk of re-offending

and also the offender's needs in terms of reintegration. The circle, comprised of approximately 4–6 trained members, is built around the offender as the core member and involving the wider community in partnership with state and voluntary agencies. The scheme provides intensive support, guidance and supervision for the offender to minimise risk and assist with the practical aspects of reintegration. The offender agrees to relate to the circle of support, pursue treatment and to act responsibly in the community. The offender has daily contact with someone from the circle each day in the high risk phase just after release which gradually diminishes (McAlinden 2007a, pp. 168–74). The circles model operates across a growing range of jurisdictions. It has been extended throughout England and Wales and Scotland and is beginning to be piloted across a number of other European jurisdictions including France, Hungary, Bulgaria, and Northern Ireland. Such schemes have had considerable success over the last decade in Canada and England and Wales in particular in protecting communities by challenging pro-offending or 'risky' behaviour prior to the commission of an offence and in supporting offenders with reintegration. (Wilson et al., 2007; Hanvey et al., 2011, pp. 150–65; Bates et al., 2012)

The ethos of circles is to manage wrongdoing within a communitarian society and informally sanction deviance by reintegration into cohesive networks rather than by formal restraint (McAlinden, 2007a, pp. 168–74). The community is involved in expressing disapproval of the sex-offending behaviour, but also in providing protection and redress for victims and in supporting offenders in their efforts to desist and reintegrate. Circles also encapsulate the 'strengths-based' philosophy. A combination of stable employment, accommodation, supportive relationships and treatment are part of a 'good lives' approach or positive reintegrative work with sex offenders (Ward and Marshall, 2004; Ward et al., 2007). They acknowledge in particular the critical contribution of the community in supporting offender rehabilitation as well as the important commitment required by the offender. By addressing both the individual and structural obstacles to reintegration, they offer a more effective mechanism for securing offender reintegration and reducing the risk of reoffending (McAlinden, 2010b).

Circle programmes should also be supplemented by public health approaches which address the needs of victims, offenders and communities affected by sexual crime. As Kemshall and Wood (2007) have made explicit, there are two main approaches to addressing risk: the 'community protection model' and the 'public health model'. The former, as noted above, is characterized with concerns about 'risk', regulation and 'precautionary logic' and epitomized in the legal and organizational frameworks for controlling sex offender risk. This model is bolstered by the 'construction and demonization of the "predatory paedophile"' (Kemshall and Wood, 2007, pp. 210–11) which has underpinned both contemporary popular and official discourses on sexual offending. In contrast, advocates of alternative public health approaches usually premise these on the failures of traditional retributive and reactive responses, particularly in terms of reducing the incidence of sexual offending and simultaneously inflating public fear and stigmatization concerning sexual offenders (Laws, 2000, p. 30). The public health model emphasizes the language of prevention and harm reduction rather than that of surveillance and risk management (Kemshall and Wood, 2007, p. 211). Key elements are the proactive (rather than reactive) management of sexual offending; challenging inappropriate behaviour; self-risk management by sex offenders; and giving the community a vested role in the day-to-day management of risk (Kemshall and Wood, 2007, p. 212).

Public health approaches, as applied to sexually harmful behaviour, identify three levels of prevention: primary, secondary and tertiary (Laws, 2000, 2008). The primary level of prevention aims to prevent sexually harmful behaviour before it occurs. This is exemplified by public education and awareness programmes which inform society about the facts and risks surrounding sexual offending, including how they are actively identified and managed. The secondary level of prevention is aimed at early identification and intervention and engaging with first-time or adolescent offenders to prevent them from progressing to more entrenched patterns of sex offending. Given the limitations of the tertiary or criminal justice level of prevention in reactively responding to a limited range of known risks, a combination of primary- and secondary-level initiatives should be developed in order to put in place more holistic and proactive responses to managing the risk posed by sex offenders (McAlinden, 2012, ch. 7). This would include a tapestry of services for victims, offenders and communities affected by sexual crime such as early staged intervention with 'vulnerable' children and families; training for professionals around a wider range of forms of sexually harmful behaviour towards children, including the risks presented by children and young people themselves; fuller provision of intervention programmes with first-time or young offenders; and further mainstream work with the offender's family as part of reintegration and release (McAlinden, 2012, pp. 266–78).

Conclusion

The notion of 'stranger danger' has dominated contemporary public discourses about the risks posed by sex offenders against children. As Cowburn and Dominelli (2001, pp. 400, 404) have argued, this concept calls for a scientific paradigm of risk assessment and management which promotes the false expectation that community safety can be achieved by ever more sophisticated and expansive precautionary modes of risk management. This chapter has advocated that the 'strengths-' or 'needs-based' model (Burnett and Maruna, 2006) of sex offender reintegration represents a more effective approach than current risk-based approaches operating alone (Ward and Maruna, 2007). An amalgam of these approaches would address the limitations of risk-based approaches and represent a more effective approach to offender reintegration and a better balance between risk management and rehabilitation (McAlinden, 2010b).

The challenges of moving 'beyond risk', however, are perhaps most acute for this specific category of offender. In particular, there are ongoing difficulties in getting the public to be accepting of a sex offender living or working in their midst. For example, in one Northern Ireland–based study of public attitudes to sex offenders, 70% of the 500 adults surveyed thought that it was unacceptable for child sex offenders to live in their local community (McAlinden 2007b, p. 52). Failure to address stereotypes surrounding the risks associated with sexual offending, including those which lie closest to home, via a government-led public education programme may ultimately act as a barrier to public acceptance of a range of viable, less punitive interventions for managing risk. In addition, new and emerging forms of sexual offending, including those presented by children and young people themselves, are beginning to emerge as the 'new frontier' of risk management and child protection. Sexually harmful or exploitative behaviours such as peer-to-peer grooming', 'sexting' and 'cyberbullying' undermine our traditional thinking about 'risks' and risk anxiety concerning children (McAlinden, 2014b). They underline the fact that children and young people may present 'as risk' as well as 'at risk.' More broadly, they also challenge us to confront our deep-seated societal and cultural assumptions about who or what constitutes a risk and how best to respond such risks.

References

Bates, A., Macrae, R., Williams, D. and Webb, C. (2012) 'Ever-increasing circles: A descriptive study of Hampshire and Thames Valley circles of support and accountability 2002-09', *Journal of Sexual Aggression* 18(3): 355–73.

Bazemore, G. (1999) 'After shaming, whither reintegration: Restorative justice and relational rehabilitation', in G. Bazemore and L. Walgrave (eds) *Restorative Juvenile Justice: Repairing the Harm of Youth Crime*. Monsey, NY: Criminal Justice Press.

Becker, H. (1963) *Outsiders: Studies in the Sociology of Deviance* (New York: The Free Press of Glencoe).

Bedarf, A. (1995) 'Examining sex offender community notification laws', *California Law Review* 83(3): 885–937.

Berry, M., Philo, G., Tiripelli, Docherty, S and Macpherson, C (2012) 'Media coverage and public understanding of sentencing policy in relation to crimes against children', *Criminology and Criminal Justice* 12(5): 567–91.

Bichard, Sir M. (2004) *The Bichard Inquiry Report*. London: Home Office.

Bottoms, A. E. (1995) 'The philosophy and politics of punishment and sentencing', in C. Clarkson and R. Morgan (eds) *The Politics of Sentencing Reform*. Oxford: Oxford University Press.

Braithwaite, J. (1989) *Crime, Shame and Reintegration*. Sydney, Cambridge University Press.

———. (2000) 'The new regulatory state and the transformation of criminology', *British Journal of Criminology* 40(2): 222–38.

Brownlee, I. (1998) 'New Labour – new penology? Punitive rhetoric and the limits of managerialism in criminal justice policy', *Journal of Law and Society* 25(3): 313–35.

Burnett, R. and Maruna, S. (2006) 'The kindness of prisoners: Strengths-based resettlement in theory and in action', *Criminology & Criminal Justice* 6(1): 83–106.

Carrabine, E., Inganski, P. Lee, M., Plummer, K. and South, N. (2004) *Criminology: A Sociological Introduction*. London: Routledge.

Castel, R. (1991) 'From dangerousness to risk', in G. Burchell, C. Gordon and P. Miller (eds) *The Foucault Effect: Studies in Govermentality*. Chicago: University of Chicago Press.

Coleman, K., Jansson, K., Kaiza, P. and Reed, E. (2007) *Homicide, Firearm Offences and Intimate Violence 2005/2006* (Supplementary Volume 1 to Crime in England and Wales 2005/2006), http://webarchive.nationalarchives.gov.uk/20110220105210/rds.homeoffice.gov.uk/rds/pdfs07/hosb0207.pdf (accessed 23 October 2014).

Cowan, D., Pantazis, C. and Gilroy, R. (2001) 'Social housing as crime control: An examination of the role of housing management in policing sex offenders', *Social and Legal Studies* 10(4): 435–57.

Cowburn, M. and Dominelli, L. (2001) 'Making hegemonic masculinity: Reconstructing the paedophile as the dangerous stranger', *British Journal of Social Work* 31(3): 399–415.

Crawford, A. (2003) 'Contractual governance of deviant behaviour', *Journal of Law and Society* 30(4): 479–505.

———. (2006) 'Networked governance and the post-regulatory state? Steering, rowing and anchoring the provision of policing and security', *Theoretical Criminology* 10(4): 449–79.

Edwards, W. and Hensley, C. (2001) 'Contextualising sex offender management legislation and policy: Evaluating the problem of latent consequences in community notification laws', *International Journal of Offender Therapy and Comparative Criminology* 45(1): 83–101.

Ericson, R. (2007) *Crime in an Insecure World*. Cambridge: Polity Press.

Ericson, R. V. and Haggerty, K. D. (1997) *Policing the Risk Society*. Oxford: Clarendon Press.

Garland, D. (1999) 'The commonplace and the catastrophic: interpretations of crime in late modernity', *Theoretical Criminology* 3(3): 353–64.

———. (2001) *The Culture of Control: Crime and Social Order in Contemporary Society*. Oxford: Oxford University Press.

Greer, C. (2007) 'News media, victims and crime', in P. Davies, P. Francis and C. Greer (eds) *Victims, Crime and Society*. London: Sage.

Grubin, D. (1998), *Sex Offending Against Children: Understanding the Risk*, Police Research Series Paper 99. London: Home Office.

Hanvey, S., Philpot, T. and Wilson. C. (2011) *A Community-Based Approach to the Reduction of Sexual Offending: Circles of Support and Accountability*. London and Philadelphia: Jessica Kingsley.

Hebenton, B. and Seddon, T. (2009) 'From dangerousness to precaution: Managing sexual and violent offenders in an insecure and uncertain age', *British Journal of Criminology* 49(3): 343–62.

Hebenton, B. and Thomas, T. (1996) 'Sexual offenders in the community: Reflections on problems of law, community and risk management in the USA and England and Wales', *International Journal of the Sociology of Law* 24(4): 427–43.

Innes, M. (2004) 'Signal crimes and signal disorders: Notes on deviance as communicative action', *British Journal of Sociology* 55(3): 335–55.

Johnstone, G. (2000) 'Penal policy making: Elitist, populist or participatory?', *Punishment and Society* 2(2): 161–80.

Kemshall, H. and Maguire, M. (2001) 'Public protection, partnership and risk penalty: The multi-agency risk management of sexual and violent offenders', *Punishment and Society* 3(2): 237–64.

Kemshall, H. and Wood, J. (2007) 'Beyond public protection: An examination of community protection and public health approaches to high-risk offenders', *Criminology and Criminal Justice* 7(3): 203–22.

Lacey, N. (2004) 'Criminalisation as regulation', in C. Parker, C. Scott, N. Lacey and J. Braithwaite (eds) *Regulating Law*. Oxford: Oxford University Press.

Laws, D. R. (2000) 'Sexual offending as a public health problem: A North American perspective', *Journal of Research and Treatment* 8(3): 243–7.

———. (2008) 'The public health approach: A way forward?', in D. R. Laws and W. T. O'Donohue (eds) *Sexual Deviance: Theory, Assessment and Treatment*. New York: The Guildford Press.

Loader, I., and Walker, N. (2007) *Civilizing Security*. Cambridge: Cambridge University Press.

Lynch, M. (2002) 'Pedophiles and cyber-predators as contaminating forces: The language of disgust, pollution, and boundary invasions in federal debates on sex offender legislation', *Law and Social Inquiry* 27(3): 529–66.

Maruna, S. and LeBel, T. P. (2002) 'Revisiting ex-prisoner re-entry: A buzz-word in search of a narrative', in S. Rex and M. Tonry (eds) *Reform and Punishment*. Devon: Willan Publishing.

McAlinden, A. (2005) 'The use of "shame" with sexual offenders', *British Journal of Criminology* 45(3): 373–94.

———. (2007a) *The Shaming of Sexual Offenders: Risk, Retribution and Reintegration.* Oxford: Hart Publishing.

———. (2007b) 'Public attitudes towards sex offenders in Northern Ireland', report prepared for Northern Ireland Sex Offender Strategic Management Committee. Belfast: NISOSMC (with Research and Regional Services).

———. (2010a) 'Vetting sexual offenders: State over-extension, the punishment deficit and the failure to manage risk', *Social and Legal Studies* 19(1): 25–48.

———. (2010b) 'From a 'risks' to a 'strengths-based' model of offender resettlement' in S. Farrall, S. Maruna, M. Hough and R. Sparks (eds) *Escape Routes: Contemporary Perspectives on Life After Punishment.* New York and London: Routledge)

———. (2012) '"Grooming" and the sexual abuse of children: Institutional, Internet and familial dimensions', *Clarendon Studies in Criminology.* Oxford: Oxford University Press.

———. (2014a) 'Deconstructing victim and offender identities in discourses on child sexual abuse: Hierarchies, blame and the good/evil dialectic', *British Journal of Criminology* 54(2): 180–98.

———. (2014b) 'Sexting and cyberbullying', in R. Atkinson, *Shades of Deviance: A Primer on Crime, Deviance and Social Harm.* London and New York: Routledge.

Moran, M. (2003) *The British Regulatory State: High Modernism and Hyper Innovation.* Oxford: Oxford University Press.

Newburn, T. and Stanko, E. A. (eds) (1994) *Just Boys Doing Business? Men, Masculinities and Crime.* London: Routledge.

O'Malley, P. (1999) 'Volatile punishments: Contemporary penality and the neo-liberal government', *Theoretical Criminology* 3(2): 175–96.

Pratt, J. (2000) 'Emotive and ostentatious punishment: Its decline and resurgence in modern society', *Punishment and Society* 2(4): 417–39.

Salter, A. (2003) *Predators, Pedophiles, Rapists, and Other Sex Offenders: Who They Are, How They Operate, and How We Can Protect Ourselves and Our Children.* New York: Basic Books.

Saraga, E. (2001) 'Dangerous places: The family as a site of crime', in J. Muncie and E. McLaughlin (eds) *The Problem of Crime,* 2nd edn London: Sage.

Scott, C. (2004) 'Regulation in the age of governance: The rise of the post-regulatory state', in J. Jorduna and D. Levi-Faur (eds) *The Politics of Regulation in the Age of Governance.* Cheltenham: Edward Elgar.

Scott, S., Jackson, S. and Beckett-Milburn (1998) 'Swings and roundabouts: Risk anxiety and the everyday worlds of children', *Sociology* 32(4): 689–705.

Shearing, C. (2000) 'Punishment and the changing face of governance', *Punishment and Society* 3(2): 203–20.

Simon, J. (1998) 'Managing the monstrous: Sex offenders and the new penology', *Psychology, Public Policy and Law* 4(1/2): 452–67.

Smith, D. W., Letourneau, E. J., Saunders, B. E., Kilpatrick, D. G., Resnick, H. S. and Best, C. L. (2000) 'Delay in disclosure of childhood rape: Results from a national survey', *Child Abuse and Neglect* 24(2): 273–87.

Spencer, D. (2009) 'Sex offender as homo sacer', *Punishment and Society* 11(2): 219–40.

Stafford, A., Parton, N., Vincent, S. and Smith, C. (2011) *Child Protection Systems in the United Kingdom: A Comparative Analysis*. London: Jessica Kingsley.

Toch, H. (2000) 'Altruistic activity as correctional treatment', *International Journal of Offender Therapy & Comparative Criminology* 44(3): 270–78.

Ward, T., Mann, R. E. and Gannon, T. A. (2007) 'Good Lives model of offender rehabilitation: Clinical implications', *Aggression and Violent Behaviour* 12(1): 87–107.

Ward, T. and Marshall, W. L. (2004) 'Good lives, aetiology and the rehabilitation of sex offenders: A bridging theory', *Journal of Sexual Aggression* 10(2): 153–69.

Ward, T. and Maruna, S. (2007) *Rehabilitation: Beyond the Risk Assessment Paradigm*. London: Routledge.

Wardle, C. (2007) 'Monsters and angels: Visual press coverage of child murders in the USA and the UK, 1930-2000', *Journalism* 8(3): 263–84.

Weaver, B. and McNeill, F. (2010) 'Public Protection in Scotland: A Way Forward?', in A. Williams and M. Nash (eds) *Handbook of Public Protection*. Devon: Willan Publishing.

Wilson, R. J., Pichea, J. E. and Prinzo, M. (2007) 'Evaluating the effectiveness of professionally-facilitated volunteerism in the community-based management of high-risk sex offenders: Part Two – A comparison of recidivism rates', *The Howard Journal* 46(4): 327–37.

Zedner, L. (2009) 'Fixing the future? The pre-emptive turn in criminal justice', in B. McSherry, A. Norrie and S. Bronitt (eds) *Regulating Deviance: The Redirection of Criminalisation and the Futures of Criminal Law*. Oxford: Hart Publishing.

Zhang, S. X. (1995) 'Measuring shame in an ethnic context', *British Journal of Criminology* 35(2): 248–62.

9

THE COLLATERAL CONSEQUENCES OF RISK

Fergus McNeill
University of Glasgow, UK

Introduction

It is hard to imagine that there exists anywhere in the world a probation or parole or youth justice service that is not concerned with preventing reoffending by people under supervision. Both morally and pragmatically, that seems a perfectly good – perhaps an essential – aspiration for such services. It follows that being able to assess and manage risks of reoffending are crucial tasks for all such services. If services are not clear and 'evidence based' in their assessment and management of risks, they risk not only failing to protect the public but also intervening illegitimately and excessively in the lives of those subject to supervision.

That said, this chapter aims to explore the adverse, unintended and collateral consequences of allowing risk assessment and management to become central and overriding preoccupations of offender supervision. The central argument is that when risk-focused discourses and practices become dominant, they can actively (if indirectly) undermine attempts to promote positive changes in the lives of people subject to supervision, and thus undermine the various social goods that may flow from such changes. At their worst, risk-based discourses and practices may paradoxically work to increase and even realize risks of reoffending.

In order to develop this argument, the chapter begins by examining the results of a number of studies of experiences of rehabilitation within correctional settings that (sometimes indirectly) explore risk practices in criminal justice and youth justice. These studies expose some of the mechanisms through which a preoccupation with risk can become counterproductive. Seeking a way out of this impasse, the chapter goes on to ask how and in what ways the need to assess, manage and reduce risks can be balanced by the need to support desistance from crime and social integration.

Risk or change?

In previous papers (Robinson and McNeill, 2004; McCulloch and McNeill, 2007; McNeill, 2011), I have argued that rehabilitation's contemporary focus on risk assessment and management – and on public protection – carries certain social and political costs and benefits. The benefits are obvious. In an era when fiscal austerity is combined with populist punitiveness (see Bottoms, 1995; Garland, 2001), it may seem to leaders of correctional services (especially those services that take place primarily in the community – probation, parole and youth justice) that they have little choice but to 'sell' their services (and defend their services from cuts) on the basis that these services can contribute significantly to the public good by reducing risks, minimizing harms and protecting people from victimization. But, as the anthropologist Mary Douglas (1992) has pointed out, there is a paradox in the promise of safety; by its very nature such a promise may serve to accentuate rather than assuage our sense of threat. And if we are really anxious, fearful and – perhaps more to the point – angry about crime, probation and parole's promises to protect may ring hollow. In reality, community-based offender supervision (at least in its current forms) cannot *guarantee* public protection, since its mechanisms and methods rely on cooperation, compliance and ultimately change – and these are not phenomena that can be straightforwardly or securely engineered. Prison walls, by contrast, can be engineered, and they are (for the most part) secure. Thus, to a certain extent, they can deliver protection not through change but through control and incapacitation, albeit at unsustainably high fiscal and social costs.

This then represents a cultural and political problem for community corrections associated with the risk agenda, but in this chapter I want to focus on a different paradox and a different problem. Here, I want to explore how rehabilitation is experienced within systems and services preoccupied with risk, and in this way to explore other unintended and collateral consequences of risk.

In a recent documentary film about desistance from crime (The Road from Crime, 2012: see: www.iriss.org.uk/resources/road-crime), Mark Johnson, founder and Chief Executive of User Voice (an ex-offender-led charity, see: www.uservoice.org) described risk as 'the archenemy of change'. He added:

> You have to allow people to fail ... the failure is actually part of the change. And we don't allow that failure. We're so risk averse ... the system is very, very dysfunctional ... If you remove a man's or a woman's hope, you create and cultivate this ground for extreme behaviour. What's the point in changing when whatever I do I am completely defeated by people that don't even know me?

These are strong and concerning claims based not only on Mark Johnson's personal experience but also on the cumulative experiences of the wide range of people subject to punishment and supervision with whom he has worked.

They are also claims that, increasingly, have been supported and elaborated by rigorous academic research. An increasing number of studies have begun to examine or reveal (directly and indirectly) the pains of penal rehabilitation in its current risk-focused guise. Thus, for example, we find evidence of burgeoning resentment amongst English prisoners towards what seems to them to be the capricious and illegitimate exercise of 'soft power' by prison psychologists involved in key decisions about prisoner progression or release (Crewe, 2009; and more generally Maruna, 2011).

It might be argued that there is nothing really new in this. In the early days of the penitentiary, after all, prisoners were often placed in silent and solitary confinement in the hope that they would repent and make peace with their Maker. For them, the pains of penitentiary reform were doubtless profound. The project of 'coercive soul transformation' may have been designed and delivered somewhat differently from that directed at the late-modern risk-bearing prisoner or probationer – but prisoners then and now were and are undeniably subjected to painful disciplinary regimes (Foucault, 1975/1977).

However, the late-modern penal subject, rather than being left to deal before God with his own sinfulness and redemption, is compelled to *display* the malleability of his or her riskiness, to take responsibility for and *perform* the reduction and manageability of his or her riskiness. At least in some risk-based systems, it is the credibility of this performance that will determine progression in and release from punishment. In those circumstances, rehabilitation is both disciplinary and punishing in particularly potent ways (see Crewe, 2009).

For example, Lacombe's (2008) ethnographic study of an English prison–based sex offender programme reveals the ways in which risk-based rehabilitation invites people serving time for sex offences to contort their perceptions and presentations of self in line with the requirements of the particular programme or process to which they are subject. Digard's (2010, 2014) English study of the experiences of post-release supervision (and sometimes recall to custody) for people convicted of sexual offences suggests that these compelled contortions continue long after release and that such forms of supposedly rehabilitative supervision have significant penal bite and are often experienced as illegitimate and procedurally unfair.

Reuben Miller's (2014) fascinating ethnography of the re-entry experiences of 25 men in Chicago's west side (principally African American men) reveals similar dynamics:

> Reentry organizations, while not acknowledging this, engage in a logic in which former prisoners 'prove' their submission to a program of personal transformation by (1) completing programs designed to broker within them an ethic of transformation; and (2) sharing in treatment groups the kinds of struggles on which they are working. Thus, a changed life is one of constant (re) evaluation, (re) discovery, and above all consistent progress toward the moving target of personal transformation. Unwillingness to transform is disciplined by service providers who facilitate reentry programs, and by former prisoners participating in these groups themselves. (Miller, 2014, p. 325)

The change in rehabilitative discourses and practices that Miller (2014) reveals centre on what he terms 'carceral devolution'. In his study, rehabilitation (and thus risk management) is devolved from the professionalized institutions of the state (principally prisons) to the para-professionalized resources of impoverished communities themselves. The re-entry organizations in these communities work on and with what they can: the ex-prisoners who come to them. The consequence is that the socio-structural dynamics of reintegration are neglected. Rehabilitation here can only be a personal project of transformation, not a social one.

Alexandra Cox's (2011, 2013) ethnographic study of 39 young people (between the ages of 15 and 24, and mainly from minority ethnic communities) involved with the juvenile and adult justice systems of an Eastern American state again tells a similar story. In a paper that vividly describes the dilemmas that the young people face in participating in treatment programmes, Cox reaches the following conclusion:

> I argue that the 'wholly individualized fully competent subject' (Ruddick, 2007: 638; see also Viego, 2007) envisaged by juvenile justice systems is a fiction, and that young people's aspirations for wholeness may result in their domination by the behavioural change practices which are said to liberate them. This form of domination encourages them to express self-discipline and control, yet provides them with few opportunities for an exercise of such forms of control ... This expression of domination is ironic: it takes place in contexts where young

people actually possess few opportunities for social mobility, and thus their enactment of domination over others can cause their further enmeshment in institutions of social control. (Cox, 2011, p. 604)

Similar dynamics and consequences of risk-based, responsibilizing rehabilitation thus seem to cross borders, systems, practices and populations.

It is important to stress that these findings about the pains of rehabilitation and re-entry are not limited to ethnographic research in the United Kingdom or the United States. For the purposes of this chapter, a key message is that the traditional absence of punitive intent in parole, probation or youth justice services in many jurisdictions does not necessarily entail an absence of 'penal bite', at least if the views and experiences of those subject to community supervision are to be taken seriously. Researchers at the RAND corporation in the United States found that there are intermediate sanctions which surveyed prisoners equate with prison in terms of punitiveness. For some individuals, intensive forms of probation 'may actually be the more dreaded penalty' (Petersilia and Deschenes, 1994, p. 306; see also Payne and Gainey, 1998; May and Wood, 2010). More recently, Durnescu (2011) has specifically explored the 'pains of probation' as experienced in Romania. Alongside deprivations of time and the other practical and financial costs of compliance, and limitations on their autonomy and privacy, probationers also reported the pain of the 'forced return to the offence' and the pain of a life lived 'under a constant threat'. The threat in question in Durnescu's (2011) study was that of breach or revocation and with it further punishment. However, the studies referred to in the last paragraph also point to the threat of failing to persuade a probation officer, a psychologist or some other professional that one's 'riskiness' can be and is being properly addressed and managed (for further evidence of the pains of supervision in the English context, see Hayes, 2015)

Perhaps presaging these developments, Edgardo Rotman (1994) drew an important distinction between anthropocentric and authoritarian rehabilitation:

> The authoritarian model of rehabilitation is really only a subtler version of the old repressive model, seeking compliance by means of intimidation and coercion. Rehabilitation in this sense is essentially a technical device to mould the offender and ensure conformity to a predesigned pattern of thought and behaviour ... The anthropocentric or humanistic model of rehabilitation, on the other hand, grants primacy to the actual human being rather than metaphysical fixations or ideologies, which long served to justify the oppressive intervention of the state. Client centred and basically voluntary, such rehabilitation is conceived more as a right of the citizen than as a privilege of the state. (Rotman, 1994, p. 292)

This distinction, and more specifically its implication that the person engaged in rehabilitation must be treated as a moral subject and a fellow citizen rather than a risk-bearing object to be manipulated or adjusted in the interests of others, is an important one.

Desistance and risk

The primarily sociological studies reviewed in the preceding section may be less familiar to readers of this book than studies of the 'evidence-based practices' that are often said to offer the best hope of making correctional interventions more effective – and they may leave practitioner-readers feeling either defensive (insisting that practice is different) or hopeless (that if this is how rehabilitation is experienced then what else can be done?). Both reactions are worth exploring. It may well be that in some systems peoples' experiences of supervision are much more positive, and indeed there is much evidence that rehabilitative supervision is often experienced as helpful, even if the methodologies of studies that support this conclusion are often relatively weak (see Durnescu, Enengl and Grafl, 2013). An obvious answer to the defensive reaction – and an obvious challenge to services and practitioners – is to encourage independent and careful study of their service users' views and to take these views seriously.

But even where it might be accepted that experiences of rehabilitative supervision resemble those described above, there are alternatives to hopelessness. Just like people, penal institutions, cultures and practices can and do change, and indeed in many jurisdictions researchers, managers and practitioners are working, in Rotman's terms, to make rehabilitation more anthropocentric and less authoritarian. One key influence in this movement (but far from the only one) is research evidence about how and why people desist from offending.

Defining desistance is not straightforward, but most discussions begin with the idea of the cessation of offending behaviour. However, since we cannot know the precise moment at which any behaviour ceases permanently, scholars have increasingly come to conceptualize and to study desistance as a process (see e.g. Bottoms et al., 2004; Maruna, 2001; Farrall, 2002; Laub and Sampson, 2003). More specifically, we can think of desistance as a process of human development that is nested within its social contexts – a process that involves moving *away* from offending and *into* compliance with law and social norms. Maruna and Farrall (2004) draw an important distinction between *primary* and *secondary* desistance; the former relates merely to behaviour whereas, the latter implies a related shift in identity. They posit that shifts in identity and self-concept matter in securing longer-term, sustained changes in behaviour as opposed to mere lulls in offending. Though the importance of this distinction has been debated by some (e.g. Bottoms et al., 2004), secondary desistance and with it substantive or committed compliance to the law (see Robinson and McNeill, 2008) is likely to be important for people who have been heavily involved in offending and/or heavily criminalized. 'Spoiled identities' may need to be shed if change is to be secured.

It may also make sense to develop the concept of *tertiary* desistance, referring not just to shifts in behaviour or identity but also to shifts in one's sense of belonging to and acceptance by a (moral) community (Kirkwood and McNeill, 2015; McNeill, forthcoming). I argue, based on developing research evidence (e.g. Laub and Sampson, 2003; Bottoms and Shapland, 2011; Weaver, 2013, 2015), that since identity is socially constructed and negotiated, securing long-term change depends not just on how one sees oneself but also on how one is seen by others and on how one sees one's place in society. Putting it more simply, desistance is a social and political process as much as a personal one.

In fact, the links between behaviour, identity and belonging are already implicit in the main explanatory theories of desistance. These are commonly divided into ontogenic theories stressing the importance of age and maturation; sociogenic theories stressing the importance of social bond and ties; and narrative theories stressing the importance of subjective changes in identity (Maruna, 2001). Recently, in a valuable review of desistance research, Bottoms (2014) has suggested a fourth set of explanatory factors that are situational in character (see also Farrall et al., 2014). Drawing on his expertise in socio-spatial criminology, as well as on desistance research, Bottoms points out that various aspects of our social environments and of our situated 'routine activities' also provide important influences on our behaviour, for better or worse. While our environments and activities are closely connected to our social bonds or ties (e.g. bonds within intimate relationships and to families, work and faith communities), they deserve attention in their own right.

Given that desistance research itself is diverse and varied, and that there is so much debate within the field (e.g. about the relative contribution of structural and subjective factors to the process), it makes little sense to talk about critical perspectives on desistance research per se. That said, some critical criminologists (e.g. Baldry, 2010) have been wary both about whether desistance research might not represent another 'responsibilizing' discourse (and therefore a discursive resource for associated oppressive practices) and about the overgeneralization of theories of desistance across diverse populations. This second observation has been recognized and has begun to be addressed seriously by desistance researchers themselves (e.g.

Calverley, 2012; Farrall et al., 2014; Glynn, 2014; Sharpe, 2012; Weaver and McNeill, 2010). The issue of responsibilization is more complex. While it is true that some desistance theorists have offered rational choice explanations of the process, most are highly critical of such perspectives. And even those desistance researchers who have come to stress the role of personal agency in desistance processes (e.g. Giordano et al., 2002; Maruna, 2001; Farrall and Calverley, 2006) tend to stress an interactionist perspective in which social structural factors continue to be seen as important. It is simply incorrect to suggest that desistance research as a whole stresses personal and familial over social responsibility; but it is important to scrutinize interpretations of desistance research for policy and practice in order to assess whether and when desistance research may be co-opted into responsibilizing discourses that neglect socio-structural causes and correlates of crime and desistance from crime.

Beyond risk: Supporting change?

Many criminologists have recently engaged with practitioners, people with convictions and others in the shared task of exploring the implications of this research for policy and practice, and in particular for how we approach the challenges of punishment and rehabilitation (McNeill, 2003, 2006, 2009, 2012; McNeill and Weaver, 2007, 2010). Desistance research has particular policy and practice relevance to the extent that policy and practice is concerned with reducing reoffending and its associated economic, human and social costs. Rather than simply seeking to explain or understand desistance, the question becomes: 'Can we enable desistance through criminal sanctions, or do they tend to frustrate it?'

In a series of publications (e.g. McNeill and Weaver, 2010), desistance-based recommendations for penal policies and practices have tended to centre on the following themes:

1. For people who have been involved in persistent offending – and who have been persistently criminalized and penalized – desistance is a complex and difficult process, so we need to be realistic about these difficulties and to expect and manage lapses and relapses.

2. Since the process is different for different people (even if there are many common threads), interventions need to be properly individualized and tailored to the circumstances of the individual and to their subjective apprehension of resources and opportunities for positive change.

3. Since desistance is relational, interventions need to work on, with and through professional and social relationships (and not just through

individualized programmes). Developing social capital (meaning networks of reciprocal relationships) is crucial to supporting desistance.

4. Since desistance often involves developing hope for the future, interventions need to work to nurture hope and motivation. Since hope seems to be connected to developing a sense of 'agency' (meaning the capacity to govern one's life), interventions should seek to identify and mobilize personal strengths and self-determination, encouraging the acquisition of a sense of agency.

5. The language of policy and practice matters; to the extent that it entrenches criminalized identities, it may frustrate desistance. We need to mind our language, as well as to ensure that we recognize and celebrate progress, so as to reinforce the development or redevelopment of positive identities.

Given our brief discussion of responsibilization above, it is interesting to note that only one of these recommendations focuses on the personal attributes of individuals (in relation to hopefulness, motivation and a sense of personal agency). The other recommendations all reflect in part some of the concerns raised by research studies like those reviewed in the preceding section. The last recommendation in particular reflects criticism of the tendency of risk discourses and practices to construct people subject to rehabilitative interventions as bundles of risk factors and deficits, as offenders, as dangerous – basically as *different* from other human beings. The suggestion is that these discourses are likely to create an epistemic frame for practice that is a barrier to shedding an offending identity rather than a positive resource for helping people do so. To give a concrete example of this, consider this brief description of a specific correctional encounter related to me by a prominent advocate of evidence-based practice:

Offender: I'm depressed.

Correctional staff member: Why?

Offender: Because I just found out I am [high risk]. Now I know I'll never make it. I was sitting next to some other lady in group, and she was a mess, and she is a [moderate risk], and the whole time she was talking, I was thinking, 'You a mess you; never gonna make it.' Then I come to find out I'm worse than she is.

I stress again, this is not to object to risk assessment per se; rather, it is to show that careless talk about risk in the context of correctional interventions is very likely to be counterproductive.

The correctional conversation above is also interesting in that it suggests that the 'offender' in question has learned to see risk as an attribute of people, not as an attribute of interactions between people, situations and environments. In the very recent chapter already referred to above, Bottoms (2014) suggests that we need to add to the list of practice prescriptions above the suggestion that practice attends carefully to the routine activities and social environments of people involved in offending. In other words, we need to provide practical supports and activities that enable and sustain change; we need to engage with situations and contexts as well as persons to support change (and, implicitly, to manage risks).

However, more broadly, and reflecting the critique offered by Miller (2014) and Cox (2011) above, some desistance researchers have argued that over the last 20 years our approaches to punishment and rehabilitation have become too narrowly focused on supporting personal change, not as a result of the influence of desistance research (which the trend predates), but rather because of the unfortunate conjunction of narrow conceptions of evidence-based practice and the managerialization of criminal justice since the late 1980s. Indeed, I have argued in previous papers (McNeill, 2012, 2014) that this has led to neglect of three other forms of rehabilitation – moral, social and judicial. The central argument in these papers is that no amount of personal change can secure desistance if change is not recognized and supported by the community ('social rehabilitation'), by the law and by the state ('judicial rehabilitation'). Without these forms of informal and formal recognition, legitimate opportunities (e.g. for participation in the labour market or in social life) will not become available, and return to offending may be made more likely. In some cases, the failure in state punishment to attend directly to the need for moral rehabilitation (the settling of debts between the offender, victim and community) may also undermine social rehabilitation. Restorative justice may have something to offer here. More generally, my position is that these four forms of rehabilitation are most often interdependent and that failing to attend to all four in correctional policy and practice reduces the likelihood of successful desistance. To put it simply: it is not (just) the person who has offended who needs to be corrected; it is the broken social relationships that lie behind offending and that are exacerbated by offending.

More recently still, I have argued that penal policy and practice needs to reconsider how it frames its goals (Kirkwood and McNeill, 2015; McNeill, 2015). Studying and supporting desistance eventually forces us to address the complex question not of what people desist *from*, but what they desist *into*. In other words, if desistance is a process or a journey, we are eventually compelled to seek to understand and articulate its destination. The concepts of citizenship, integration and solidarity may have much to offer in addressing this question; perhaps a positively framed set of goals for criminal sanctions operationalizing these concepts (and a positive set of metrics for judging their successes) may help us move beyond an increasingly fruitless preoccupation with risk and reoffending.

The unlikely analogy of plumbing might help to make clear the differences between these positive and negative perspectives. Most of the time, when we think about plumbing – and when we call plumbers – it is because we are concerned about flaws (or leaks) in our plumbing systems. We know that, left unattended, even very minor leaks have the capacity to destroy the fabric of our homes and to diminish their value. Major leaks can do serious damage very quickly and can make life in our homes intolerable. A good plumber, we tend to think, is one who fixes leaks swiftly and efficiently – minimizing our losses and restoring our comforts.

But there is another way to think about plumbing; the way that architects, for example, might think about it. For them, plumbing is a central design feature in any property, the purpose of which is to bring two of the necessities for human life – heat and water – to wherever they are needed (and, of course, to remove some of the waste that human life inevitably produces). Perhaps for architects, the 'true' purpose of plumbing is to make human life comfortable in a given space and thus to allow its human dwellers to thrive.

My suggestion is that, much of the time, when we think and talk about criminal justice and specifically risk-based rehabilitation in criminal justice, we think and talk as if its institutions are like leak-repair or leak-prevention services. In contrast, I argue that perhaps *we should judge rehabilitation not so much by the evils (or harms) they reduce as by the goods they promote*. In other words, perhaps we should learn to think and practice rehabilitation like architects of justice (see McNeill, 2015).

Conclusion

To sum up, the following table uses the practice prescriptions of desistance research discussed above to highlight some of the key tensions between approaches to rehabilitative interventions focused on managing risk and those focused on supporting desistance:

Table 9.1 Desistance Based and Risk Based Practice

Supporting desistance (at its best)	Managing risk (at its worst)
Realism (expects and manages lapses)	Demands compliance
Individualizes	Dividualizes (i.e. treats people as instances of 'types', not as persons)
Works in, with and through relationships	Works on the individual, uses relationships to manage risk
Builds and sustains hope	Manages fear
Builds strengths	Addresses deficits
Supports agency	Applies external controls/interventions
Develops social capital/integration	Manages social control/containment/exclusion
Provides positive recognition	Reinforces negative labelling

Binary oppositions, like the ones set out here are always problematic. I am not arguing that all (or even most) risk-based practices contain the attributes listed in the left-hand column. I am also not arguing that it is an inevitable consequence of thinking about and focusing on risk that these attributes emerge. I *am* arguing that the careless absorption of risk discourses into the ways that we think about and work with people in the criminal and juvenile justice systems creates a danger that these problems emerge – and the evidence in the first section of this paper suggests that this is not as uncommon as we might wish.

Perhaps most fundamentally, when we construct and treat people as bundles of risks, we risk neglecting their strengths, their potential and, ultimately, their humanity. As well as being a failure of professional ethics (since it is a failure to offer the 'respect for persons' that is so often said to lie at the heart of social work values), this likely has practical consequences. When people involved in justice pick up on being constructed and treated in this way, the possibilities of constructive engagement with them diminish. Who amongst us would wish to extend our trust to someone who defined and treated us only with reference to our vulnerabilities and deficiencies?

Some sociologists have used the terms 'symbolic violence' and 'misrecognition' to refer to what happens when one person or group *imposes* such definitions and understandings on others. Perhaps if we could have complete confidence in our classification instruments and skills, then it might be more problematic to object to the imposition of these constructions. But we do not and cannot have this confidence – and so, with a cruel irony, to construct and classify people in this way is arguably offensive at best and dangerous at worst … and it begs the question of who is posing risks to whom.

References

Baldry, E. (2010) 'Women in transition: from prison to...?' *Current Issues in Criminal Justice* 22: 253.

Bottoms, A. (1995) 'The philosophy and politics of punishment and sentencing', in Clarkson, C. and Morgan, R. (eds) *The politics of sentencing reform*. Oxford: Clarendon.

———. (2014), 'Desistance from crime', forthcoming in Z. Ashmore and R. Shuker (eds) *Forensic Practice in the Community* London: Routledge.

Bottoms, A., Shapland, J., Costello, A., Holmes, D. and Muir, G. (2004) 'Towards desistance: Theoretical underpinnings for an empirical study', *The Howard Journal* 43(4): 368–89.

Bottoms, A. and Shapland, J. (2011) 'Steps towards desistance among male young adult recidivists', in S. Farrall, M. Hough, S. Maruna and R. Sparks (eds) *Escape Routes: Contemporary Perspectives on Life after Punishment*. London: Routledge.

Calverley, A. (2012) *Cultures of Desistance: Rehabilitation, reintegration and ethnic minorities*. International Series on Rehabilitation and Desistance. London: Routledge.

Cox, A. (2011) 'Doing the programme or doing me? The pains of youth imprisonment', *Punishment and Society* 13(5): 592–610.

———. (2013) 'New visions of social control? Young peoples' perceptions of community penalties', *Journal of Youth Studies* 16(1): 135–50.

Crewe, B. (2009) *The Prisoner Society: Power, Adaptation and Social Life in an English Prison*. Oxford: Oxford University Press.

Digard, L. (2010) 'When legitimacy is denied: Sex offenders' perceptions and experiences of prison recall'. *Probation Journal* 57(1): 1–19.

———. (2014) 'Encoding risk: Probation work and sex offenders' narrative identities', *Punishment and Society* 16(4): 428–47.

Douglas, M. (1992) *Risk and Blame: Essays in Cultural Theory*. London: Routledge.

Durnescu, I. (2011) 'Pains of probation: Effective practice and human rights', *International Journal of Offender Therapy and Comparative Criminology* 55: 530–45.

Durnescu, I., Enengl, C. and Grafl, C. (2013) 'Experiencing supervision' in McNeill, F. and Beyens, K. (eds) *Offender Supervision in Europe*. Basingstoke: Palgrave.

Farrall, S. (2002) *Rethinking What Works with Offenders: Probation, Social Context and Desistance from Crime*. Cullompton: Willan Publishing.

Farrall, S. and Calverley, A. (2006) *Understanding Desistance from Crime*. Maidenhead: Open University Press.

Farrall, S., Hunter, B., Sharpe, G. and Calverley, A. (2014) *Criminal Careers in Transition: The Social Context of Desistance from Crime. Clarendon Studies in Criminology*. Oxford: Oxford University Press.

Foucault, M. (1975/1977). *Discipline & Punish*. (English trans. 1977), London: Allen Lane.

Garland, D. (2001) *The Culture of Control*. Oxford: Oxford University Press.

Giordano, P. C., Cernkovich, S. A. and Rudolph, J. L. (2002) Gender, crime, and desistance: Toward a theory of cognitive transformation. *American Journal of Sociology* 107(4): 990–1064.

Glynn, M. (2014) *Black Men, Invisibility and Crime: Towards a Critical Race Theory of Desistance*. International Series on Rehabilitation and Desistance. London: Routledge.

Hayes, D. (2015) 'The impact of supervision on the pains of community penalties in England and Wales: An exploratory study', *European Journal of Probation* 7(2): 85–102.

Kirkwood, S. and McNeill, F. (2015) 'Integration and Reintegration: Comparing pathways to citizenship through asylum and criminal justice' *Criminology & Criminal Justice,* first published on March 16, 2015 as doi: 10.1177/1748895815575618.

Lacombe, D.(2008) 'Consumed with sex: The treatment of sex offenders in risk society', *British Journal of Criminology* 48(1): 55–74.

Laub, J. and Sampson, R. (2003) *Shared Beginnings, Divergent Lives: Delinquent Boys to Age Seventy*. Cambridge, MA: Harvard University Press.

McCulloch, P. and F. McNeill (2007) 'Consumer Society, Commodification and Offender Management', *Criminology and Criminal Justice* 7(3): 223–42.

McNeill, F. (2003) 'Desistance based practice', in W-H. Chui and M. Nellis (eds) *Moving Probation Forward: Evidence, Arguments and Practice* (pp. 146–62) Harlow: Pearson Education.

———. (2006) 'A desistance paradigm for offender management', *Criminology and Criminal Justice* 6(1): 39–62.

———. (2009) *Towards Effective Practice in Offender Supervision*. Glasgow: Scottish Centre for Crime and Justice Research, available at: www.sccjr.ac.uk/documents/McNeil_Towards.pdf.

———. (2011) 'Probation, credibility and justice', *Probation Journal* 58(1): 9–22.

———. (2012) 'Four forms of 'offender' rehabilitation: Towards an interdisciplinary perspective', *Legal and Criminological Psychology* 17(1): 18–36.

———. (2014) 'Punishment as rehabilitation' in G. Bruinsma and D. Weisburd (eds) *Encyclopedia of Criminology and Criminal Justice* (pp. 4195–206), Springer Science and Business Media: New York. DOI 10.1007/978-1-4614-5690-2, (A final draft version of this paper is available open access online at http://blogs.iriss.org.uk/discoveringdesistance/files/2012/06/McNeill-When- PisR.pdf.) Accessed on 28.7.15.

———. (2015) 'Positive criminology, positive criminal justice?', in Ronei, N. and Segev, D. (eds) *Positive Criminology*. London: Routledge.

McNeill, F. and Weaver, B. (2007) *Giving Up Crime: Directions for Policy*. Edinburgh: Scottish Consortium on Crime and Criminal Justice.

———. (2010) *Changing Lives? Desistance Research and Offender Management*. Glasgow: Scottish Centre for Crime and Justice Research, available at http://blogs.iriss.org.uk/discoveringdesistance/files/2012/12/Changing-Lives.pdf.

Maruna, S. (2001) *Making Good*. Washington, DC: American Psychological Association.

Maruna, S. and Farrall, S. (2004) 'Desistance from crime: A theoretical reformulation', *Kvlner Zeitschrift fur Soziologie und Sozialpsychologie* 43: 171–94.

May, D. and P. Wood (2010) *Ranking Correctional Punishments: Views from Offenders, Practitioners and the Public*. Durham, NC: Carolina Academic Press.

Miller, R. (2014) 'Devolving the carceral state: Race, prisoner reentry, and the micro politics of urban poverty management', *Punishment and Society* 16(3): 305–35.

Payne, B., and Gainey, R. (1998), 'A qualitative assessment of the pains experienced on electronic monitoring', *International Journal of Offender Therapy and Comparative Criminology* 42: 149–63.

Petersilia, J. and Deschenes, E. (1994) 'Perceptions of punishment: Inmates and staff rank the severity of prison versus intermediate sanctions', *The Prison Journal* 74(3): 306–28.

Robinson, G. and McNeill, F. (2004) 'Purposes matters: The ends of probation', in G. Mair (ed.) *What Matters in Probation Work*. Cullompton: Willan Publishing.

———. (2008) Exploring the dynamics of compliance with community penalties, *Theoretical Criminology* 12(4): 431–49.

Rotman, E., (1994) 'Beyond punishment', in Duff, A. and Garland, D. (eds) *A Reader on Punishment*. Oxford: Oxford University Press.

Ruddick, S. (2007) 'At the horizons of the subject: Neo-liberalism, neo-conservatism and the rights of the child: Part two: Parent, caregiver, state', *Gender, Place & Culture* 14(6): 627–40.

Shapland, J. and Bottoms, A. (2011) 'Reflections on social values, offending and desistance among young adult recidivists', *Punishment & Society* 13(3): 256–82.

Sharpe, G. (2012) *Offending Girls: Young Women and Youth Justice*. Abingdon: Routledge.

Viego, A. (2007) *Dead Subjects: Toward a Politics of Loss in Latino Studies*. Durham, NC: Duke University Press.

Weaver, B. (2013) *The Story of the Del: From Delinquency to Desistance*, PhD thesis, Glasgow: University of Strathclyde.

———. (2015) *Offending and Desistance*. London: Routledge.

Weaver, B. And McNeill, F. (2010) 'Travelling hopefully: Desistance research and probation practice', in Brayford, J., Cowe, F. and Deering, J. (eds) *What Else Works? Creative Work with Offenders*. Cullompton: Willan.

10

PROBATION, RISK AND THE POWER OF THE MEDIA

Wendy Fitzgibbon
London Metropolitan University, UK

Abstract: Media representation of offenders strongly influences community perceptions of offender-related risks as well as risk management practices within the criminal justice system. This chapter examines how weak, fragmented communities are both vulnerable to media moral panic and impede desistance strategies based on viable non-criminal social networks, with a resultant reinforcing of the focus on risk management and public protection. The influence of this on workers and practice within the criminal justice system will be examined, as well as broader consequences such as stigma and marginalization of offenders.

Introduction

The probation service often appears to be misunderstood and criticized by the public in terms of its role and its effectiveness. Public knowledge and confidence in the ability of probation staff to supervise offenders to minimize their risk has been identified in recent years as a problem. The obstacles faced by probation in terms of public confidence are clearly illustrated in Table 10.1 extracted from the British Crime Survey 2009 by Smith (2010, p. 18).

Two things stand out. First, that police get much higher confidence ratings than other branches of the criminal justice system, and second that out of all areas of criminal justice, irrespective of levels of public confidence, only probation and the prison service did not improve their positions between 2002–3 and 2007–8.

Table 10.1 Proportion of the public who think different parts of the Criminal Justice Service are doing a good or excellent job, 2002–03 to 2007–08, England and Wales

	2002–3	2007–8
Police	48	53
Prisons	25	25
Magistrates	26	31
Probation	24	23
CPS	23	30
Judges	25	30
Youth Court	14	16

Table 10.2 Public confidence in effectiveness of criminal justice, 2010–11

Confident (percent):	Very	Fairly	Not very	Not at all
Police are effective at catching criminals	8	58	28	6
CPS is effective at prosecuting	6	45	36	13
Courts are effective at dealing with cases promptly	5	38	41	15
Courts are effective at giving punishments which fit the crime	3	23	41	32
Prisons are effective at punishing offenders	3	25	41	30
Prisons are effective at rehabilitating offenders	2	19	48	32
Probation service is effective at preventing reoffending	2	22	51	26
CJS as a whole is effective	3	40	43	14

More recent data extracted from the 2010–11 Crime Survey for England and Wales reinforces this picture. The table above (from Hough et al., 2013, p. 31) attempts to measure degrees of public confidence in various parts of the criminal justice system.

In these figures probation appears to score lowest in terms of lack of public confidence, though the percentage of respondents feeling that probation is 'fairly' effective is slightly higher than for prisons. Again, police score by far the highest ratings in terms of public confidence. What then, if any, is the role of the media in what Maruna and King (2008, p. 339) aptly characterize as probation's 'distinct public relations problem'?

The process of risk amplification

The tragic death of 17-month-old 'Baby Peter' Connelly and the violent murder of two French research students by Dano Sonnex and Nigel Farmer (Fitzgibbon, 2011) provided graphic illustrations of how the media are able to systematically frame high-profile calamities to the detriment of both social work and probation. Often this is seen simply as a process of moral panic in which print and broadcast media are able to exaggerate and magnify the risk of such incidents and vilify hard-working probation officers and social workers in order to gain an audience. To obtain a better understanding of some of the less obvious factors at work, it might be useful to start with a brief look at the less turbulent, but no less important, area of how the media deals with some types of physical risks – issues like climate change or health risks from genetically modified food. It is in this area of investigation that government agencies have invested in systematic studies.

The study by Judith Petts and others for the Health and Safety Executive (HSE) (Petts et al., 2001) discusses two models of media amplification of (physical) risk. First, the Social Amplification of Risk Framework (SARF) is a linear model that starts with a 'risk-related event' to which initial responses by the public are then 'subject to predictable changes as they are filtered through the various "amplification" stations' (Petts et al., 2001, p. 1). The latter can include, besides the media itself, individual scientists, politicians, government agencies and activist groups.

The SARF model focuses on physical risks (air pollution, GM food) which may affect large populations, but the perspective is useful in that, first, the media are seen as building on already established public fears rather than creating them (as in crude versions of moral panic theory), and second, there will be other stakeholders than the media who will contribute to the amplification process. Thus the Sonnex and Baby Peter incidents could be taken as 'risk events' which were then taken up not just by the media but also by sections of the political elite – in particular the ministers of the relevant departments (Jack Straw and Ed Balls) who, as stakeholders, had their own input into the amplification process, notably the sacking of the head of Haringey Children's Services, Sharon Shoesmith, and the resignation of the Chief Probation Officer for London, David Scott. This then provided a resource for the media to highlight, magnify and re-frame the issues as failures by social work and probation (Fitzgibbon, 2011). It is fair to say that neither probation nor social work stood a chance to participate as counterbalances in the amplification process.

This model moves beyond the simple 'media-orchestrated moral panic' view. Indeed, the HSE was of the view that 'the media can only amplify or attenuate risk if they capture or resonate with an existing public mood, and even then the media are not alone in this function' (Petts et al., 2001,

p. ix). This is in line with critical studies of moral panic theory, in particular the classic study by Hall et al. (1978) of media panic over street theft (mugging), in which not only the media but police and courts entered into the amplification process.

The second model considered by the HSE research is a modification of the SARF model, namely the Model of Risk Communication (MRC). Derived from Bourdieu's (1998) view of public communication as a field of play and competition, this refines the account of the amplification process with a more dynamic structure of mutual interaction 'in which key players continually launch initiatives and respond to each others' moves ... [entering into] ... exchange relations with journalists, bargaining information, images or announcements against publicity.' The media 'operate as the central space in which battles over the identification, definition and management of risk are fought out' (Petts et al., 2001, p. 4).

This model places greater stress on a process of *continuous* interaction. The lay public participates in this process by actively interpreting and discussing information rather than passively receiving it as in the original SARF model. Other key participants from the outset include (depending on the nature of the issue) government, corporations, advocacy and campaigning groups, all of whom may have differential access to and influence on the media determined by the resources at their disposal for 'defining the situation'. The latter include relations of legitimacy and trust in the eyes of the public.

Again, this model fits most immediately struggles around such issues as risks to the public from GM foods and the various interplays between food multinationals, anti-GM activists, government and media. We are invited to look at the power relations (e.g. between eco-activists and the big food multinationals) in a competitive process of attempting to define the field and develop policy initiatives. But the notion of continual interaction between a number of actors with differing degrees of power, derived from both control and access to the media on the one hand and legitimacy and trust in the community on the other, makes obvious sense.

In the Sonnex case, for example, it would lead to a focus on the power relations between probation, the political elite, the media and community groups, and it provides a framework for the study of the relatively weak position of probation vis-à-vis other actors, both due to a lack of an independent (from the Ministry of Justice) institutional voice and from the very nature of its mode of operation, in particular the adoption of the so-called risk agenda.

In criminology, the nearest to this is the well-known Left Realist 'Square of Crime' (Lea, 1992, 2002), which sees the process of crime control as a frame of interaction between offenders, victims, communities and criminal justice agencies. To analyse the situation facing probation and risk management, we can construct a modified version of the square, incorporating what we judge to be the principal actors in the relationship between probation and the media. This framework can incorporate some of the insights from the MRC approach, in particular noting that, contrary to SARF or moral panic theory, it is not simply a question of the media seizing on and amplifying a 'risk event' and being able to outwit probation in doing so. Rather, from the outset, a process of interaction in which modes of operation and access to various types of resources between all components of the 'square' comes into play.

This approach also, it is important to note, clashes with simplistic notions of a single focus of power (e.g. the coercive state which somehow directly dictates to the media and overpowers other potential actors). As David Garland has recently pointed out, the capacity of the state to directly dictate penal policy differs between countries and is related to factors such as the relative autonomy of penal state organs (e.g. the judiciary, prison and probation administration) within the state itself and the cultural as well as material resources at the disposal of various actors (see McNeill, 2013). This of course in no way rules out the possibility that the eventual outcome of interaction between seemingly autonomous participants is structured *in the final instance* as a reflection of the power of the state or powerful interests allied to it. It is rather that such power relations can only be seen as the *outcome* of interaction rather than presupposed at its *outset*.

This is the approach that is adopted here. What follows attempts to set out the relations between the main actors – probation, the media, the political system (in particular the interests of the dominant political elite), the communities within which offenders and their victims are situated and the particular character of the latter themselves in the context of risk management. The chapter concludes by attempting to assess the overall outcomes of the interaction process.

Probation and the media

Media coverage is never simply informative. Generations of social scientists have attempted to assess the role of the mass media in influencing and shaping public opinion rather than simply investigating 'facts' and reflecting the opinions that various sections of the public already have (Chibnall, 1977; Cohen and Young, 1981; Critcher, 2009; Greer, 2011).

What is important is that abandoning the SARF model of the 'event' then amplified as part of a moral panic in favour of a process that is, at the outset, interactive and enables an understanding not just that the media may have a political agenda but that there are structural contradictions between the media and probation (and social work for that matter) which derive from the distinct modes of operation of probation and the media and which cannot easily be resolved.

Many practitioners feel, quite rightly, that the media tend to be only interested in probation when something has gone demonstrably wrong – such as a serious further offence (SFO) committed by an offender under their supervision (Fitzgibbon, 2011, 2012). It is easy to see this as simply a right-wing punishment politics predominating in the 'red top' print media. Such politics characterizes community sentences as 'walking free', so that an offender outside prison committing an SFO is taken as vindication of the view that the person should really have been behind bars all along. Such politics among sections of the print media may well exist, but behind its success lies an important structural issue related to the very different modes of operation of probation and the media.

Probation starts from its successes, the hundreds of ex-offenders who are kept out of trouble and integrated back into a non-criminal way of life. Probation does not start from the fact that occasionally individuals under its supervision commit SFOs. It is a measure of success that such things are relatively rare. But this is precisely where the media starts. Journalists focus on the event (the SFO) and then search for answers to questions about this particular event: how did this happen and who is to blame? There are quite different, and conflicting, notions of risk at work here. Probation starts from the low risk of SFOs, and when one such occurs is always in a difficult position, being forced to say things like These things are rare, but we cannot of course guarantee absolutely that they will never happen. We will attempt to plug the holes identified by our inquiry into this particular case and ensure it is unlikely to recur.'

But the media works in a different way. The humdrum everyday success of the Probation Service is not news: the SFO is. The media focuses on the particular event, *not* to argue that it is rare, but to point out that it *has happened*. The media then derives its own conceptions of risk not from the aggregate rehabilitation statistics, but from this single event. It could happen again and any one (of our readers) might be the victim next time. In place of actuarial risk statistics, we have Murphy's Law: if it can happen, it will happen. That is the logic of the media focus on the particular event. The fact that such a level of security and risk reduction as that demanded by the media could only really be achieved in prison (Maruna and King, 2008) can of course be seen as vindication of right-wing punishment politics and the belief that serious offenders should remain in prison rather than be released on licence. Probation is at a disadvantage.

The discussions noted above on physical risk have identified similar issues with media coverage. Thus Jenny Kitzinger notes that

> TV news, radio reports and the press, for example, do not cover 'risk' as formally defined (as a multiple of likelihood and impact), they cover stories: disasters, crises, controversies and Inquiries. (Kitzinger, 2009a, p. 7)

The 'research methodology' of journalism with regard to the reporting of risks is summarized thus by Kitzinger:

> Key factors impacting on media involvement include the 'body count' (how many people are killed at once) and who is at risk (is it someone audiences care about?). Journalists will also consider whether the threat can be given a 'human interest angle', how it can be made personally relevant to their audiences and where a threat occurs or disaster strikes. (Kitzinger, 2009b, p. 2)

Sociologist Frank Furedi (2006) in his discussion of public fear distinguishes between *theoretical* risk (the calculus of probabilities by experts) and *speculative* risk. Experts produce actuarial statistics of theoretical risks, calculations of certain chance of a particular type of event occurring. The media, he argues, replaces this with a quite different notion of speculative risk based around the individual event which *has* happened and therefore it should have been foreseen that it *would* happen. Thus 'exceptional events such as the abduction of a child are turned into a normal risk' (Furedi, 2006, p. xvii).

And once the perpetrator of the exceptional event, such as child abduction, is identified (and the media rush in before the evidence is conclusive), the event is turned into a person, and risk leaves entirely the realm of statistical probabilities and becomes inhered in an *individual* person or type of person. This then enables the media to fuel moral panics, suggesting that the phenomenon is far more widespread than it actually is and that the institutions responsible for protecting us from such events have suffered more spectacular failure than they actually have.

This effect of media focus may be growing in intensity. Greer and McLaughlin (2012) see the rise of what they call 'attack journalism' based on a 'cluster of trends: the decline in deference to institutional authority; conflicting moralities; ideological divisions; the emergence of celebrity culture; an accommodating legal context; and technological developments that have revolutionized the communications marketplace' (Greer and McLaughlin, 2012, p. 397). Competition from other news sources increases the pressure on print media to demonstrate its 'relevance'. A similar point is made by David Hayes (see Hayes, 2013, p. 25).

Finally, this journalistic methodology also perhaps explains why police (detectives) have historically had a better relationship with the media than has probation. The detective is not regarded as responsible for allowing a murder or child abduction to take place, but rather for apprehending the perpetrator. Neither detectives nor journalists find it necessary to defend their actions by pointing to the rarity of such events. It is true that the police in general may be criticized if crime rates rise steeply, but investigating detectives are judged more by the successful clear-up of those crimes which have occurred. They are vulnerable to media criticism if an investigation of a high-profile case is bungled, but normally detectives and journalists operate in very similar ways. The focus is on acquiring information about individuals, the detective to get a 'result' and the journalist to get a 'scoop'. Information exchange between detectives and crime journalists has, for this reason, a long history.

For probation, however, it is only the failure which will attract journalists' interest. The popular media does not carry stories about how gritty and determined probation officers successfully rehabilitated a former murderer, bank robber or drugs trafficker and kept them out of crime. Indeed, such is the strength of the focus on probation only when it fails that current (2014) moves to privatize the service were actually justified by government partly by reference to the high reoffending rates of short-term prisoners who do *not even fall under probation responsibilities!* (Fitzgibbon, 2013)

Media and community

Communities in which crimes occur and in which offenders are supervised by probation are not solely dependent on the media for information and opinion about matters concerning crime, and there are important restraints on the power of media to orchestrate moral panics. Opinions and information, shared between community members in the normal processes of interaction – at work, in pubs and recreational activities and through family and friendship networks – act as important alternatives to print and broadcast media and impose checks on the ability of the latter to construct images and narratives of fear and risk. Thus the 'lay public's responses to the media are continually negotiated and refined through everyday conversation and argument ... [such that] ... the media can only amplify or attenuate risk if they capture or resonate with an existing public mood, and even then the media are not alone in this function' (Petts, 2001, p. ix).

In traditional close-knit communities, for example, people might know criminals and their families, know who was on probation and know how they were progressing. Media stereotypes conflicting with such experience would be harder to establish. People would be likely to have their own judgements about risk based on more than a passing experience of the offender and how typical he or she was in comparison with other offenders. These would be communicated to probation and other agencies (police, schools, etc.) so that there would be less likelihood of a conflict of views into which the media could gain a foothold. People would also be more likely to know the local probation officers, as they did the local police, and when someone on licence did commit a further offence, a more balanced judgement could be made about precisely what such an incident indicated as to levels of risk. In these circumstances the risk calculations made by ordinary people are much more likely to approximate those deployed by agencies such as probation.

But this type of community cohesion is steadily weakening under the impact of economic change (Dorling et al., 2008). There is a steady accumulation of evidence regarding community fragmentation. A 2008 survey by the Joseph Rowntree Trust on public perceptions of social problems (Watts, 2008) found that community decline featured prominently, with people often expressing feelings that 'the less people know their neighbours, the less they care about the neighbourhood and the more they feel alienated and scared' (Watts, 2008, p. 9).

More recent research by the Princes Trust (2010) points to a continuation of these trends, particularly among young people. The research – a poll of 2226 young people aged 16–24 – found that more than a third did not feel part of their local community, and almost a third did not feel that there was a future for them in their own area. There was also a breakdown of communication between age groups, with more than half of respondents (54%) indicating that they 'rarely' or 'never' spoke to people over the age of 40 in their local community, while more than two-thirds (68%) 'rarely' or 'never' spoke to those over 60 years of age. Almost a quarter (23%) felt ignored by older people, while almost half (46%) thought older people were scared of young people.

As people living in a locality become more isolated and interact less outside the household (leaving aside the issues of interaction in online internet communities), the greater the influence of the media in defining the levels of risk presented by individuals on probation. It is important to note that there are two distinct processes at work. First, as channels of information outside the media dry up, people become more dependent on the media for information, including about risk of crime (Jewkes, 2004). People are pulled towards the media.

But, additionally, the more isolated from community-based networks of information and discussion they become, the more people's concepts of risk and fear assimilate in any case to the paradigm of speculative risk deployed by the media. The community starts to work in the same way as the media. When a crime takes place, particularly if the offender is on probation, people have little recourse to local knowledge of other offenders who were successfully rehabilitated and went on to make good. Furedi's notion of speculative risk becomes the natural recourse not only for the media but for the population as well. There is just the *individual instance* on which to base their judgements, and people have no alternative but to derive their notions of risk from that instance, unchecked by any wider knowledge of similar events (see Altheide, 2002). People increasingly lack a 'reliable indication of what constitutes a realistic level of concern, anxiety or alarm' (Hier, 2008, p. 178). This inevitably widens the gap between public conceptions of risk and the actuarial measures deployed by bureaucratic organizations, including probation. The latter appear complacent, distant and uncaring about people's fears and concerns. By contrast, people are driven into the hands of a media which is reacting in exactly the same way and which gives a voice, a coherence and a sense of shared concern to people's fears. The media provide a temporary feeling of solidarity through a moral outrage directed at the 'authorities' who manifestly failed in their task of protection. The evidence that they have failed is provided by the single incident quite irrespective of the fact that a total security against *any* instances could only be guaranteed by incarceration (Maruna and King, 2008).

Total security is replaced by 'total risk', which is seen to be inherent less and less in any calculus of probabilities and increasingly in the characteristics of individuals themselves – either as threatening 'others', what Furedi called 'nearby strangers' or as an attribute of permanent victimhood such that 'to be at risk is no longer only about what you do, or the probability of some hazard impacting on your life – it is also about who you are. It becomes a fixed attribute of the individual' (Furedi, 2006, p. 5).

Communities, offenders and victims

But there is a second problem: there are flaws at the heart of the notion of risk that strengthen the position of those who focus on the individual incident. The key feature of actuarial statistics, as is well known, is that they are based on group characteristics. People with this or that life history and social indicators (poverty, education level, job history, drug use, family stability and so on) are statistically more or less *likely* to commit offences than people with different characteristics. The conclusion is based on the offence rate for the group over a given time period. This leaves risk analysis wide open to the well-known *actuarial fallacy* which mistakenly assumes that the future behaviour of particular individuals within the group can be inferred from the characteristics of the group to which they are assigned on the basis of risk indicators (see Fitzgibbon, 2007, 2011; Littlechild, 2008; Robinson, 2003). When an event – such as an SFO – occurs, this just goes to show that the risk level cannot indicate what is actually going to happen as regards the behaviour of an individual. But it is very difficult for probation to say, 'We could not predict that this *individual* would do this' when the event has happened. By contrast, it is very easy for the public and the media to conclude that probation is neither focused on, nor capable of delivering, public protection (McCulloch and McNeill, 2007).

This problem is compounded by the fact that individual risk levels are dynamic rather than static. Not only is it not possible to say what people will actually do from their risk score, but their risk score may fluctuate over time. Julia Davidson, discussing child sexual abusers, asks: 'can risk assessment tools really indicate likely re-offending among a group whose behaviour is erratic and unpredictable?' (Davidson, 2008, p. 170). This fact can then lead the agency to defend itself by reference to the limitations of the assessment measures. 'At least if re-offending occurs the responsible criminal justice agency can claim that assessment and management protocol was followed; the re-offending then becomes "accidental" and not a consequence of agency incompetence or ineptitude' (Davidson, 2008, p. 170).

This nicely captures the point that agency orientation to management based on actuarial risk calculations reinforces negative public perception of the agency. When the SFO occurs, the public and the media are saying to probation, 'Why did you, with all your paraphernalia of risk management, not prevent this from happening?' Probation and similar agencies (such as child protection social work) reply, 'We followed the procedures'. It is a dialogue in which probation loses every time because – so it appears – it will not face the fact that it let the individual incident happen. If, as in cases such as Sonnex, the risk levels changed and these changes were not noted and properly responded to, then the complexity is compounded. Individual incidents cannot be *anticipated* from risk scores, particularly if the risk scores themselves are incorrect! In the face of such complexities, the public's preference for speculative risk appears understandable.

Discussions of the difficulty of correctly estimating risk of reoffending on the basis of risk calculators such as OASys (Offender Assessment System, used by the Probation Service in England and Wales) have sometimes concluded that traditional casework-based social work skills – increasingly under threat in probation – which prioritized the practitioner's relationship with and knowledge of the offender were, in fact, necessary to fill in the risk score templates in any meaningful fashion (Horsfield, 2003). This makes an important concession to the notion of speculative risk in that it prioritizes detailed knowledge of individual cases rather than statistical group characteristics. A detailed knowledge of, and relationship with, Sonnex would have enabled an experienced probation officer (or psychologist) to see the danger and initiate a recall to prison before the SFO could be committed (Fitzgibbon, 2011).

A further illustration of how speculative risk tends to win out is the issue of the rationality of fear. When probation, or similar agencies, respond to a SFO by saying, 'This type of thing is mercifully rare', not only does this appear as distant from public concerns but also contains within it a hidden set of assumptions about how worried the public should actually be. The 'correct level' of fear and anxiety (and fear is crucial to media involvement and moral panic) cannot be inferred from the statistical risk calculations in any direct way.

This issue sometimes comes up in studies of the fear of crime. There is a well-known problem of what it means to characterize levels of fear of crime as irrational, and the assumption that 'there is such a thing as objective and expertly derived crime statistics against which people's perceptions can be measured: an approach which also assumes some objective measure of "rationality", so that people can be regarded as "properly afraid", "too afraid" or "not afraid enough" of crime' (Lupton and Tulloch, 1999, p. 508). Levels of fear, as measured in victimization surveys, characterized as 'irrational' can then be attributed to media moral panics (Grabosky, 1995). We cannot summarize the debate here, but sophisticated studies of fear of crime have replaced attempts to calculate the degree of individual 'rationality' or 'irrationality' in relation to statistical measures of risk of crime with an understanding of how fear of crime is a component of both individual biography and more general issues of insecurity and isolation (see Lupton and Tulloch, 1999; Hollway and Jefferson, 1997; Gray et al., 2012; Walklate and Mythen, 2008). Within such a conceptualization, there is no such thing as the *'right level of fear'*. Furedi (2007) takes up this issue, referring to the historical sociologist Norbert Elias, who famously observed that 'the strength, kind and structures of the fears and anxieties that smoulder or flare in the individual never depend solely on his own "nature" ... [but are] ... always determined, finally by the history and the actual structure of his relations to other people' (Elias, 1982, p. 327 quoted in Furedi, 2007).

Crucial is the structure – or lack of it – of relations with other people: the community and its victims. The victim is 'someone like us', but in the strong community, where the victim is known, this means he or she is someone we can help. Where victim and offender know each other and the community knows both, the potential restorative justice paradigm is most feasible.

But where the community is fragmented and fearful of the offender as 'other', the victim will more likely achieve iconic status as representation of public fears, and the community (quite irrespective of the media) will be most likely to seek retribution/revenge – the mirror image of restorative justice – precisely because the offender has placed everyone 'at risk' and has, in effect, committed the offence against everyone. This is not so strange considering that criminal law defines the offence as against the law rather than the victim, with the latter 'only' being involved as the chief prosecution witness.

The implications for probation and the predominating notions of risk are immediately obvious. Probation is in the invidious position of asserting purely statistical levels of risk in the aftermath of an SFO which has been responded to by people in fragmented communities with high levels of insecurity and anxiety for which the SFO, particularly if it involves murder, acts as the 'sum of all fears'. Probation appears uncaring and arrogant in apparently accusing ordinary folk of reacting 'irrationally'. This leaves the field clear for the media, focusing on the act rather than its 'statistical unlikelihood', to become the people's tribune in the face of incompetent and distant bureaucratic authority.

Media, offender and victims

A particularly brutal murder naturally attracts the attention of the print and broadcast media. In a democracy the public has a right to know about such events. There may be frictions between media inquiry and other responses such as police or official investigations. There may also be frictions between journalists and the right to everyday privacy of relatives of the victims or practitioners from the criminal justice and other agencies involved in the cases. Interests conflict, but nevertheless it is fundamental to an open society that the media has a right to investigate the facts, form opinions and broadcast its conclusions.

But basically the relation between the media and the offender encapsulates and reproduces the dynamic explored above, in terms of the relations between media and probation and between media and the community. The media's focus on the event replicates the standpoint of the fragmented community, of the offender as speculative risk made flesh and the victim as iconic of all people of that category who are confirmed as 'at risk'. The whole method of the media is that of speculative risk – the focus on the individual event, the offender and the iconic victims. The occasional conflict between journalists and the police is a reflection of the fact that both institutions work in the same way – they focus on the event. This is replicated in the media but also in the community, which should warn against any hasty notions of moral panic 'created by the media'. It should, perhaps, be more appropriately conceptualized as an exaggeration of what is already there.

All this is graphically illustrated by the Sonnex affair and more recently by the Baby Peter case. The initial failure in the latter case was, of course, Haringey Children's Services. But the conviction and subsequent release on parole of Peter's mother, Tracey Connelly, shifted the responsibility to probation.

Sections of the media, reworking and amplifying the speculative risk-retribution/revenge paradigm, were able to link Connelly's release with a direct attack on the theoretical/actuarial risk paradigm deployed by probation:

> I believe in many circumstances people can change and they can be redeemed. But I absolutely cannot believe that any woman who watched her toddler son being brutally tortured and did nothing to save him can be "danger free" after a pathetic four years in jail... And if she was prepared to act like this with her own child, God only knows what she could do to someone else's.
>
> All the rest of us can do is hope and pray we never find out. Because it is a risk our probation service is more than happy to take. (Phillips, 2013)

And

> THE vile mum who allowed Baby P to be tortured to death will be given tips on hiding her true identity ahead of her imminent release.
>
> Probation officers have ruled Tracey Connelly is no longer a danger to the public and a parole board is expected to set her free this week. (Armstrong, 2013)

Probation is used as the whipping boy, regardless of its success or thoroughness, by not only the media and the public but also, as will be discussed below, by politicians in an attempt to gain legitimacy in their electorate's eyes.

Politics, the media and probation

The most important development in recent years in relation to cases like Baby Peter and Dano Sonnex is the changed nature of the political and social context. The fallout from the media hysteria surrounding both the

Baby Peter and the Sonnex cases included high-profile, precipitate action by government ministers against senior managers: Sharon Shoesmith, head of Haringey social services, and David Scott, head of London Probation Area.

To understand these events, it is necessary to stand back and view some of the profound changes that have taken place in the role of both social services and probation over the last few decades. There are two key policy and political developments which ultimately underpin these fundamental changes.

The first is the shift from welfare to security. Crime and violence have, since the 1970s, become high on the political agenda. Despite recent falls in actual crime levels, public concern and fear of crime remains at high levels. Part of that anxiety is a fear of a 'feral underclass' of permanently unemployed social deviants who are regarded, by the middle-class tax-paying public in particular, less as fellow citizens in a comprehensive universalist welfare state than as a 'risk group' or dangerous population against whom it is the duty of the state to provide security and protection.

In criminal justice terms, such developments imply what Garland (2001) has referred to as the decline of *penal welfare*. The traditional welfare aim of the rehabilitation of the offender has been decisively displaced by that of public protection. In the political programme of the previous, New Labour government, this was epitomized by the title of the 2002 white paper *Justice For All*, which declared the aim of government policy to be 'to rebalance the system in favour of victims, witnesses and communities' (Home Office et al., 2002, p. 3).

The primacy of public protection had a particular effect on probation (and also on social services). In the context of greater public dependence on these services 'over-selling the promise of public protection poses serious risks for offender management services by creating a dynamic that drives up consumer demand for more controlling and incapacitating measures' (McCulloch and McNeill, 2007, p. 223). At the same time it raises the costs of failure: the public must be absolutely protected at all times. Given the 'uncomfortable truth that the potential for the commission of serious further offences cannot be eradicated' (Burke and Collett, 2009, p. 221), the likelihood of major public and media backlash against probation when failures do occur is enhanced.

None of this is to imply that the particular cases of Baby Peter or Sonnex were not avoidable tragedies: they were. The point is a more general one: that the increasing demand for infallibility in public protection has occurred in the context of the progressive deskilling and declining professional status of large parts of probation and social work as a result of targets and formulaic risk assessments resulting from New Public Management–inspired changes in these agencies. This combination of the declining status of probation officers and social workers (from part of a respected body of skilled professions to overworked and underpaid 'public protection' security guards) and the increasing demands of the public and the media for absolute protection are bound to produce a situation in which failures, however small in number, give rise to high-profile media panics. To this toxic mix must be added a final ingredient: the changed nature of politics.

The latter can be characterized as the hollowing out of democracy, reflected in a futile and superficial attempt by the political elite to engage the public via media communications and public relations in the absence of any authentic dialogue and engagement. Referring to such phenomena as increasingly low voter turnout at elections and declining membership of political parties, some political scientists have argued that we are witnessing 'the twin processes of popular and elite withdrawal from mass electoral politics' Mair (2006, p. 25). The effective convergence of the major parties' manifestos have blurred political ideologies and weakened hitherto strong linkages to social groups and interests. So people, particularly the young, see politics as having less impact on their lives (Franklin, 2004). Add to this the fragmentation of poor communities and their social networks and the greater reliance on the media for a sense of collectivity and for information, and it can be understood how media moral panics and alarm over specific events tend to become a substitute for the articulation of political opinions and interests.

Governments themselves have increasingly sought a 'direct' relationship with the population unmediated by parties and the clash of interests but relying increasingly on opinion polls, focus groups and, of course, the mass media. This was the factor, according to Mair (2006), which lay behind Tony Blair's increasingly 'presidential' style of leadership in which policies would often be announced to the media before being announced and discussed in parliament.

The upshot is that ministers pay increasing attention to the media rather than the political process. This dictates a quick, high-profile reaction to events. The space in which Parliament, let alone specialist inquiries reporting to Parliament, can deliberate and formulate policy *before* government ministers have acted is turned on its head. It is the quick, often hastily conceived reaction of ministers in the media which then sets the terms for, and may activate, other pressures upon the various inquiries which may follow. Combine these changes with those already mentioned – the public demand for total protection and the deskilling and decline of professional status of both managers and practitioners in probation and social services – and we have the ingredients for the high-profile ministerial reactions which followed the Baby Peter and Sonnex incidents and which more generally in the New Labour administration 'allowed rhetorical toughness rather than reason and evidence to dominate both guiding principles and policy' (Vanstone, 2010, p. 284; see also Fulwood, 2010).

Thus in both the Sonnex and Baby Peter cases, it seemed inevitable that government response to the media outrage would take the form of ministers turning ferociously on both the practitioners and the senior managers involved. The government's media-driven damage limitation exercise through high-profile dismissals and resignations had the effect of attempting to define the issues, both in child protection and probation, as essentially managerial: matters of the failure of senior management to effectively supervise (Fitzgibbon, 2011). Thus politicians attempt to use high-profile events and their reaction to them as a shortcut to a form of communication between the political elite and public utilizing the media 'event' rather than a legitimate process of democratic deliberation reaching the public by extending into communities.

Probation and the community

To what extent can probation recover from the advantage possessed by the media in the fragmented community? The central problem is that it is in the very nature of probation, unlike prison, that the SFO *can happen*. The first possible strategy is obviously, therefore, to make probation as much like prison as possible. This is self-defeating. As Maruna and King pointed out:

> If people serving community sanctions are demonized as hate figures needing to be degraded and demeaned, then why are they serving community penalties in the first place when prison would do quite nicely? No matter how tough the work or how humiliating the bib is, community penalties simply cannot compete with the iron bars, high walls and razor wire of the prison in the battle for being the 'toughest' penalty. (Maruna and King, 2008, p. 346)

This strategy – no community sentences and no parole licences – would combine the toughness of punishment with the elimination of risk. But it would not assuage the type of media campaign mentioned above in the case of Connelly. When does anyone who has ever committed a serious offence cease to be a danger to the public? They might, whatever the risk assessments, do it again. This takes us off into the debate about whole life sentences which would turn the penal system into something that in democratic societies – outside the far right – would be regarded as unthinkable.

A second strategy envisages probation attempting to win over communities to its perspectives and thus undermine the viability of 'attack journalism'. Governments have thought about this problem. A Home Office study in 2002 (Chapman et al., 2002) suggested that more information about the work of probation would increase public confidence and undermine media negativity. Rod Morgan, when serving as Chief Inspector of Probation, suggested in 2000 that '[l]ocal publicity packages could be produced which tell the good stories which abound within the Service of victims reassured, offenders' lives transformed, community service beneficiaries satisfied and employers of ex-offenders convinced that their decision to offer employment was right' (HMIP press release, 18 June 2000, quoted by Teague, 2002, p. 34). In a similar vein Julia Davidson (2008, p. 170) argues that, regarding sexual offenders, 'the Probation Service would do better to open a dialogue with the community about offender reintegration and risk, exploring levels of community tolerance to risk and reoffending.'

Yet from what has been said above, such strategies are likely to have limited impact. In general, the public might benefit from more information about the work of probation, but when an SFO occurs, the dynamics of conflict between theoretical and speculative risk analysed above are likely to kick in to the detriment of probation and to the advantage of media criticism and public fears.

Conclusion: Back to casework?

But there is another strategy that is perhaps less politically acceptable in the present climate, but possibly more effective than the 'more information' approach. A move back to casework and a focus on the relationship between individual client and practitioner – periodically re-emphasized in probation practice – combined with an orientation to desistance through re-integration into community networks would enable two changes in the position of probation.

First, the relationship between known offenders and *their probation officers* could be given a higher public profile. SFOs might be less likely if an offender was under the supervision and casework relationship of a skilled practitioner known in the community. If an SFO did occur, then the community would have some knowledge of the steps that the probation officer had taken to try and prevent this happening, and people would feel less like they were dealing with an impersonal bureaucracy that they knew little about. The probation officer, as part of the desistance strategy, would have had a higher local profile and would have been working with community groups and networks to try and get the offender into non-criminogenic relationships, as suggested in the work by Maruna and others (Maruna and Immarigeon, 2004; Farrall and Maruna, 2004). Both the community and the probation service would have a much more detailed knowledge of the situation, and this would do much to reduce the conflict between theoretical and speculative risk discussed above.

But the other side of the coin, of equal importance, is to get the community itself involved. The isolation and fragmentation of many deprived communities – the basis of fear of 'others' and of the centrality of the media – means that positive steps have to be taken to create community cohesion. It goes without saying that such projects are well beyond the remit of probation. But it is also vital that probation plays, and is seen to play, a positive part in community activism aimed at renewal.

There are success stories. Most local authority-based youth and community organizations understand that '[y]oungsters moving out of custody into accommodation and a placement in education, training or employment are less likely to reoffend' (Jarvis and Reed, 2014, p. 14). They also understand that the best situation is to get all sections of the community involved, including parents, ex-gang leaders, ex-offenders as well as social services, local authority agencies, police and probation. When open discussion about alternatives is taking place freely between agencies and the community, including ex-offenders and victims (with the understanding that most offenders are also themselves victims), then the networks of personal experience and relationships which act as an *alternative* to media power can be re-established. But this involves probation fundamentally changing direction: away from technocratic risk assessment and surveillance and back towards comprehensive community-based social work with offenders.

References

Altheide, D. (2002) *Creating Fear: News and the Construction of Crisis*. New York: Transaction.

Armstrong, J. (2013) 'Baby P. mum taught how to hide her i.d. Tracey Connelly gets parole advice', *Daily Mirror*, 7 October.

Bourdieu, P. (1998) *On Television and Journalism*. London: Pluto Press.

Burke, L. and Collett, S. (2010) 'People are not things: What New Labour has done to Probation', *Probation Journal* 57(3): 232–49.

Chapman, B., Mirrlees-Black, C. and Brawn, C. (2002) *Improving Public Attitudes to the Criminal Justice System: The Impact of Information*. London: Home Office Research, Development and Statistics Directorate

Chibnall, S. (1977) *Law and Order News*. London: Tavistock.

Cohen, S. and Young, J. (1981) *The Manufacture of News: Deviance, Social Problems and the Mass Media*. London: Constable.

Critcher, C. (2009) 'Widening the focus: Moral panics as moral regulation', *British Journal of Criminology* 49(1): 17–34.

Davidson, J. (2008) *Child Sexual Abuse: Media Representations and Government Reactions*. Routledge.

Dorling, D., Vickers, D., Thomas, B., Pritchard, J. and Ballas, D. (2008) *Changing UK: The Way We Live Now*. Sheffield: Social And Spatial Inequalities (SASI) group, Department of Geography, University of Sheffield.

Elias, N. (1982) *The Civilizing Process: State Formation and Civilization*. Oxford: Basil Blackwell.

Farrall, S. and Maruna, S. (2004) 'Desistance-focused criminal justice policy research: Introduction to a special issue on desistance from crime and public policy', *The Howard Journal of Criminal Justice* 43, 358–67.

Fitzgibbon, W. (2007) 'Risk analysis and the new practitioner: Myth or reality?', *Punishment and Society* 9(1): 87–97.

———. (2011) *Probation and Social Work on Trial: Violent Offenders and Child Abusers*. Basingstoke: Palgrave MacMillan.

———. (2012) 'In the eye of the storm: The implications of the munro child protection review for the future of probation', *Probation Journal* 59(1): 7–22.

———. (2013) 'Riots and probation: Governing the precariat', *Criminal Justice Matters* 93(1): 18–19.

Fulwood, C. (2010). Criminal justice and New Labour: A personal valediction. *Probation Journal* 57(3): 286–290.

Furedi, F. (2006) *Culture of Fear Revisited*. London: Bloomsbury Academic.

———. (2007) 'The only thing we have to fear is the "culture of fear" itself', *Spiked Online*, available at www.spiked-online.com/newsite/article/3053#. VHuq74vA7eQ (accessed 30 November 2014).

Garland, D. (2001) *The Culture of Control: Crime and social order in contemporary society*. Oxford: Oxford University Press.

Grabosky, P. N. (1995) *Fear of Crime and Fear Reduction Strategies*. Australian Institute of Criminology.

Gray, E., Jackson, J. and Farrall, S. (2012) 'In search of the fear of crime: Using interdisciplinary insights to improve the conceptualisation and measurement of everyday insecurities', in Gadd, D., Karstedt, S. and Messner, S. (eds) *The SAGE Handbook of Criminological Research Methods* (pp. 268–81) London: Sage.

Greer, C. (2011) *Crime News*. London: Routledge.

Greer, C. and McLaughlin, E. (2012) 'Media justice: Madeleine McCann, intermediatization and "trial by media" in the British press', *Theoretical Criminology* 16(4): 395–416.

Hall, S., Critcher, C., Jefferson, T., Clarke, J. and Roberts, B. (1978) *Policing the Crisis: Mugging, the State, and Law and Order*. London: Macmillan.

Hayes, D. (2013) Reading between the Lines. English Newspaper Representations of Community Punishment. *European Journal of Probation* 5(3): 24–40.

Hier, S. P. (2008) 'Thinking beyond moral panic: Risk, responsibility, and the politics of moralization', *Theoretical Criminology* 12(2): 173–90.

Hollway, W. and Jefferson, T. (1997) 'The risk society in an age of anxiety: Situating fear of crime', *The British Journal of Sociology* 48(2): 255–66 (accessed 23 March 2014).

Home Office (2002) *OASys User Manual v.2*. London: National Probation Directorate.

Horsfield, A. (2003) 'Risk assessment: Who needs it?', *Probation Journal* 50(4): 374–79.

Hough, M., Bradford, B., Jackson, J. and Roberts, J. (2013) *Attitudes to Sentencing and Trust in Justice: Exploring Trends from the Crime Survey for England and Wales*. London: Ministry of Justice.

Jarvis, D. and Reed, S. (2014) 'To stop youth crime before it starts, we need to shift power to communities', *New Statesman,* 14 March.

Jewkes, Y. (2004) *Media and Crime: A Critical Introduction*. London: Sage.

Kitzinger, J. (2009a) 'The ultimate neighbour from hell? Stranger danger and the media framing of paedophiles', in B. Franklin (ed.) *Social Policy, the Media and Misrepresentation*. London: Routledge.

———. (2009b) 'Risk, news coverage and public responses', conference paper, *Managing the Social Impacts of Change from a Risk Perspective*, Beijing 15–17 April.

Lea, J. (1992) 'Left realism: A framework for the analysis of crime', in Young, J. and Matthews, R. (eds) *Rethinking Criminology: The Realist Debate*. London: Sage.

———. (2002) *Crime and Modernity*. London: Sage.

Littlechild, B. (2008) 'Child protection social work: Risks of fears and fears of risks: Impossible tasks from impossible goals?', *Social Policy & Administration* 42: 662–675.

Lupton, D. and Tulloch, J. (1999) 'Theorizing fear of crime: Beyond the rational/ irrational opposition', *British Journal of Sociology* 50(3): 507–23.

Mair, P. (2006) 'Ruling the void: The hollowing of Western democracy', *New Left Review* 42.

Maruna, S. and Immarigeon, R. (2004) *After Crime and Punishment*. Cullompton: Willan.

Maruna, S. and King, A. (2008) 'Selling the public on probation: Beyond the bib', *Probation Journal* 55(4): 337–51.

McNeill, F. (2013) 'Offender supervision and the penal state' www.offender supervision.eu/blog-post/offender-supervision-and-the-penal-stat> (accessed 16 January 2014).

McCulloch, T. and McNeill, F. (2007) 'Consumer society, commodification and offender management', *Criminology and Criminal Justice* 7(3): 223–42.

Petts, J., Horlick-Jones, T. and Murdoch, G. (2001) *Social Amplification of Risk: The Media and the Public*. London: HMSO.

Phillips, A. (2013) 'Four years is not enough', *Daily Mirror*, 2 October.

Prince's Trust (2010) 'Young people and their communities: A report by The Prince's Trust', www.princes-trust.org.uk/docs/MA_One_in_three_survey_ Oct10%20.doc> (accessed 5 March 2014).

Robinson, G. (2003) 'Risk and risk assessment', in W. H. Chui and Nellis, M. (eds) *Moving Probation Forward* (pp. 108–29) London: Pearson: 108–29.

Sjoberg, L. and Wahlberg, A. (2000) 'Risk perception and the media', *Journal of Risk Research* 3: 31–50.

Smith, D. (2010) *Public Confidence in the Criminal Justice System: Findings from the British Crime Survey 2002/03 to 2007/08*. London: Ministry of Justice.

Teague, M. (2002) 'Public perceptions of probation', *Criminal Justice Matters* 49(1): 34–35.

Vanstone, M. (2010) 'New Labour and criminal justice: Reflections on a wasteland of missed opportunity', *Probation Journal* 57(3): 281–85.

Walklate, S. and Mythen, G. (2008) 'How scared are we?', *British Journal of Criminology* 48(2): 209–25 (accessed 24 March 2014).

Watts, B. (2008) *What Are Today's Social Evils? The Results of a Web Consultation*. York: Joseph Rowntree Foundation.

Young, J. (1999) *The Exclusive Society: Social Exclusion, Crime and Difference in Late Modernity*. London: Sage.

SECTION 3

WAYS FORWARD

11

PUTTING RISK IN ITS PLACE

Craig Schwalbe
Columbia University, USA

Gina Vincent
University of Massachussetts, USA

Introduction

Worldwide, risk assessment has emerged as an accepted 'best practice' for offender management and case planning in juvenile and criminal justice systems. In the United States, risk assessment emerged during the early twentieth century, where Ernest Burgess was credited with the first actuarial studies of risk assessment with incarcerated men in Illinois (1928, 1936). Nevertheless, risk assessment did not become firmly established as an integral part of the justice system until the development of the structured decision-making model (SDM; Baird, 1984; Howell, 2003). Since then, predictive validity has been the preoccupation of scholars, driven to establish that risk classification systems could in fact distribute justice-involved adolescents and adults into groups that varied in their risk of recidivism. To date, risk assessment instruments have been adopted worldwide, and studies involving risk assessment have been published in China (Zhang and Liu, 2014), Japan (Takahashi et al., 2013), and throughout Europe, Australia and North America (Singh et al., 2011).

Accompanying the widespread adoption of risk assessment has been a chorus of criticism. Some critics question the contribution of risk assessment to just and fair justice system decision-making. Feminist scholars and others concerned with gender equity argue that current risk assessment models reflect the experiences of justice-involved men but do not adequately represent risk processes that are idiosyncratic to women, for example (Van Voorhis et al., 2010). Others have correctly noted that rather than muting the effect of race on justice system decision-making, risk assessment can in fact hide the influence of race under a façade of rationality (Cabaniss et al., 2007). A second criticism concerns the validity of the risk assessment enterprise. These scholars either (a) doubt the research methodologies employed to derive risk assessment in the first place, or (b) critique the risk factor perspective as 'backward facing', and not relevant to the task of preventing the recurrence of juvenile and criminal offending (Haines and Case, 2009). A third criticism raised against risk assessment is that it further entrenches labelling processes that undermine the rehabilitative purposes of justice system interventions. The institutionalization of the language of risk (e.g. 'high risk') creates reasonable resistance among justice-involved adolescents and adults against the label, and also creates further roadblocks to their eventual desistance from crime as labels become adopted internally and also by the justice system itself.

Accepting the veracity of at least some of these critiques, our position is that the criticisms in and of themselves do not diminish the promise of risk assessment. Risk assessment instruments, being built on a foundation of 100 years of empirical research on risk processes that influence offending trajectories, can contribute to justice system interventions in meaningful ways. However, the critiques point to the next frontier of research and scholarship needed to realize this promise. Whereas the last 30 years of risk assessment research have been dominated by matters of predictive validity, the next era of risk assessment research will be dominated by matters of implementation. Indeed, many of the criticisms raised above can be answered, if not fully, then at least partially, by attention to this neglected area. The remainder of this chapter addresses five challenges that risk assessment systems need to overcome to maximize the contribution of risk assessment to offender management and case planning:

1. Risk assessment and the challenge of inequality

2. Reliability and the justice system lottery

3. Case conceptualization and the clinical validity of risk assessment

4. Practice models and de-labelling high-risk offenders

5. Stakeholder buy-in and implementation

In each section, the chapter draws conclusions based on the current state of research and practice, and outlines critical unanswered questions that will focus the next era of risk assessment development and implementation. In the end, the chapter concludes with a proposal to establish comprehensive implementation systems that draw lessons from nascent research on risk assessment implementation and lessons learned from the growing field of implementation science.

Risk assessment and the challenge of inequality

Among those who argue that risk assessment introduces a façade of rationality into justice system decision-making are those who express concerns about the intersection of gender, race and risk-based decisions. These concerns are well founded. Unequal treatment by legal systems around the world, based on gender biases and racial and ethnic discrimination, has been documented for decades (Bishop and Frazier, 1988; Chesney-Lind and Sheldon, 1998). Standardized decision-making tools like risk assessment are intended to mute or eliminate the impact of race, ethnicity and gender by focusing decision-makers on correlates of repeated and chronic offending that are neutral with respect to race, ethnicity and gender. Whether risk assessment lives up to this promise is a topic worthy of debate.

The promise of risk assessment is to reduce the impact of biased personal discretion on critical justice system decision-making. Theoretically, risk assessment accomplishes this goal through several mechanisms. One mechanism is to make explicit the rationale for decisions, muting the role of unacknowledged extra-legal factors and biases on decision-making. Another mechanism is by countering cognitive tendencies that tend to reduce prediction accuracy. First explicated in 1974 by Tversky and Kahneman, the heuristics and biases tradition in psychology identifies the routine errors that people are prone to make when making 'judgments under uncertainty' (Kahneman, 2011; Tversky and Kahneman, 1974). Among these errors are tendencies to resist changes to first impressions when presented with alternative evidence, the tendency to favour strong intuitive impressions rather than empirical patterns and trends, and the tendency to violate rules of probability when making predictions by overvaluing vivid idiosyncratic information and by ignoring population base rates. Risk assessment practices force decision-makers to broaden the range of factors considered when making risk-based decisions and link their determinations of risk to empirical evidence about the contribution of specific risk factors as well as recidivism base rates. Indeed, there is evidence that risk assessment does achieve these ends to a greater or lesser degree. Anecdotal evidence from our experience suggests that probation officers who introduce risk assessment instruments broaden the array of risk factors they assess when making risk-based decisions. Moreover, empirical data suggest that actuarial and structured risk assessment instruments reduce over-classification of youths to high-risk groups, with a corresponding decrease in rates of secure institutional placements (Hoyt et al., 2002).

There exist at least three additional sources of bias that can influence decisions based on risk assessment findings and that have particular importance for the role of risk assessment in reducing biases grounded in gender and race/ethnicity. These sources of bias are structured into the design of risk assessment instruments themselves as well as embedded into the sociopolitical context in which risk assessment instruments are implemented. These biases include unmeasured variable bias, structural bias and perceptual bias.

Unmeasured variable bias occurs when risk assessment instruments fail to include risk factors that mark critical risk processes for diverse groups of justice-involved people, based on gender, race or ethnicity. The problem arises when the original research that identified key risk factors for recidivism fails to adequately represent all groups of offenders. The growth of gender-responsive risk assessment is illustrative of concern for this type of bias. Notwithstanding the findings of several broad-based meta-analyses demonstrating that current risk assessment instruments have on average equivalent predictive validity for males and females, some scholars are developing 'gender-responsive' risk assessment instruments that include risk factors such as exposure to trauma and psychosocial stressors that are hypothesized to influence the offending of females differently from males. The results of this line of research are supplemental assessments that correct gender biases in traditional risk assessment instruments, as well as stand-alone risk assessment instruments developed specifically for female offenders (Van Voorhis et al., 2010).

The second type of bias that influences risk assessment is structural biases. Structural biases are those psychosocial phenomena that are extrinsic to the risk assessment process but that influence risk assessment findings. Risk factors associated with school performance, behaviour and attendance are clear examples. In the United States, there exists widespread disproportionality across race/ethnicity in matters such as the use of serious punishments like suspension and expulsion, and in indicators of poor academic performance like graduation rates, grades and test scores (Losen and Skiba, 2010). As nearly all risk assessment systems for youthful offenders include an assessment of school behaviour and academic performance, probation officers and others who are responsible for making decisions about risk routinely contend with structural biases in their offender management and decision-making, whether they are aware of this or not. Structural biases lead to unequal treatment by inflating risk scores and exposing justice-involved youths and adults of colour to more aggressive justice system interventions.

The third type of bias influencing risk assessment is implicit biases. Implicit biases are latent discriminatory attitudes about race and gender that influence conclusions by probation officers and other justice system stakeholders about individual offenders (Mahzarin, Banaji and Greenwald,

2013). For example, qualitative research with probation officers reveals their higher expectations of recidivism for minority youths (Graham and Lowery, 2004) and the view that 'girls are seen as being very difficult to work with. Whether the officers blame or sympathize, they perceive the girls as being troubled and troublesome' (Gaarder, Rodriguez and Zatz, 2004, p. 558). Implicit biases may influence the risk assessment process in at least two ways. First, implicit biases may contribute to risk assessment overrides when these are allowed (Chappell, Maggard and Higgins, 2012). Second, implicit biases may influence how individual risk factors are judged during the assessment process itself. For example, some research suggests that minority families are often perceived to be less cooperative with probation than white families (Schwalbe and Maschi, 2010; Smith, Rodriguez and Zatz, 2009).

While we do not believe that risk assessment implementation can possibly relieve the justice system of all of its oppressive practices and biases, risk assessment instruments should in the first place do no harm, that is, should not make inequality based on gender and race/ethnicity worse, and in the second place should strive to make at least incremental contributions to the goal of equity and fairness. Achieving this objective requires consideration of how risk assessment instruments can be designed, implemented and utilized in practice. For instance, when faced with structural biases that elevate risk levels (e.g. differential rates of school suspension), there is little to no research available to guide how the justice system should respond. Should they consider structural oppression as a mitigating factor in override decisions? Should they incorporate structural biases into their case management practices (e.g. advocating for more favourable school policies and practices)? In regard to implicit biases, there is a marked absence of data to establish the significance of the problem in the risk assessment context. Assuming that implicit biases do in fact influence risk assessment practices, research is needed to identify strategies for muting these biases in the assessment process. Possible avenues for achieving this objective include training strategies that explicitly include discussions and activities to make probation officers aware of biases they may hold, and also designing risk assessment instruments in a manner that primes unbiased judgements through the strategic inclusion of formal strengths assessment, for example.

Reliability and the justice system lottery

Whereas accuracy or predictive validity has been the overriding concern of risk assessment scholarship since the first Burgess risk assessment studies (1928, 1936), the application of risk assessment in practice demands reliability. Reliability implies that when assessed by two probation officers with the same risk assessment instrument, measured risk for an individual offender will be the same. Reliability is key to the transparency and fairness of any decision-making systems that hinge on the outcome of risk assessment. Fortunately, a small number of studies report that risk assessment reliability improves when trained probation officers employ structured risk assessment (Schwalbe, Fraser and Day, 2004; Schmidt, Hoge and Gomes, 2005; Vincent et al., 2012).

Reliability hinges on two aspects of effective implementation. First, probation officers need high-quality training on the risk assessment instrument itself to ensure that they have a reasonably consistent understanding of the individual risk indicators that make up the risk assessment instrument and a consistent understanding of the thresholds that move individuals from lower to higher risk categories. By and large, there have been few examples reported in the literature of training and ongoing support systems dedicated to sustaining the reliability of probation officers who conduct risk assessment. Into this void, the Models for Change project of the MacArthur Foundation recommends that staff training in risk assessment be followed with booster training every six months and with periodic small scale inter-rater reliability tests to enable supervisors to provide feedback to line staff who are primarily responsible for completing risk assessment (Vincent et al., 2012).

Second, reliable risk assessment demands high-quality data about the justice-involved youths or adults being assessed. Thus, a critical unexamined aspect of the risk assessment process is the manner in which assessment data is gathered by probation officers. Whereas some risk assessment systems include semi-structured interview guides, and some jurisdictions have developed broad-based assessment packages for youths in terms of risk, mental health and substance abuse (e.g. juvenile assessment centres), many justice professionals collect risk assessment information based on interviews of uncertain quality. Therefore, there are no controls in most jurisdictions to ensure that information collected during the process of risk assessment instrument is of high quality.

To further strengthen the reliability of risk assessment in practice, quality assurance systems are needed to monitor assessment consistency and quality. Following the lead of the Models for Change project (Vincent, Guy and Grisso, 2012), the field needs to establish strong guidelines detailing the organizational investments required to sustain risk assessment reliability and counter the tendency of probation officers to drift in their risk judgements. The frequency of booster sessions and inter-rater reliability tests presents empirical questions that are ripe for experimental tests. One might ask whether semi-annual booster sessions are sufficient to sustain reliability with and without supplemental inter-rater reliability tests to gauge the level of organizational investment needed. In terms of assessment quality, attention is needed for the assessment strategies that probation officers use to collect information about risk and needs from youths, family members and others. The increasing availability and accessibility of technology raises the possibility of strengthening the assessment process by integrating standardized self-report questionnaires into the semi-structured interview process. The result could be a two-stage assessment process, whereby youth and parent responses to a computer-assisted self-report survey of risks and needs is used to generate a personalized semi-structured interview guide to be implemented by probation officers. By incorporating semi-structured interview questions strategically as follow-up questions, assessment efficiency can be gained, as probation officers would focus on key strengths and risk factors identified in the self-report surveys while simultaneously ensuring that probation officers are focusing on the full range of risk and needs that may be acting in an individual case.

Case conceptualization and the clinical validity of risk assessment

For risk assessment to influence client outcomes, they must be incorporated into the clinical thinking of probation officers, judges and other actors. Clinical thinking in this context means the way probation officers establish a 'theory of the case', or a causal story about the case, or a rationale for how risk assessment links to a set of interventions chosen to reduce risk, prevent recidivism and improve client well-being. In the language of psychiatry, psychology and social work, risk assessment instruments should be involved in the case conceptualization process (Christon, McLeod and Jensen-Doss, 2015).

Presently, the risk-need-responsivity framework provides the most widely adopted approach to case conceptualization (Andrews and Bonta, 2010). Using a public health approach, the RNR framework invites probation officers to match keystone risk factors with specific evidence-based interventions. The simplicity of this approach can motivate action on the part of probation officers and justice systems in at least two ways. At the individual level, the matching approach to case conceptualization provides a clear rationale for referral decisions. At the agency level, the matching approach provides a clear rationale for the development of services, programmes and interventions to fill gaps. To date, a growing number of research studies lend support to the matching approach. Across studies, client outcomes improve when they are referred to services that match their criminogenic needs (Andrews and Dowden, 2006).

While the matching approach to case conceptualization is provocative in its simplicity, we have two concerns. First, the evidence supporting the matching process is preliminary and insufficient to support a mechanistic case-planning system that somehow dictates that clients with a specific risk profile should be required to participate in specific services. The current state of research in this area should be understood to support justice system attention to criminogenic needs in the intervention process. That is, justice system interventions that intend to prevent recidivism should focus efforts on dynamic risk factors known to be associated with outcomes like recidivism. Second, we are concerned that the matching approach to case conceptualization can limit creative problem-solving. Principally, the matching approach fosters a categorical approach to case planning and referral practices leading to the conclusion that each jurisdiction needs to have formal evidence-based interventions available to address each assessed need presented by clients. The problem is that the distribution of service types across jurisdictions and communities, much less the distribution of named evidence-based practices, is uneven. Thus the matching approach to case conceptualization does not foster the kind of creative case planning needed to serve the broad range of clients that appear in the justice systems.

The strengths perspective and the positive youth development movement provide an alternative framework for linking risk assessment with case conceptualization (Barton and Butts, 2008). The positive youth development framework directs probation officers to consider how community assets, client strengths and compensatory protective factors can be leveraged in the service of risk reduction and asset promotion. To be sure, the ideas of risk assessment and positive youth development are not typically joined in a case conceptualization model or as a practice model. However, both were developed to reduce problematic, high-risk behaviours, and both are grounded in the ecological framework that considers the transactional relationships between individuals and their environments that conspire to influence the likelihood of prosocial and antisocial outcomes.

The strengths perspective and the positive youth development framework direct probation officers to question how mechanisms of risk, protection and assets interact in the lives of individual clients, rather than simply identifying categorical service needs (Fraser, 2004). A case conceptualization model that merges risk, protection and assets considers how these can interact in an individual case to improve the likelihood of positive outcomes. In the presence of measured risk, protective factors and assets operate in the following ways that can be leveraged for case planning:

1. They can have a direct effect on risk reduction. For example, favoured teachers can be enlisted informally to provide extra support to youths who exhibit academic problems.

2. They can interfere with a risk process. For example, clients who exhibit a strong capacity for self-control can learn skills and strategies for coping with 'hot' emotions that can be implicated in aggression or other antisocial behaviour.

3. They can create opportunities to avoid risk processes entirely. For example, the availability of local employers who are willing to 'take a chance' on clients who otherwise have limited access to the labour market.

The advantages of blending risk assessment with the strengths perspective and youth development framework for case conceptualization include the following. First, they are conceptually compatible. They are grounded in the eco-systems perspective and can be easily integrated with multiple theoretical frameworks and models, including traditional criminological theories such as social learning theory and control theories, as well as contemporary criminological theories such as reintegrative shaming and restorative justice. Second, the ideas of client strengths and assets are already present and accepted among many in the justice field. Thus, incorporation of the strengths perspective and positive youth development is compatible with current practice in many places.

We are aware of very few efforts to engage probation officers in the process of case conceptualization beyond the matching approach (Haque and Webster, 2013; Minoudis et al., 2013). To advance the field, a concerted effort is needed to conceptualize how risk assessment can be integrated into the clinical thought process that probation officers and other justice professionals use to understand how mechanisms of risk operate in individual cases. By offering the strengths perspective and youth development framework as an alternative case conceptualization approach, we have shed light on an important limitation of risk assessment – that risk assessment cannot be the only assessment completed by probation officers. Indeed, a comprehensive assessment system is needed to account for the needs of a chosen case conceptualization framework.

Practice models and de-labelling high-risk offenders

The manner in which risk assessment is incorporated into the problem-solving process and into the relationship between probation officers and individual offenders has been virtually ignored in the literature. To our knowledge, there is no expert guidance, much less empirical evidence, about how probation officers should discuss risk assessment processes or findings with their clients. Without question, a discussion of risk assessment findings can be alienating when clients detect a labelling process (e.g. 'I am not "high risk"'). Evidence from research on labelling and stigma suggests that both contribute to trajectories of chronic offending and deeper penetration into the justice system (Bernberg, Krohn and Rivera, 2006). What is clear from this research is that the implementation of risk assessment within a justice setting should not amplify the effects of labelling and stigma that are omnipresent in the lives of justice-involved adults and adolescents, and that a well-implemented risk assessment instrument should ultimately provide tools to buffer the effects of labelling and stigma. Thus, careful attention to policy and practice issues implicated in the implementation of risk assessment is warranted.

Labelling and stigma influence chronic offending through at least two processes (Link, 1989). First, social stigma and public labelling impact behaviour by imposing constraints on opportunity structures available to adolescents and adults involved in the justice system. These limited opportunity structures serve to exclude labelled individuals from full participation in society. Exclusionary pressures can be formally imposed, as when formal background checks are used to screen potential job candidates, or informal, as when parents of prosocial youth monitor their friendship networks to minimize exposure to delinquent peer networks. Second, social stigma and labelling can be internalized, leading justice-involved adolescents and adults to make active choices that reinforce trajectories of chronic offending. The selection of peer networks is an example, where data supports the process of homophilly, or the process of selecting peers that are similar in key attributes (antisocial behaviour in the present case).

At all levels, justice system interventions need to be structured such that they expand opportunities for prosocial engagement and contribute to prosocial identity formation. Risk assessment cannot on its own influence the labelling and stigmatizing impact of justice system involvement on adolescents or adults, without reference to the manner in which implementation takes place in the real world. To date, the most common approach to risk assessment implementation with implications for labelling and stigma is through its support of diversion for low-risk offenders (Schwalbe et al., 2012). Diversion is an effort to exclude groups of offenders from formal justice system processing, thereby avoiding official labels such as 'delinquent' or 'criminal'. Warn-and-release programmes as well as formal psychosocial programmes can be employed in this manner either at the point of arrest, whereby individuals who are apprehended for a delinquent or criminal act are diverted directly, or at the point of justice system intake, where diversion occurs prior to formal court procedures taking hold. Most programmes utilize legal criteria to determine diversion eligibility, including results of formal risk assessment.

For justice-involved youths and adults who penetrate the justice system more deeply through probation involvement, the degree to which risk assessment can dampen the deleterious labelling processes inherent to the justice system may depend in part on the language of risk assessment. The language of risk assessment can threaten to label and stigmatize justice-involved youths and adults when the labels are treated as character flaws that adhere within individuals. In fact, it is a misuse of the language of risk assessment to describe a client as 'high risk'. Precisely speaking, clients are classified into groups that share a certain propensity to reoffend. It is the group that carries the label, not its individual. Because classification is inherently probabilistic and uncertain, individual offenders have choices about whether or not to adopt or reject the label.

Further, the stigmatizing effect of risk assessment may also hinge on the practice models that probation officers and others employ. Risk assessment itself is not a practice model. Practice models provide a framework for problem-solving and a road map for how probation officers and clients implement a change process. Moreover, it is the practice model that dictates how risk assessment conclusions are incorporated into the intervention process. For example, probation officers trained in the task-centred model will use risk assessment findings to identify issues or problems to work on and identify positively framed goals to guide their problem-solving efforts (Trotter, 2006). Probation officers trained in motivational interviewing help clients to amplify their ambivalence about an individual risk factor in an effort to activate change processes (Clark, 2005). Probation officers who operate from a solution-focused framework use knowledge of risk factors to identify exceptions – times when risk factors or risk processes are not activated – in order to identify potential solutions that will reduce risk in the long run. Finally, probation officers who employ a cognitive behavioural approach will use risk assessment findings as the basis for identifying and challenging antisocial beliefs, teach cognitive coping skills and engage in problem-solving processes (Bonta et al., 2011).

A common thread across all of the practice models mentioned above is the notion of collaboration. Each assumes that the probation officer has established a collaborative relationship with the client. What about probation officers who operate from a sanction/threat orientation that emphasizes authoritarian deterrence-based approaches? While deterrence generally has been discredited as an ineffective basis for justice system effects on clients, there is some evidence that deterrence processes are at play in probation and that deterrence is an effective change mechanism for at least some offenders (Maxwell and Gray, 2000). Does risk assessment necessarily amplify labelling processes in this context? What is the role of risk assessment in a deterrence-based approach? At its best, risk assessment, especially risk assessment based on dynamic risk factors, can help probation officers to target their sanction threats to issues or problems that research has identified as marking clients for higher probabilities of reoffending. So rather than offering sanction threats for general compliance, or for legal conditions, sanction threats can be targeted to such issues as substance abuse treatment (e.g., 'Stop using drugs or else ...'), peer involvement (e.g. 'Avoid negative friends or else ...'), and the effectiveness of parental supervision (e.g. 'Listen to your parents or else ...'). Arguments about the effectiveness of sanction threats notwithstanding, the question for our present discussion is whether or not risk assessment increases labelling processes when probation officers employ deterrence approaches.

While a comprehensive review of probation practice models is beyond the scope of this chapter, a discussion about risk assessment, practice models and labelling processes suggests the following implications for research and practice. First and foremost, the practice model into which risk assessment is inserted needs to be fully articulated. This ensures that the role of risk assessment is completely understood within its intervention context. Full articulation of the practice model also ensures that risk assessment does not become the goal in and of itself, but that the goal of risk assessment is to contribute to a more comprehensive approach to offender management. Second, into whichever practice model is chosen, the threat of labelling through the language of risk needs to be addressed. To militate against social stigma and labelling, probation officers and justice system stakeholders need training to avoid the misuse of the language of risk assessment. Finally, among a limited set of practice models that have been incorporated into the justice system at the level of probation and parole, models that maximize client choice and that emphasize collaboration in the change process are probably most capable of buffering the threat of labelling and stigmatization from risk assessment.

Stakeholder attitudes and buy-in

To date, there has been very little discussion of the attitudes and perspectives of line staff and local stakeholders who are responsible for carrying out risk assessment policies. The emerging fields of implementation science and diffusion of innovation suggest that the perspectives of these local stakeholders are critical to the successful implementation of risk assessment into the routine practice of juvenile and criminal justice. While research in this area is sparse, available studies about critical attitudes of local stakeholders point to ways forward for the next phase of the risk assessment project.

Not surprisingly, research reveals that local stakeholders often express ambivalence to risk assessment. For example, writing as early as the mid-1990s, Schneider, Ervin and Snyder-Joy (1996) described results of a mixed methods study, whereby prevailing attitudes of probation and parole officers (N = 179) towards risk assessment were negative, or neutral at best. The study was carried out in Oklahoma's department of corrections after a 15-year process of selecting and implementing risk assessment instruments. Less than half of research participants reported that risk assessment instruments were helpful or useful for the system, except for ensuring that high-risk cases get intensive supervision (53% agreed), and to provide uniformity to supervision state-wide (57% agreed). Paradoxically, few participants agreed that the system would be better off without risk assessment (23%) despite reporting unfavourable attitudes towards risk assessment overall.

More recent research continues to elaborate on the theme of ambivalence among line staff and local stakeholders. Miller and Maloney's (2013) survey of risk assessment utilization provides a framework for understanding the differential attitudes of probation officers. A little less than half of their survey respondents (48%) reported utilizing risk assessment for decision-making about risk-based and need-based decisions. A substantial minority (40%) completed required risk assessment as a matter of bureaucratic requirements but did not reference risk assessment in their risk-based and need-based decisions. A small group, 12%, were described as risk assessment cynics – they completed instruments as required, but self-reported that they manipulated risk assessment findings to suit their positions.

While Miller and Moloney (2013) and Schneider, Ervin and Snyder-Joy (1996), among others (Guy, Nelson and Fusco-Morin, 2014; Shook and Sarri, 2007), catalogue ambivalent attitudes towards risk assessment by probation and parole officers, these studies also identify conditions that are associated with more favourable attitudes. Across several studies, the buy-in and support of agency leadership and judges emerged as a key correlate of risk assessment support (Guy et al., 2014; Miller and Maloney,

2013; Schneider et al., 1996; Shook and Sarri, 2007). The strongest correlate of positive attitudes towards risk assessment among Miller and Maloney's sample was confidence in the risk assessment tools, while the strongest correlate of positive attitudes among Schneider, Ervin and Snyder-Joy's survey respondents was confidence in their ability to rehabilitate offenders and prevent recidivism.

In our experience, key stakeholder support can be eroded by other themes not yet reported in empirical research. For instance, some probation officers report that they are unable to detect in their own practice how the process of risk assessment adds to their management of offenders. In many cases, system actors carry the perception that the results of risk assessment are obvious. To be sure, some clients are obviously low risk, while others are obviously extremely high risk. The difference between these poles in terms of client presentation is readily detected without the assistance of a risk assessment instrument, notwithstanding empirical findings that show reductions in overall rates of high-risk designations when risk assessment instruments are used. Probation officer beliefs that they can detect risk level without the aid of formal risk assessment instruments can be a barrier to stakeholder buy-in.

Another belief reported by some probation officers is that risk assessment instruments reduce discretion. The purpose of any structured decision-making system, of which risk assessment instruments are often a part, strives to increase the transparency of decision-making, and to rationalize the decision-making process by applying a consistent set of rules that do not depend fully on the idiosyncratic judgments of decision-makers. The multiple benefits of structured decision-making include increasingly fair decisions that are less subject to decision-maker biases and also the potential to conform decision rules to justice approaches that have documented effectiveness. However, human beings resist perceived threats to freedom, and structured decision-making systems compete with other forces that tend to influence decisions, including organizational culture and politics at the local level.

The foregoing summary of stakeholder attitudes and buy-in suggests the following for practice and research to strengthen the acceptance of risk assessment by probation officers and judges. First, the benefits of risk assessment for specific system-wide goals should be emphasized. For instance, some jurisdictions will implement risk assessment in an effort to reduce rates of institutional placement, whereas others will implement risk assessment to allocate scarce resources. Still others will strive to align themselves with risk-need-responsivity principles in which low-risk youths are screened out of most intensive contacts and interventions. Second, the relationship between risk assessment and discretion in the case-planning process should be directly discussed, particularly as it relates to the process of case conceptualization discussed above. When implemented within a positive youth development framework, risk assessment instruments in and of themselves do not diminish the creativity required to plan risk reduction and asset-promoting interventions. Rather, the risk assessment process can provide a platform for identifying key needs upon which to design individualized intervention approaches. Finally, research on risk assessment acceptance and utilization suggests that probation officers need support that increases their perceived treatment efficacy, and need instruction to showcase how risk assessment instruments can contribute to the successful management of a case.

Conclusion

In the face of these implementation challenges, one needs to ask the question – why retain risk assessment? The answer to this question comes first from data. Research on the psychology of decision-making finds repeatedly that human beings struggle in tasks that involve forecasting future outcomes. In contemporary justice systems, nearly all decisions have some reference to the prevention of recidivism; few decisions are solely dedicated to punishment. Further, research on the risk-need-responsivity paradigm is growing to show that reference to risk and criminogenic needs works. Justice-involved youths and adults who have few risk indicators are prone to worse outcomes when they are engaged vigorously and deeply in justice system interventions; justice-involved youths and adults who have many risk indicators have better outcomes when they are exposed to evidence-based interventions that are individually targeted to their profile of criminogenic needs.

With this data as a backdrop, the field is ready to grapple with questions about effective implementation. The review above provided an overview of five implementation challenges facing the field. Each is important in its own right, and each is interrelated with the others. In the end, what are required are multidimensional implementation systems and programmes that impact multiple elements of the risk assessment process within a comprehensive package of training and support. Elements of a multidimensional implementation system will include at a minimum:

1. Valid and reliable risk assessment technology, including risk assessment instruments and assessment aids like semi-structured interview guides and self-report questionnaires. The assessment aids should be specifically tailored to obtain the most valid information possible about the risk profiles of justice involved youths and adolescents.

2. Training programmes that include sufficient experiential learning opportunities to develop reasonably consistent risk ratings across staff. An adequate dose of training has not been established, and is probably dependent in part on the prior education and experience of the trainees as well as the specific risk assessment instrument itself.

3. An explication of how risk assessment findings can be integrated into the case planning process in the service of practice models that guide a change process. Whether jurisdictions opt for case planning processes based on matching measured needs with services within an assessment-referral model, or select a case conceptualization model based on an integration of risk assessment with positive youth development principles and a task-centred approach, these processes should be explicit.

4. An ongoing quality assurance system that includes supportive supervision of risk assessment practices as well as periodic reliability tests. Quality assurance is needed to prevent drift and to sustain high levels of reliability.

5. Training in how risk assessment practices interface with the structural and implicit biases that influence justice system decision-making. This training should also alert trainees to the language of risk assessment so as to mitigate against stigma and labelling risks associated with risk classification.

References

Andrews, D. A. and Bonta, J. (2010) 'Rehabilitating criminal justice policy and practice', *Psychology, Public Policy, and Law* 16: 39–55.

Andrews, D. A. and Dowden, C. (2006) 'Risk principle of case classification in correctional treatment: A meta-analytic investigation', *International Journal of Offender Therapy and Comparative Criminology* 50: 88–100.

Baird, C. (1984) *Classification of Juveniles in Corrections: A Model Systems Approach.* Madison, WI: National Council on Crime and Delinquency.

Banaji, M. R. and Greenwald, A. G. (2013) *Blindspot: Hidden Biases of Good People.* New York: Delacorte Press.

Barton, W. H. and Butts, J. A. (2008) *Building on Strengths: Positive Youth Development in Juvenile Justice.* Chicago, IL: Chapin Hall Center for Children.

Bernberg, J. G., Krohn, M. D. and Rivera, C. J. (2006) 'Official labelling, criminal embeddedness, and subsequent delinquency: A longitudinal test of labelling theory', *Journal of Research in Crime and Delinquency* 43: 67–88.

Bishop, D. M. and Frazier, C. E. (1988) 'The influence of race in juvenile justice processing', *Journal of Research in Crime and Delinquency* 25: 242–63.

Bonta, J., Bourgon, G., Rugge, T., Scott, T., Yessine, A. K., Gutierrez, L. and Li, J. (2011) 'An experimental demonstration of training probation officers in evidence-based community supervision', *Criminal Justice and Behavior* 38: 1127–48.

Burgess, E. W. (1928) *Factors Determining Success or Failure on Parole*. Springfield, IL: Illinois State Board of Parole.

———. (1936) 'Protecting the public by parole and by parole prediction', *Journal of Criminal Law and Criminology* 27: 491–502.

Cabaniss, E. R., Frabut, J. M., Kendrick, M. H. and Arbuckle, M. B. (2007) 'Reducing disproportionate minority contact in the juvenile justice system: Promising practices', *Aggression and Violent Behavior* 12: 393–401.

Chappell, A. T., Maggard, S. R. and Higgins, J. L. (2012) 'Exceptions to the rule? Exploring the use of overrides in detention risk assessment', *Youth Violence and Juvenile Justice* 11: 332–48.

Chesney-Lind, M. and Sheldon, R. G. (1998) *Girls, Delinquency, and Juvenile Justice* (2nd edn.). Belmont, CA: West/Wadsworth.

Christon, L. M., McLeod, D. and Jensen-Doss, A. (2015) 'Evidence-based assessment meets evidence-based treatment: An approach to science-informed case conceptualization', *Cognitive and Behavioral Practice* 22: 36–48.

Clark, M. D. (2005) 'Motivational interviewing for probation staff: Increasing the readiness to change', *Federal Probation* 69: 22–28.

Fraser, M. W. (ed.) (2004) *Risk and Resilience in Childhood*. Washington, DC: NASW Press.

Gaarder, E., Rodriguez, N. and Zatz, M. (2004) 'Criers, liars, and manipulators: Probation officers' views of girls', *Justice Quarterly* 21: 547–78.

Graham, S. and Lowery, B. S. (2004) 'Priming unconscious racial stereotypes about adolescent offenders', *Law and Human Behavior* 28: 483–504.

Guy, L. S., Nelson, R. J., Fusco-Morin, S. L. and Vincent, G. M. (2013) 'What do juvenile probation officers think of using the SAVRY and YLS/CMI for case management, and do they use the instruments properly?', *International Journal of Forensic Mental Health* 13: 227–41.

Haines, K. and Case, S. (2009) *Understanding Youth Offending: Risk Factor Research, Policy and Practice*. Cullompton: Willan Publishing.

Haque, Q. and Webster, C. D. (2013) 'Structured professional judgement and sequential redirections', *Criminal Behaviour and Mental health* 23: 241–51.

Howell, J. C. (2003) *Preventing & Reducing Juvenile Delinquency: A Comprehensive Framework*. Thousand Oaks, CA: Sage.

Hoyt, E. H., Schiraldi, V., Smith, B. B. and Zeidenberg, J. (2002) *8 Pathways to Juvenile Detention Reform: Reducing Racial Disparities in Juvenile Detention*. Baltimore, MD: The Annie E. Casey Foundation.

Kahneman, D. (2011) Thinking, fast and slow. New York: Farrar, Straus and Giroux.

Link, B. G., Cullen, F. T., Struening, W., Shrout, P. E. and Dohrenwend, B. P. (1989) 'A modified labelling theory approach to mental disorders: An empirical assessment', *American Sociological Review* 54: 400–23.

Losen, D. J. and Skiba, R. J. (2010) *Suspended Education: Urban Middle Schools in Crisis*. Montgomery, AL: Southern Poverty Law Center.

Maxwell, S. R. and Gray, M. K. (2000) 'Deterrence: Testing the effects of perceived sanction certainty on probation violations', *Sociological Inquiry* 70: 117–36.

Miller, J. and Maloney, C. (2013) 'Practitioner compliance with risk/needs assessment tools: A theoretical and empirical assessment', *Criminal Justice and Behavior* 40: 716–36.

Minoudis, P., Craissati, J., Shaw, J., McMurran, M., Freestone, M., Chuan, S. J. and Leonard, A. (2013) 'An evaluation of case formulation training and consultation with probation officers', *Criminal Behaviour and Mental Health* 23: 252–62.

Schwalbe, C. S. and Maschi, T. M. (2010) 'Patterns of contact and cooperation between juvenile probation officers and parents of youthful offenders', *Journal of Offender Rehabilitation* 49: 398–416.

Schmidt, F., Hoge, R. D. and Gomez, L. (2005) 'Reliability and validity analysis of the Youth Level of Service/ Case Management Inventory', *Criminal Justice and Behavior* 32: 329–44.

Schneider, A. L., Ervin, L. and Snyder-Joy, Z. (1996) 'Further exploration of the flight from discretion: The role of risk/need instruments in probation supervision decisions', *Journal of Criminal Justice* 24: 109–21.

Schwalbe, C. S., Fraser, M. W., Day, S. H. and Arnold, E. M. (2004) 'North Carolina Assessment of Risk (NCAR): Reliability and predictive validity with juvenile offenders' *Journal of Offender Rehabilitation* 40: 1–22.

Schwalbe, C. S., Gearing, R. E., MacKenzie, M. J., Brewer, K. B. and Ibrahim, R. (2012) 'A meta-analysis of experimental studies of diversion programs for juvenile offenders', *Clinical Psychology Review* 32: 26–33.

Shook, J. J. and Sarri, R. C. (2007) 'Structured decision making in juvenile justice: Judges' and probation officers' perceptions and use', *Children and Youth Services Review* 29: 1335–51.

Singh, J. P., Grann, M. and Fazel, S. (2011) 'A comparative study of violence risk assessment tools: A systematic review and metaregression analysis of 68 studies involving 25,980 participants', *Clinical Psychology Review* 31: 499–513

Smith, H., Rodriguez, N. and Zatz, M. (2009) 'Race, ethnicity, class, and noncompliance with juvenile court supervision', *The Annals of the American Academy of Political and Social Science* 623: 108–20.

Takahashi, M., Mori, T. and Kroner, D. G. (2013) 'A cross-validation of the Youth Level of Service/Case Management Inventory (YLS/CMI) among Japanese juvenile offenders', *Law and Human Behavior* 37: 389–400.

Trotter, C. (2006) *Working with Involuntary Clients* (2nd edition). Thousand Oaks, CA: Sage.

Tversky, A. and Kahneman, D. (1974) 'Judgment under uncertainty, heuristics and biases', *Science* 185: 1124–31.

Van Voorhis, P., Wright, E. M., Salisbury, E. and Bauman, A. (2010) 'Women's risk factors and their contributions to existing risk/needs assessment: The current status of a gender-responsive supplement', *Criminal Justice and Behavior* 37: 261–88.

Vincent, G. M., Guy, L. S., Fusco, S. L. and Gershenson, B. G. (2012) 'Field reliability of the SAVRY with juvenile probation officers: Implications for training', *Law and Human Behavior* 36: 225–36.

Vincent, G. M., Guy, L. S. and Grisso, T. (2012) *Risk Assessment in Juvenile Justice: A Guidebook for Implementation*. Chicago, IL: MacArthur Foundation.

Zhang, J. and Liu, N. (2014) 'Reliability and validity of the Chinese Version of the LSI-R with probationers', *International Journal of Offender Therapy and Comparative Criminology* (Advance online publication). doi:10.1177/0306624X14538396.

12

DYNAMIC AND PROTECTIVE FACTORS IN THE TREATMENT OF OFFENDERS: A RECONCEPTUALIZATION

Tony Ward
Victoria University of Wellington, New Zealand

Imogen McDonald
Victoria University of Wellington, New Zealand

Introduction

A promising approach to the explanation of crime and evidence-informed assessment and intervention, is to focus on factors that have been reliably linked to the onset and reoccurrence of offending. An additional requirement is that factors associated with offending are currently a focal point of theoretical and empirical research in the forensic and correctional domains. In fact, a cornerstone of evidence-based practice is that correctional interventions have been shown to reduce reoffending rates by virtue of their impact on the causes of crime. We suggest that work on dynamic risk factors meets these requirements and they can be reasonably construed (after some conceptual reworking) as proximate causal factors that are reflections of basic human needs. For example, the dynamic risk factor of intimacy deficits can be conceptualized as arising from the need of human beings to form close social relationships. In the case of intimacy failure, the person concerned lacks the necessary psychological and contextual resources to meet this need in prosocial and personally fulfilling ways. As a consequence of the absence of the required personal and social capabilities to establish and maintain intimate relationships, some individuals commit sexual offences (Ward, Polaschek and Beech, 2006). Other types of dynamic risk factors can also be theoretically traced back to motivational, cognitive and behavioural capacities such as the capacity for self-regulation (or agency), emotional identification and control, social learning, causal and inductive (generalizing) reasoning, group identification, status and resource seeking, and identity formation.

The problem with basing the (proximate) explanation of crime on dynamic risk factors is that such an account fails to adequately reflect human agency and the goal-directed nature of action. What you typically end up with is a list of factors that predict recidivism but reveal little or no understanding of how they actually cause offending in part or collectively. This is in part because criminal justice researchers are preoccupied with risk assessment and prediction, and therefore, heavily favour psychometric models of offending over causal ones (Ward, 2014). In our view this is a mistake and is likely to lead to theoretical and practice dead-ends very quickly; additionally, it conflates risk prediction with causal explanation (Ward, 2015). A more fruitful strategy is to shift the research focus and concentrate instead on the goal-directed nature of human functioning and the constituents of human agency. The question then becomes: What type of goals (and their motivational and cognitive underpinnings), strategies, plans and contexts are associated with the violation of significant social and moral norms?

Dynamic risk factors are pseudo explanations and, in our view, their importation into explanatory and treatment planning contexts is rapidly leading the field into theoretical and practice dead-ends. It is timely to think about other ways of understanding both dynamic risk and protective factors.

In this chapter we first outline the concepts of dynamic risk factors and protective factors. The ability of these concepts to function as explanations of crime (and its desistance) is critically evaluated and their relationships to proximate causes explored. A major problem identified is that dynamic risk factors are *composite* constructs and are summaries of psychosocial and social characteristics and processes. Due to this hybrid nature they do not actually refer to real factors at all. A similar problem holds for protective factors, although the issue here is more one of vagueness than failure to genuinely refer. Second, the Agency Model of Risk (AMR) is systematically outlined and its grounding in psychological, biological and cultural processes is discussed. We do not pretend that the AMR represents the final word on the conceptualization of risk and protective factors. Rather, our intention is to offer one possible way of thinking about them and by doing so to open up a conceptual space for new theoretical work. Third, we demonstrate how dynamic risk factors and protective factors, once distributed across the components of human agency, contribute to the occurrence of crime. In this chapter we concentrate our analysis on sexual offenders, although our argument extends to all types of offenders.

Dynamic risk factors

Researchers in the correctional and sexual offending fields have paid considerable attention in recent years to the development and validation of risk assessment measures and protocols (Mann, Hanson and Thornton, 2010; Ward, 2014). The identification of risk factors and risk assessment has been prioritized in the field and increasingly practitioners and researchers have used them to explain sexual offending and to guide treatment. In brief, risk assessment is the process of using risk factors (i.e. any variable that is measurable and predictive of harmful outcomes) to estimate the likelihood of a person committing another offence in the future (Cooke and Michie, 2013). The process of risk assessment may differ in terms of its degree of structure and reliance on professional judgement and/or a set of explicit rules. The nature of the risk factors used in research and clinical assessment varies in a number of ways including their degree of changeability (static vs. dynamic), duration (stable vs. acute), content (e.g. relational style, attitudes and biomarkers), form (risk vs. protective) and function (causal, contributing or contextual).

Dynamic risk factors in general terms are conceptualized as 'enduring factors linked to the likelihood of offending that can nevertheless be changed following intervention' (Beech and Craig, 2012, p. 170). A subset of dynamic risk factors have been called *criminogenic needs*, essentially offender or social characteristics which are causally related to individuals' criminal behaviour and that if modified or managed in some way result in lower reoffending rates (Andrews and Bonta, 2010). In an important recent paper, Mann, Hanson and Thornton (2010) identified a number of what they called *psychologically meaningful* risk factors that were considered to be prima facie causes of sexual offending and validated predictors of recidivism. The list of supported meaningful risk factors for child sexual abuse included sexual preferences for children, emotional congruence with children, general self-regulation problems, emotional deregulation, offence-supportive attitudes, poor cognitive problem-solving, and lack of adult intimate relationships. Mann et al. (2010, p. 210) concluded that:

> Assessment and treatment for sexual offenders should focus on empirically established causal risk factors. In this review, we propose a definition of psychologically meaningful causal risk factors as propensities and outline the types of evidence required to identify them. Although the causal role of such factors has yet to be established, we believe that the causal factors for sexual recidivism will ultimately be drawn from variables similar to those included in our list. We believe that it is these variables that should be emphasized in treatment.

Critical comments

While the use of dynamic risk factors for *risk prediction* purposes is perfectly acceptable, there are significant problems with employing them to explain offending, individually or collectively. Furthermore, this difficulty is compounded when they are incorporated into clinical case formulations. There are two major difficulties in our view: (a) dynamic risk factors are actually psychometric, *composite* constructs, and therefore a mixture of causal elements and clinical attributes; (b) because they are composite factors, they do not actually exist or genuinely refer to psychological and social processes (Ward and Beech, 2015). And because they strictly do not exist, it is meaningless to investigate their relationship with protective factors and other risk- and offence-related variables. This is a radical claim and completely undermines the correctional field's current preoccupation with constructing explanatory and case formulation models based on dynamic risk factors. They are not useful in explaining offending because they are essentially summaries or placeholders for diverse predictive factors. An explanation refers to the mechanisms generating phenomena and is essentially backward looking: why did x occur? What caused it? However, prediction is forward looking and asks the question: will x occur? Causation is irrelevant. We will examine each of the above problems in turn.

First, dynamic risk factors are composite factors in at least three distinct senses. They are frequently discussed in the literature and appear in psychometric models as a *type* of construct, whereas in fact they are a collection of dynamic risk factors; thus the general category label is simply a placeholder. For example, de Vries Robbé (2014) unpacks the general category of dynamic risk factors evident in sex offenders into such elements as sexual preoccupation, deviant sexual interests, offence-supportive attitudes, emotional congruence with children, impulsiveness, poor cognitive problem-solving, grievance/hostility and lack of concern for others (pp. 43–44). The difficulty is that later in his monograph he outlines a proposed explanatory model that uses the general term 'risk factors', in which he explores their relationship to violence and protective factors (p. 152). At best this use of the term is misleading, while at worse it conflates levels of constructs. A further problem related to the composite nature of dynamic risk factors is that each specific factor is typically broken into further features, some of which causally exclude each other. For example, in his recent summary of risk and protective factors in adult male sexual offenders, Thornton (2013) listed sexual violence and sexual interest in children as subdomains of the general dynamic risk factor of sexual interests. The problem is that the 'umbrella', so to speak, of deviant sexual interests consists of qualitatively different variables, which arguably refer to distinct causal processes and their associated problems. Finally, the description of dynamic risk factors is vague and seems to include both trait and state aspects. For example, the stable dynamic factor of general self-regulation includes negative emotionality (a mental state) and poor problem-solving (a trait or enduring psychological feature). Thus dynamic risk factors are really psychometric instruments that contain heterogeneous features and in this sense are summaries or composite constructs.

Second, the problem of dynamic risk factors' composite nature has serious implications for its usefulness in both theory construction and clinical case formulations, once their construct validity status is evaluated. We argue that taking into account their composite nature, and the mixture of causal elements and clinical attributes, they do not genuinely refer to processes and structures in persons and the world, and therefore, do not exist. Dynamic risk factors are of instrumental value in risk assessment contexts, but once they are incorporated into explanations and clinical case formulations, they exceed their existential warrant, so to speak. They then become fictitious entities. Because dynamic risk factors do not strictly exist, it is meaningless to investigate their relationship with protective other risk and offence-related variables. Borsboom (2005, p. 158) captures this issue nicely when he asserts:

> If term is treated as referential but has no referent, then one is reifying terms that have no other function than that of providing a descriptive summary of a distinct set of processes and attributes. For instance, one then comes to treat a name for a group of test items as if it were a common cause of the item responses. That of course is a mistake.

If no attribute answers the referential call, the test is not valid for measuring that attribute no matter how useful the test may be for prediction, selection or how well it may fulfil other functions.

Finally, because dynamic risk factors lack construct validity and therefore do not genuinely refer to real psychological and social processes, there is little point investigating their relationship to protective factors: outside a risk prediction context. In the context of risk prediction, pragmatic considerations can override those of truth and explanatory robustness. However, this is not the case when it comes to the construction of etiological explanations and their subsequent application in treatment planning (Ward and Beech, 2015).

Protective factors

A significant amount of attention has been paid to resilience in children who have experienced maltreatment, which includes physical, sexual and emotional abuse, and neglect (Cicchetti and Toth, 2005). Previous research has demonstrated that there is a large range of negative outcomes associated with maltreatment in childhood. These include anxiety, depression and social withdrawal in adolescence (Lansford et al., 2002), low self-esteem and difficulty in interpersonal relationships in adult females who have experienced childhood sexual abuse (Browne and Finkelhor, 1986) and increased likelihood of violent offending in males who have been abused as children (Dutton and Hart, 1992). In this context, resilience is described as being fostered by protective factors (Mrazek and Mrazek, 1987), which are the factors that protect individuals from the negative outcomes that are typically associated with maltreatment. Common protective factors in the child maltreatment literature include personality traits, intelligence, stable caregiving and supportive family and peer relationships (Afifi and MacMillan, 2011). Some researchers have proposed that we should turn our attention towards protective processes rather than focusing solely on protective factors. Rutter (1987, p. 137) claimed that 'instead of searching for broadly based protective factors, we need to focus on protective mechanisms and processes'. For example, rather than focusing on the protective factor of high self-esteem, we should examine *how* and *why* some people manage to maintain high self-esteem in the face of adversities when perhaps others are unable to do this.

Further distinctions have been made between protective factors and other similar, yet distinct, concepts. For example, Cutuli and Masten (2009) distinguished between protective factors and promotive factors, otherwise known as assets. Promotive factors have been described as positive outcomes in general, regardless of the presence of risk. An example of a promotive factor is healthy brain development, which predicts general positive life outcomes. Alternatively, protective factors 'moderate risk, showing a special effect when adversity is high' (Cutuli and Masten, 2009, p. 841). Some factors have been described as promotive in low-risk contexts but take on more protective functions in the face of adversity. For example, the presence of good parenting is a promotive factor, but it may also take on a further protective function for a child experiencing adversity.

Protective factors in the offending literature

Interest in protective factors in the forensic area has only developed recently, and there has been very little discussion surrounding the notion of protection in the offending domain (de Vries Robbè, de Vogel, Koster and Bogaerts, 2015). One of the key areas that the concept of protection has been applied to is offender risk assessment. Forensic risk assessment is used in correctional settings to examine the level of reoffending risk that an offender poses, usually focusing on the likelihood of an individual committing further violent or sexual offences upon release (Beech and Craig, 2013). Risk assessment tools typically assist clinicians in determining an individual's level of recidivism risk (high, medium or low), with some tools also assisting in the development of appropriate treatment approaches (Mann et al., 2010). Forensic assessment has been criticized for an almost exclusive focus on risk and risk factors (i.e. factors that increase the likelihood of offending), while paying little to no attention to the concept of protection. This over-emphasis on risk has been criticized for a range of reasons; for example, Rogers (2000) argued that one-sided risk assessments are inherently inaccurate and therefore of limited utility due to the exclusion of protection, likely resulting in a range of negative outcomes for offenders, such as the unwarranted removal of freedoms through more severe restrictions, while important and scarce resources (e.g. treatment) may be wrongly allocated to individuals who may not need them. Furthermore, professionals working with offenders may come to develop an overwhelmingly negative view of their clientele, leading to high levels of pessimism and further negative outcomes. In order to combat the negative consequences of this exclusive focus on risk, Rogers argues that protective factors should be introduced in the assessment process.

De Vries Robbè, Mann, Maruna and Thornton (2015) define protective factors as social, interpersonal and environmental factors, and psychological and behavioural features, that lower an individual's risk of reoffending. They propose that, like risk factors, it is possible to distinguish between static and dynamic protective factors. Further, they suggest that it is useful to differentiate between a protective factor as an underlying propensity (e.g. a psychological characteristic) versus an observable manifestation of that propensity (such as employment, which may be a manifestation of underlying propensities such as work ethic and social skills).

In a recent monograph de Vries Robbè (2014) developed an explanatory model which attempted to depict how protective factors exert their effects. In his model, there are four main mechanisms by which protective factors have an impact on risk: *the risk-reducing* effect, the *moderator* effect, the *main* effect and the *motivator* effect. According to the risk-reducing effect, some protective factors reduce risk directly by causally altering risk mechanisms in some way. The second effect, the moderator or buffering effect, is hypothesized to occur when protective factors lessen the strength of the relationship between a risk factor and subsequent offending (i.e. violence). These factors influence the likelihood that specific risk factors will lead to offending, rather than changing the risk factor directly. Next, de Vries Robbè proposes that the main effect pathway works by protective factors having a general positive effect, offering overall protection rather than influencing specific risk factors, which then leads to a reduction in offending. Finally, a final mechanism of protection, termed 'the motivator effect', occurs when protective factors exert a positive influence on each other. For example, the static factors of intelligence and secure attachment may be able to enhance or facilitate the later development of other protective factors, such as empathy, work, social network and motivation for treatment.

In his model, de Vries Robbè (2014) proposed that these mechanisms are not necessarily mutually exclusive, with the majority of the protective factor causal pathways impacting on individuals at the same time; or furthermore, he states that protective factors may work through different mechanisms for different people, or at different points in time. For example, a social network may directly lessen the risk factor of stress by providing a supportive environment while also acting as a moderator by assisting the individual to stay away from substances that might enhance risk, even if he does not believe the substance is likely to be harmful. Additionally, social networks may have a direct effect on offending by improving the quality of someone's life, therefore decreasing the likelihood of offending. Finally, social networks might facilitate other protective factors, such as treatment motivation, because of the presence of supportive social relationships.

Although research on protective factors for offenders is still in its early stages, researchers in some areas have attempted to identify the specific factors that facilitate desistance from offending. The Structured Assessment of Protective Factors (SAPROF) was developed for the assessment of risk in violent offenders; however, this scale has also demonstrated its usefulness in assessing sexual offenders. In a recent study, de Vries Robbè, de Vogel, Koster and Bogaerts (2015) used the SAPROF to assess sexually violent offenders and found that the scale was significantly predictive of sexual reoffending at follow-up (AUC = 0.76 after three years). In another recent paper, de Vries Robbè, Mann, Maruna and Thornton (2015) identified a range of possible factors that appear to protect individuals specifically from sexually offending. These factors included some taken from the SAPROF for violence risk (such as self-control, coping and work); opposites of risk factors (such as moderate intensity sexual drive, sexual preference for adults and a preference for emotional intimacy for adults); and protective factors from the desistance literature (such as enhanced sense of personal agency and having found a place within a social group or network). While a range of these factors are reflected in the SAPROF domains, de Vries Robbè et al. (2015) have suggested that it may be beneficial to include *healthy sexual interests*, a protective factor specific to sexual offending, that is not included in the SAPROF when assessing sexually violent offenders.

Critical comments

There are a number of conceptual and theoretical difficulties in de Vries Robbè's model of protective factors and their relationship to dynamic risk factors. In our view, they all have their source in a failure to appreciate the differences between risk prediction and explanation.

A general problem concerns the way protective factors are defined by de Vries Robbè and his colleagues, namely as 'characteristics of an offender, or alternatively, his or her environment or situation, that reduce the risk of future violent behaviour' (p. 26). According to this definition, the term 'protective factor' refers to anything that is associated with decreased levels of offending, including maturation, treatment and social support for a start. This definition markedly differs with the original conceptualization of protective factors in the psychopathology and child maltreatment area. For example, in the child maltreatment area, Afifi and MacMillan (2011, p. 268) define protective factors as follows: 'A protective factor may influence, modify, ameliorate, or alter how a person responds to the adversity that places them at risk for maladaptive outcomes.' Broadening the concept of protective factors is conceptually problematic, as it makes it harder to distinguish between protective factors, maturational effects, therapy-induced change or desistance events (Durrant and Ward, 2015). In other words, the concept is so all-encompassing that it is arguably vacuous.

Each of the four proposed causal pathways specified in the model is conceptually problematic. First, the assertion that protective factors can alter the nature of dynamic risk factors and therefore reduce re-offending is confusing. In his model of protective factors and the way they impact on risk, de Vries Robbè (2014) classified protective factors as being either the healthy opposite of risk factors, or 'unipolar' (i.e. without an opposite). Let's look at the first option. He has argued that opposing factors may co-occur; for example, an individual may be exposed to negative social influences (the risk factor) and positive social influences (the opposing protective factor) simultaneously. But that amounts to stating that an individual has a characteristic *and lacks* it at the same time, clearly logically impossible and causally doubtful. If this is countered by stating that they are different *types* of social influences, then each operates, in effect, as a *separate* risk or protective factor, and therefore they are not really opposites. Granted, a person may be mixing with antisocial peers while also having social ties with a church group. But in this case, one is not the opposite of the other at all. If you try to resolve this issue by stating that the opposition occurs between *broad* prosocial and antisocial influences, then it is apparent the term is so vague that it is not picking out specific causal factors at all. It is theoretically vacuous. It is simply a way to group different types of causal influences. The dilemma of falseness versus vacuity runs through every type of risk–protective factor opposite pair; it is endemic to the model, and as far as we can see, is a fatal flaw. The only way to make sense of this to interpret the opposite claim in terms of a shift from a risk factor to a protective factor – its opposite – over time as a result of therapy or via some process such as a maturation. While this avoids the contradiction, it reflects a different relationship between the two, as depicted by de Vries Robbè. Under this interpretation, there is no causal interaction between a risk factor and its opposite protective factor, but rather a change in a risk factor over time. Quite a different claim.

The above analysis concluded that it is not logically or practically possible for protective factors to causally alter their opposites – dynamic risk factors – within a given individual. Perhaps what is meant by de Vries Robbè is that if you take sex offenders as a *group*, then protective factors can change the nature of some dynamic risk factors, just not their specific opposites. So, for example, although adaptive sexual interests cannot coexist with maladaptive sexual interests, perhaps it is possible they could cause changes in another dynamic risk factor such as intimacy deficits. Just how that could occur remains to be spelt out in terms of causal mechanisms. While this is plausible, it only applies to treatment contexts or maturation. Obviously, at the time an offence occurred, the presence of the protective factor – in this case adaptive sexual interests – did not prevent an offence from occurring. Thus, saying that protective factors – as the opposites of dynamic risk factors – can alter the nature of another dynamic risk factor is not that illuminating. Furthermore, protective factors do not alter or change dynamic risk factors; they are essentially replacements for them.

The second way in which protective factors are thought to impact on dynamic risk factors is through their moderating effect. The example de Vries Robbè (2014) gives is that of self-control and its moderating effects on negative attitudes and alcohol abuse. However, it is not immediately apparent exactly how a good level of self-control lessens the impact of either problem, without having a lot more information concerning the crime-supportive attitudes in question or an account of the reasons why the person has substance abuse problems. For example, some sex offenders have excellent self-control and demonstrate sophisticated planning and emotional control in the commission of their offences (Fortune, Bourke and Ward, 2015). A more general point is that to say that the relationship is one of *moderation* is to assume that the dynamic risk factor and its associated mechanisms still exist (unlike in the first pathway when they have been altered or eliminated) and that the protective factor somehow attenuates or blocks its influence. But given that, for example, substance abuse is often linked to impulsivity, the claim is that an individual (a) has good self-control, which lessens the impact of his (b) poor self-control, at the same time. Again, this is contradictory and causally doubtful. And in the case of negative attitudes, the assertion seems to be that self-control, a self-regulatory capacity, somehow blocks or lessens the impact of this cognitive factor. It is not clear how this could work or even if it makes sense. The source of all these problems is that de Vries Robbè has constructed a risk prediction model, not an explanatory one, and has conflated the two.

The third type of relationship between protective factors and dynamic risk is hypothesized to depend on the existence of well-being or lifestyle promotive factors such as work, leisure activities and life goals. Unfortunately, de Vries Robbè does not provide specific examples of what leisure activities may involve nor what life goals may be appropriate. Further, there is no explanation concerning *how* these factors could directly reduce offending, just that they do. An explanatory model should not only include the factors that are associated with or predictive of an outcome; it should also include an explanation for *how* or *why* this happens. Furthermore, it seems to us that what are being referred to here are desistance factors which have their own set of associated causal mechanisms such as changes in self-narratives or the existence of social supports.

The final causal pathway outlined in de Vries Robbè's explanatory model of the relationship between protective factors and level of risk is that of the 'motivator effect'. This concerns the potential for some protective factors, such as secure attachment or intelligence, to enhance (i.e. increase the likelihood they will occur and/or their level) other protective factors such as work or empathy. The problem with this hypothesized pathway is that it is simply too vague, and, for some factors, is conceptually confused. For example, secure attachment is likely to be associated with a number of personal strengths such as good social skills, high levels of empathy and strong emotional regulation capacities. It is hard to grasp why, if someone has all these skills, he or she would commit an offence. Or if the person did, then surely his or her risk level would be low? Furthermore, if the ability to be empathic or to have good mentalizing ability is a component of secure attachment (as it seems to be), it is actually part of what it *means* to be securely attached. It is then rather odd to say that someone who is securely attached and therefore has good empathy skills (along with other strengths) will develop strong empathy skills! We think that this pathway is subject to objections such as these because it is theoretically undeveloped, along with the model as a whole. While de Vries Robbè's model of protective factors and their relationship to dynamic risk factors and offending might be useful for predicting reoffending and ascertaining individuals' level of risk, it is not adequate as an explanatory model.

Conclusions

We have critically examined the concepts of dynamic risk factors and protective factors and concluded that they are problematic and are of little value in the context of explanation, and therefore have little to offer in intervention planning. This is especially worrying because assessment and case formulation in the correctional and forensic domains seem to revolve largely around the detection of dynamic risk factors, and the classification of offenders and their problems amounts to formulating risk profiles. What is needed is a way of reconceptualizing dynamic risk and protective factors that explicitly links them to the causes of offending.

The agency model of risk

Even though there are serious theoretical problems with both sets of concepts, it seems likely that dynamic risk factors, in particular, track at least some of the causal processes that generate offending. Otherwise, it is hard to account for their success in predicting recidivism rates and in guiding some aspects of treatment. Furthermore, it is reasonable to assume that constituents of dynamic risk factors exert a causal influence and are, in part at least, proximate explanations of crime.

We seem to have arrived at something of an impasse: while dynamic risk factors do not appear to genuinely refer to real psychological or social processes, they are markers for crime-related processes. They excel in risk prediction contexts but in their traditional form are not good candidates for causal explanations of offending and therefore should not be used – unmodified – in clinical case formulations. This is because pragmatic considerations regulate the development of predictive measures, and in the offending area they are typically summaries of multiple variables and therefore do not cohere well as theoretical constructs. The trouble is that they are currently used in both these ways. The problem as we see it is that researchers and clinicians have no viable alternative. They want to hang onto the benefits of a dynamic risk factor framework, and protective factors to a lesser extent, but are unclear how to resolve the theoretical problems outlined above. We believe the answer resides in stepping outside a purely risk assessment and management lens to focus on the components of human agency. *Agency* refers to a person's capacity to plan action and control his or her behaviour. More specifically, it involves the ability to manage multiple and sometimes competing goals in ways that enable individuals to sustain their functioning, repair any damage (often at a biological level through internal physiological processes), avoid harm and threats, and implement plans that are cohesive and responsive to any relevant contexts – social, physical and cultural (Christensen, 2012; Christensen and Hooker, 2000).

The agency model of risk

Dynamic risk factors in the correctional and forensic domains are intended to predict harm related to reoffending, typically to victims and the community. Protective factors are features that lessen the chances of risk factors having this effect, or more generally, if present, they reduce the likelihood of offending occurring. As stated above, it is a good idea to *turn* things around and start with the personal and contextual factors that both dynamic risk factors and protective factors refer to. In our view, a promising way to understand both is by reference to human agency and the multiple systems that constitute agency and make it possible. That is, we propose that dynamic risk and protective factors refer to the components of agency: goals, plans and strategies, implementation and evaluation, and the subsequent revision of goals and plans. Furthermore, in our model there are three levels of agency, each associated with its own distinct set of goals, plans and strategies, and each capable of influencing the others types of agency (see below): system level, social role and personal (Christensen and Hooker, 2000; Colombetti, 2014). As proposed earlier, dynamic risk factors do not exist other than as summaries of different variables, and because protective factors are defined in terms of harmful (risk associated) outcomes, they do not have conceptual meaning aside from this context.

Thus, risk factors once broken down into their causal elements can be viewed as psychological and social processes (i.e. those associated with goals, plans, strategies and action implementation) that adversely impair functioning and hence disrupt persons' internal and external relationships to their social, cultural and physical environments. This disruption can be at multiple levels and even be confined to incorrect actions within a single practice (e.g. relationship repair). Protective factors, once broken down into their core elements, work in multiple ways across the various levels of agency to inhibit and/or disrupt dysfunctional systems, and to restore normal functioning. Sometimes the constraints exerted by protective factors may be external, such as the construction of supportive social networks around high-risk offenders. Strengths are conceptualized as internal and external capacities that enable offenders to flourish in certain environments, which can be used also to motivate them and recruited to function as protective factors in some situations.

In the AMR there are two major sources of causal influence, the agent and the context (environment). We have used the term 'agent' to better capture the self-regulation of persons and the term 'contexts' because it more adequately reflects the fine-grained nature of environments that activate, and are responsive to, the agent's goals. In the AMR there are bidirectional relationships between the agent and the environment, which is intended to convey their dynamic interactions and reciprocal causation. The temporal scale may reflect real (immediate) time processes and ongoing contact as well as portraying extended sequences of interactions.

We will start with the agent side of the relationship and make a few general comments to begin with. The first thing to note is that there are three primary components involved in the initiation of action: selection of goal(s) (what is the purpose of the action? What outcomes does the agent desire to achieve?); the construction of a plan and selection of the strategies required to realize the plan (this will involve norms that specify effective strategies and how best to integrate goals, strategies and norms within a coherent action sequence); and the implementation and evaluation of the plan (Did the plan result in the desired outcomes? If not why not? How can it be revised in the light of its failure to achieve the desired result?). Second, the three components of the action sequence have bidirectional relationships with each other. Third, there are three levels of agency within the AMR: systems level, social roles and personal identity, each conceptually linked to distinct sets of goals, strategies and implementation practices.

The Agent. The capacity for agency is inherent in all living things; however, in human beings the level of sophistication is much higher due to their ability to intentionally structure learning and physical environments (i.e. niche construction – Sterelny, 2012). The origins of this enhanced agency capacity arguably reside in the possession of language and cognitive plasticity. A consequence of this suite of competences is that human beings can think counterfactually about their past and possible future and regulate action through the application of complex mental models and the acquisition of cultural cognitive and behavioural tools. According to the AMR, basic human needs and their elaboration into explicit norms and their accompanying strategies create an array of scripts and action templates. Emotions are fast appraisal systems that inform the organism about its current goal status and progress, and therefore can function as effective action organizers and prompts. Furthermore, norms are linked to specific emotions, which are viewed as internal cues indicating that things are going well or badly. For example, a sex offender may have an insecure attachment style and feel anxious when in the presence of adults. The activation of feelings of anxiety or fear could cause him to feel vulnerable and to seek out children for support. As a consequence of this goal state, he may engage in the sexual abuse of a child but consider this as a caring and mutually beneficial encounter. Thus there is a close causal connection between attachment-related beliefs, emotions and needs, current environmental cues and the formation of a plan to sexually abuse a child. The activation of a goal can unconsciously affect an offender's subsequent behaviour and result in a complex sequence of actions that lead to high-risk situations. The goal-dependent actions are represented in long-term memory in the form of cognitive scripts and contain information that guides the offending behaviour. They specify the conditions under which an offence plan can be enacted, including the creation of access to possible victims and the use of strategies to groom and subdue them. These scripts can be enacted without conscious intention and with minimal awareness of the overall goal (Colombetti, 2014; Maise, 2011).

Thus, at times goals can be automatically activated and embedded within action plans or offence scripts that come with specified strategies. However, on other occasions offenders will construct new plans in response to unique motivational states and environmental cues, once they have formulated their goals – although the initial goal formulation may not be explicit (Haung and Bargh, 2014).

The implementation of a plan always occurs within a particular environment in response to internal and external cues and in this respect is ecologically responsive. In other words, offenders do not simply come up with general plans that ignore the context in which they live and overlook the various social and physical affordances inherent in these contexts. Once plans are constructed, individuals carry them out and evaluate the degree to which they are successful in achieving their goals. The bidirectional causal relationships depicted in the AMR rest on the assumption that each component of the action sequence can influence the others, both during and following the completion of the action and its subsequent evaluation. For example, if an individual is experiencing trouble constructing a workable plan, he may adjust his goals; or partway through the execution of an offence, he might abandon the original plan and refine it. In other words, although we have conceptually divided the sequence into three major components, in actuality they are seamlessly integrated.

The final key feature of the agent component of the AMR is the existence of levels of agency. For purposes of illustration, we have included three agency levels in the model but readily acknowledge that this is more for didactic purposes, and we are not committed to there being only three, or even these particular three. The important point is that each level is associated with different types of action sequences in response to varying internal and environmental cues. The level of *system agency* is meant to deal with threats to the physical nature of agents; for example, when feeling threatened or when intoxicated or unwell. We suggest that the activation of this level of agency will determine the types of goals and plans constructed, and itself is likely to be triggered by unique contextual cues, for example the presence of a threat to safety. The agency level *of social roles* is associated with particular social institutions and contexts. For example, a sex offender might be working as a therapist and in this role blurs the boundaries between his professional and personal interests. He takes advantage of a patient and sexually assaults her, possibly rationalizing it as part of therapy. Another example is that of rape in wartime. A soldier might see victims as the enemy and incorrectly justify his sexually abusive actions as legitimate acts of war. In other words, in both examples the offence-related goals, strategies, plan and implementations are strongly connected to specific social contexts and identities. The *personal* level of agency concerns individuals' overall sense of identity and their core normative commitments. It seeks to fashion connections between global (implicit or explicit) plans for living and individuals' most heavily weighted values. For example, an offender might conceive of himself as a sensitive, somewhat empathic person who is distrustful of adults. He seeks the company of children because they are perceived as less rejecting and more considerate. This could provide an emotional and social context for sexual offending to occur, in the presence of normal human needs for sex and intimacy. Another example is a man who views himself as 'a fighter', someone determined not to be 'pushed around' by what he perceives as 'dominating females'. Such an individual is predisposed to mistakenly interpret assertive behaviour by women as deliberate snubs and worthy of violent retaliation (e.g. rape). In all of the three levels of agency, there are possible interactions, and any one individual could move between them depending on the external contexts and his motivational state.

The Context. The AMR is a dynamic interactional model of human action and states that sometimes the initial causes of offending may be external, such as the presence of offending opportunities (Smallbone and Cale, in press). Other examples include being a member of a gang or part of a paedophilic network or experiencing the loss of a romantic partner. However, on its own the presence of contextual cues will not be enough to initiate offending. In addition, there is likely to be a corresponding shift in the agent's goals and, prior to this, his motivational state and cognitive functioning. The individual will need to interpret what is happening around him and form some type of offence-related goals. Following the setting of goals, he requires the construction of a plan and strategies that will enable him to overcome any conflicting personal motivations and that give access to a potential victim and means of overcoming resistance.

On the other hand, desistance factors such as the presence of social support, employment, intimate relationships and being afforded the chance to 'knife off' an offending identity and lifestyle can decrease the chances of recidivism (Maruna, 2001; McNeill, 2006).

A unique feature of the AMR is its implication that at times environments may effectively override a person's inhibitions against harming others; for example, because of the presence of powerful emotional states in threat situations or due to the social framing of a situation by other people (e.g. racial riots). Given human beings' strong, arguably innate, need for social connection and responses to threats, they may be especially susceptible to malign influences in certain kinds of contexts (Durrant and Ward, 2015). In addition, subcultures that strongly promote norms that dehumanize or alienate individuals could also create external contexts that increase the chances of crime occurring. The tendency for people to seek out and create environments that resonate with their interests and attitudes is likely to facilitate such an effect.

Thus from the viewpoint of the AMR, social and cultural contexts can either activate individuals' underlying crime-supportive attitudes, beliefs and goals or in some causes actually *create* them. The rejection of certain ethnic subgroups or people with certain characteristics by a community may alienate and insulate them from prosocial influences and create enormous resentment and norms that endorse antisocial behaviour. What starts out as primarily an environmental explanation of crime ends up shaping and entrenching cognitive and behavioural characteristics that predispose individuals to harm others.

But– and this is a crucial point – irrespective of where the causal influences originate, the commission of an offence requires the presence of *both* an agent(s) and an external context that supports criminal actions. The degree to which one or the other dominates in a subsequent explanation is a function of the presence of conflicting goals, persistence of offence-supportive or unsupportive attitudes and beliefs, and contexts that either encourage prosocial behaviour or funnel individuals in to adopting offending lifestyles.

Dynamic risk factors, protective factors and the AMR

From the viewpoint of the AMR, dynamic risk factors can be deconstructed into psychological and social processes that are distributed across components of the action sequence; that is, they *exist* as components of action, not as things in themselves. Protective factors in correctional contexts are simply action components that function as *brakes* on, or *eradicators* of, problematic action components, whereas strengths refer to any prioritized goals and capacities of persons and contexts and thus do not need to be specifically mentioned in a causal risk model.

Practice implications

The AMR provides an account of how dynamic risk factors could be causally related to the occurrence of crime, and by extension to the initial onset of offending. The fact that it is built upon the concept of agency and action components underlines the importance of goal-directed behaviour for both biological organisms and for persons. The relational aspect of the model acknowledges the important causal role of the social, cultural and physical environment in facilitating and shaping offence-related proclivities, while also pointing to the way human beings' niche construction abilities create offence-supportive contexts.

The AMR is a conceptual model of dynamic risk factors and protective factors transposed into components of human action, and provides a useful way of thinking about the link between risk and explanation. It can help practitioners analyse the relationships between person and contextual variables and points to the dynamic, interactional nature of offending (and all human action). The traditional formulation of dynamic risk factors – and protective factors – is theoretically problematic and unable to explain the onset and reoccurrence of offending. What is lacking is an understanding of how the causal processes that constitute dynamic risk factors (criminogenic needs) exert an influence on individuals and their environment. The AMR can clarify this.

Conclusions

There is theoretical and practice gridlock in the correctional and forensic domains because of an increasing reliance on dynamic risk factors to guide assessment and intervention with individuals who have committed crimes. The dilemma for clinicians is that on the one hand, they want to engage in evidence-based practice, but on the other, current models centred on dynamic risk factors result in formulaic approaches to working with individuals. The current trend to build protective factors into the assessment matrix does not help much, as they are conceptually almost as problematic as dynamic risk factors. One way forward is to utilize an agency model of risk such as the one outlined in this chapter to create a conceptual link between dynamic risk and protective factors, and individuals' offence-reacted goals, strategies and contexts. Such models are nuanced and make room for multiple levels of analysis while understanding that desistance from offending ultimately requires the chance for people to live meaningful and fulfilling lives.

References

Andrews, D. A. and Bonta, J. (2010) *The Psychology of Criminal Conduct*. New Providence, NJ: Anderson Publishing.

Bartel, P. A. and Forth, A. E. (2005) 'Structured assessment of violence risk inyouth', *Mental Health Screening And Assessment In Juvenile Justice*: 311–23.

Beech, A. R. and Craig, L. (2012) The current status of static and dynamic factors in sexual offending risk assessment. *Journal of Aggression and Peace Research*, 4: 169–85.

Beech, A. R. and Mitchell, I. J. (2005) 'A neurobiological perspective on attachment problems in sexual offenders and the role of selective serotonin re-uptake inhibitors in the treatment of such problems', *Clinical Psychology Review* 25: 153–82.

Borsboom, D. (2005) *Measuring the Mind: Conceptual Issues in Contemporary Psychometrics*. Cambridge, UK: Cambridge University Press.

Christensen, W. (2012) 'Natural sources of normativity', *Studies in the History and Philosophy of Biological and Biomedical Sciences* 43: 104–12. doi:10.1016/j.shpsc.2011.05.009.

Christensen, W. D. and Hooker, C. A. (2000) 'An interactivist-constructivist approach: to intelligence: Self-directive anticipative learning', *Philosophical Psychology* 13: 5–45.

Cicchetti, D. and Toth, S. L. (2005) 'Child maltreatment', *Annual Review of Clinical Psychology* 1: 409–38.

Colombetti, G. (2014) *The Feeling Body: Affective Science Meets the Enactive Mind*. Cambridge, MA: The MIT Press.

Cooke, D. J. and Michie, C. (2013) 'Violence risk assessment: From prediction to understanding- or from what? To why?', in C. Logan and L. Johnstone (eds) *Managing Clinical Risk: A Guide to Effective Practice* (pp. 3–25). Abingdon, UK: Routledge.

Cutuli, J. J. and Masten, A. S. (2009) 'Resilience', in *Encyclopaedia of Positive Psychology*. Chichester, UK; Malden, MA: Wiley-Blackwell.

de Vogel, V., de Vries Robbé, M., de Ruiter, C. and Bouman, Y. H. (2011) 'Assessing protective factors in forensic psychiatric practice: Introducing the SAPROF', *International Journal of Forensic Mental Health* 10(3): 171–7.

de Vries Robbe, M. (2014) Protective Factors: Validation of the Structured Assessment of Protective Factors for Violence Risk in Forensic Psychiatry, PhD thesis, Radboud University Nijmegen, Netherlands.

de Vries Robbé, M., de Vogel, V. and de Spa, E. (2011) 'Protective factors for violence risk in forensic psychiatric patients: A retrospective validation study of the SAPROF', *International Journal of Forensic Mental Health* 10: 178–86.

de Vries Robbé, M., de Vogel, V., Koster, K. and Bogaerts, S. (2015) 'Assessing protective factors for sexually violent offending with the SAPROF', *Sexual Abuse: A Journal of Research and Treatment* 27: 51–70.

de Vries Robbé, M., Mann, R. E., Maruna, S. and Thornton, D. (2015) 'An exploration of protective factors supporting desistance from sexual offending', *Sexual Abuse: A Journal of Research and Treatment* 27: 16–33.

Dutton, D. G. and Hart, S. D. (1992) 'Evidence for long-term, specific effects of childhood abuse and neglect on criminal behavior in men', *International Journal of Offender Therapy and Comparative Criminology* 36: 129–37.

Dyer, J. G. and McGuinness, T. M. (1996) 'Resilience: Analysis of the concept', *Archives of Psychiatric Nursing* 10(5): 276–82.

Farrington, D. P. and Loeber, R. (2000) 'Some benefits of dichotomization in psychiatric and criminological research', *Criminal Behaviour and Mental Health* 10: 100–22.

Haung, J. Y. and Bargh, J. (2014) 'The selfish goal: Autonomously operating motivational structures as the proximate cause of human judgment and behavior', *Behavioral and Brain Sciences* 37: 121–34.

Heffernan, R. and Ward, T. (in press) 'The conceptualization of dynamic risk factors in child sex offenders: An agency model', *Aggression and Violent Behavior*.

Jones, N. J., Brown, S. L., Robinson, D. and Frey, D. (2015) 'Incorporating strengths intoquantitative assessments of criminal risk for adult offenders the service planning instrument', *Criminal Justice and Behaviour* 42(3): 321–38.

Lansford, J. E., Dodge, K. A., Pettit, G. S., Bates, J. E., Crozier, J. and Kaplow, J. (2002) 'A 12-year prospective study of the longterm effects of early child physical maltreatment on psychological, behavioral, and academic problems in adolescence', *Archives of Pediatrics and Adolescent Medicine* 156: 824–30.

Lodewijks, H. P., Doreleijers, T. A., De Ruiter, C. and Borum, R. (2008) 'Predictive validityof the Structured Assessment of Violence Risk in Youth (SAVRY) during residential treatment', *International journal of law and psychiatry* 31: 263–71.

Mann, R. E., Hanson, R. K. and Thornton, D. (2010) 'Assessing risk for sexual recidivism: Some proposals on the nature of psychologically meaningful risk factors', *Sexual Abuse: A Journal of Research and Treatment* 22: 191–217.

Maise, M. (2011) *Embodiment, Emotion, and Cognition.* Basingstoke, UK: Palgrave Macmillan.

Martinez-Torteya, C., Anne Bogat, G., Von Eye, A. and Levendosky, A. A. (2009) 'Resilience among children exposed to domestic violence: The role of risk and protective factors', *Child Development,* 80: 562–77.

Maruna, S. (2001) *Making Good: How Ex-Convicts Reform and Rebuild Their Lives.* Washington, DC: American Psychological Association.

McNeill, F. (2006) 'A desistance paradigm for offender management', *Criminology & Criminal Justice* 6: 39–62.

Miller, H. A. (2006) 'A dynamic assessment of offender risk, needs, and strengths in a sample of pre-release general offenders', *Behavioral Sciences & the Law* 24: 767–82.

Mrazek, P. J. and Mrazek, D. A. (1987) 'Resilience in child maltreatment victims: Aconceptual exploration', *Child Abuse & Neglect* 11: 357–66.

Smallbone, S. and Cale, J. (in press) 'Situational theories', in T. Ward and A. R. Beech (eds) *Theories of Sexual Offending*. Oxford, UK: Wiley-Blackwell.

Sterelny, K. (2012) *The Evolved Apprentice: How Evolution Made Humans Unique*. Cambridge, MA: MIT Press.

Thornton, D. (2013) 'Implications of our developing understanding of risk and protective factors in the treatment of adult male sexual offenders', *International Journal of Behavioral Consultation and Therapy* 8: 62–5.

Ward, T. (2014) 'The explanation of sexual offending: From single factor theories to integrative pluralism', *Journal of Sexual Aggression* 20: 130–41.

———. (2015) 'The detection of dynamic risk factors and correctional factors', *Criminology & Public Policy* 14: 105–11.

Ward, T. and Beech, A. R. (2015) 'Dynamic risk factors: A theoretical dead-end?' *Psychology, Crime & Law* 21: 100–13.

Ward, T., Polaschek, D. and Beech, A. R. (2006) *Theories of Sexual Offending*. Chichester, UK: John Wiley.

Werner, E. E. and Smith, R. S. (1992) *Overcoming the Odds: High Risk Children from Birth to Adulthood*. Cornell University Press.

Yesberg, J. A. and Polaschek, D. L. (2015) 'Assessing dynamic risk and protective factors in the community: Examining the validity of the Dynamic Risk Assessment for Offender Re-entry', *Psychology, Crime & Law* 21: 80–99.

13

AN UNFINISHED ALTERNATIVE: TOWARDS A RELATIONAL PARADIGM

Beth Weaver
University of Stathclyde, UK

Allan Weaver
North Ayrshire Council, UK

Abstract: In recent years, studies of desistance from crime – and of their implications for criminal justice practice – have begun to challenge 'the risk paradigm'. That challenge has been cast principally in terms of the ways in which desistance can be supported (and therefore risk of reoffending reduced), with research suggesting, for example, the critical importance of motivation, relationships and social contexts in the human development processes associated with leaving crime behind. However, more recently, desistance research has begun to raise questions about the end point or destination implied: what comes after desistance? This chapter argues that a focus on social relations, trust and reciprocity is essential – both practically and normatively – to processes of change and to supporting them. That focus in turn requires the development of co-productive approaches to practice that take more seriously the lived realities of the struggle for change, and the experiential expertise of those engaged in that struggle.

Introduction

In the past two decades, 'desistance research' has emerged as a significant field in criminology and has (to a greater or lesser degree) caught the attention of British policymakers, probation and social work practitioners.

Whether it has adequately informed policy and practice, whether it has been properly understood, is a moot point. Most discussions of what it means to desist begin with the idea of the cessation of offending behaviour. As such, academic enquiry has sought to reveal the processes through which the transition from offending to non-offending occurs, what it entails and how we might interpret what this means for penal policy and practice. In an exploration of the implications of desistance research for practice, McNeill (2006) identified a fundamental difference in emphasis between the dominant risk paradigm and the desistance paradigm. Whereas the risk paradigm, or at least its configuration as 'what works?' in policy and practice, focuses primarily on professional intervention, McNeill argues that 'desistance-based perspectives stress that the process of change exists before, behind and beyond the intervention' (McNeill 2012, p. 3). Yet, with notable exceptions (i.e. Farrall et al., 2010; Barry 2013a) our collective preoccupation with how change happens has, however, led us to neglect what happens *after* change occurs. Similarly, notwithstanding the adoption of a vocabulary of desistance, there is little evidence to suggest that policy and practice have progressed beyond existing emphases on personal or self-change (Barry, 2013a & b; McNeill, 2012, 2014) to pursue the more challenging task of supporting social integration.

The structural impediments to social integration are multifarious and include 'the economic (e.g. getting and keeping a job), the relational (e.g. rebuilding relationships with a spouse and family members after the shame of conviction) and the emotional (e.g. learning which social contexts will be accepting of ex-offenders, and which rejecting)' (Farrall et al., 2010, p. 548). Such analyses bring into view the lived realities of individuals' struggles for change and the limitations of existing social policies and penal practices to impact the cumulative, structural disadvantages and obstacles to social integration experienced by many. While desistance research casts new light on the dynamics of the change process and on the means through which change might be supported, even desistance-focused discourses of practice have focused either on what the desister does or on what professionals do; what is missing is an appreciation and elaboration of the non-professional relational contexts of offending and desistance and how these contexts are suffused with concerns linked to the character and obligations of reciprocity in social groups. This underlines the need to attend to these relational contexts and to consider how these contexts might also shape and influence approaches to practice and, as part of that, inform the development of the kinds of assets and reflexive relational networks that can support not just desistance but also social integration.

Such an approach requires us to move beyond the individualistic approaches that dominate not just community sanctions or supervision but also approaches to punishment and crime control more broadly. In an examination of the exercise of power and shifts in responses to risk in contemporary times, governmentality theorists have documented and analysed the retreat from welfarist, government-led, collective approaches to risk management and the provision of welfare and security to neo-liberal politics (Rose, 1996). Individuals are responsible for exercising choice in a prudential manner (see O'Malley, 1992, 1996); they are responsible for their own self-governance, providing for their own security and navigating and managing risks with the assistance of a plurality of independent experts and private businesses (see Robinson, Chapter 1 of this volume). This compound of autonomization, individualization and responsibilization is manifest in a retreat from approaching risk as a shared concern, a retreat from the perspective of risk causation as a social phenomenon and a retreat from seeing the best defence against risk as located in collective solutions, characterized by Rose (1996) as 'the death of the social'. In turn, approaches to 'reducing re-offending' have become similarly individualistic and responsibilizing, reliant on cognitive-behavioural, professionally led interventions designed to manage and minimize the risks associated with offending (Barry 2013). Indeed, Barry (2013, p. 349) argues that, for the most part,

> interventions ... are no longer about delivering justice *per se* but about what Rose (2000) describes as 'moralizing techniques of ethical reconstruction in the attempt to instil the capacity for self-management.' (p. 336)

The responsibility for change, then, is placed squarely on individuals as if their offending occurred freely and in isolation.

In echoes of Habermas' (1987) related argument about the colonization of the 'lifeworld' by the 'system', Archer (2011) observes that the market exchange and political command relations that ensue from this state-market complex operate with an instrumental or systems rationality which has had the effect of fragmenting and disrupting human relations. We hold that the relational paradigm, advanced here, which is underpinned by a politics of fraternity (in the form of collective action, cooperation and mutual aid) (see Donati, 2011) represents an alternative to the established 'risk paradigm', to the 'state-market binominal' (Donati, 2015, p. 16). Indeed, there is increasing evidence of the emergence of new social forms, of innovations in modes of governance, rooted in the 'the life-world', which is the work of civil society.

> [T]he emerging social forms are arising in those areas where the Market and State generate gaps ... [and these] discontinuities are coming about under the aegis of a new 'relational thinking'. (Donati, 2015, p. 17)

In progressing beyond, then, a focus on personal or self-change, this chapter proceeds to elaborate the centrality of social relations in the desistance process to illuminate how and why a focus on social relations, trust and reciprocity is essential, both practically and normatively, to supporting social integration. We suggest that this focus in turn requires the development of co-productive approaches to practice that take more seriously the lived realities of the struggle for change and the experiential expertise of those engaged in that struggle (Weaver, 2013a). We then present one 'unfinished alternative' (Mathiesen, 1974) for co-producing change, in the form of a mutual-aid based group, whose underpinning principles might usefully inform the development of a diverse range of practices oriented to enhancing opportunities for social participation and integration.

Supporting integration: Solidarity, subsidiarity and social reciprocity

Elsewhere, one of us has reported empirical findings exploring the role of a co-offending peer group in shaping and influencing each other's offending and desistance trajectories (Weaver and McNeill, 2014; Weaver, 2015). The study involved the analysis of the life stories of a friendship group of six men in their 40s who offended together in their youth and early adulthood to reveal the individual, relational and structural contributions to the desistance process, through an exploration of the relationships between these men (who once co-offended) and the wider social relations in which they individually and collectively participated over the life course (for an account of the methodology, see Weaver, 2015). Where these relationships once contributed to their collective involvement in offending, these particular friends also supported each other, albeit to differing degrees and with different effects, to pursue constructive changes in their lifestyles.

In elaborating the means through which the group acted as a resource for enabling and supporting each other's process of change, this study showed how, for different individuals, these relations triggered reflexive evaluation of their priorities, behaviours and lifestyles. It was observed that one's social networks can be a context that triggers this evaluative review through a process of comparing and measuring one's self against that of one's associates, refracted through the lens of 'the looking glass self' (Cooley, 1922). In other words, people's perceptions of how they think other people see them can motivate the initiation of behavioural or lifestyle changes. It was similarly identified that individuals' observation of change in significant others also had the effect of triggering this process of personal reflexivity through an appraisal of *their* behaviour and how different they and their lives had become, which motivated individuals to make changes in their own behaviours and/or lifestyles. The observation of change in their friends – with whom they had a fraternal relationship and shared experiences – enhanced their receptivity to their influence in the hope that similar outcomes could be achieved by them. Moreover, it was also observed that, as an outcome of a more relational mode of reflexivity, their commitment to the maintenance of these significant relationships motivated these individuals-in-relation to make reciprocal adjustments or modifications to their behaviours as a collective so as to respect and support each other's shifting lifestyle choices. While these friends responded differently to changes to their structural conditions and relational contexts, they also provided each other with mutual support to change by sharing with each other their own experiences of trying to change and, in that sense, acted as guides to each other; they provided each other with practical and emotional support; and they shared their personal and social resources, which included access to new social networks and employment.

Among these men, change was further enabled and facilitated through the reciprocal informal exchanges that take place between *family* and the social relations that manifest through work and (for some) faith and other civic groups. These relations do not cause, nor are they conditional on, behavioural change; social relations can only exert influence where the individual is receptive to that influence. What all these types of social relations have in common is that they all incorporate shared expectations of reciprocity that imply degrees of interdependency, manifest as mutual support. This notion of reciprocity or mutual exchange is central to Donati's (2011) conceptualization of social relations. It is the engine, or what he terms, the 'generating mechanism of social relations', in that it is the practice of reciprocity that generates and re-generates the bond of the relationship, motivated by the maintenance of the emergent relational goods of trust, loyalty, confidence or caring, for example. This reciprocal orientation is also the source of collective intentionality in larger groups. Those social relations that are most causally influential in the desistance process are characterized by solidarity and subsidiarity, or in other words, a sense of 'we-ness' (Weaver 2013b). Put simply, subsidiarity is a way to supply the means or a way to move resources to support the other without making him or her passive or dependent but in such a way that it allows and assists the other to do what is required in accordance with his or her personal priorities. Critically, in the context of this discussion, subsidiarity cannot work without *solidarity* (sharing a common or mutual responsibility through reciprocity, which implies interdependence and trust) (Donati, 2009). In general terms, the manner of relating, characteristic of these relations of reciprocity, manifest as mutual helping performed in accordance with the principles of solidarity and subsidiarity, has much to offer in terms of informing contemporary penal practice 'beyond the risk paradigm'. The implication of this is that if correctional practice is to support desistance, it must extend far beyond its traditional concerns (i.e. with professionally led interventions focused on changing individuals) and into a deeper engagement with means and processes that enable the (re) connection of the individual to the kinds of assets and reflexive relational networks that can facilitate not just desistance but social integration. This implies re-establishing 'the circuit of social reciprocity' (Donati, 2009, p. 227) and in so doing, learning from the experiential expertise of those engaged in that struggle. Such an approach is in alignment with the aspirations of co-production (Weaver, 2011, 2012).

Co-producing change

Supporting social integration requires, at the very least, the building of and interaction with social and community networks to enable change and the mobilization of their resources in the development, delivery and innovation of penal practice (Weaver, 2011, 2013c). Co-production is a term for such collaborative efforts, reflecting, in this context, the interdependent relationship between professional service providers, service users and communities as co-producers in enabling change (Pestoff, 2012).

Co-production as both a term and a concept is, however, beleaguered by different definitions, by disagreement about how it should be interpreted and operationalized, and by a limited empirical evidence base. Bovaird and Loeffler (2013) define co-production as *'the public sector harnessing the assets and resources of users and communities to achieve better outcomes'*. While this is somewhat operationally vague, and while it does not specify the contributions of the third sector, it retains an emphasis on reciprocity; it incorporates recognition of the relationships that exist between the various co-producers or stakeholders; it focuses on outcomes and not just services; and it encompasses an active role for both service users and for communities.

In seeking to explain the different dimensions of co-production, some academics have delineated typologies which distinguish between individualistic forms of co-production and group and collective forms (Brudney and England, 1983, pp. 63–64, in Needham, 2008; see also Bovaird and Loeffler, 2008). Individual co-production produces outcomes that benefit the individual participants and this, according to Bovaird and Loeffler (2008), is presently the dominant co-productive strategy. This understanding of co-production, and its operationalization in practice, is more akin in many respects to 'personalization' (in the form of increased personal choice and control across and within existing service provision) with an emphasis on supporting individual empowerment and self-help. By contrast, group forms of co-production denote a greater level of communication and collective involvement than individual forms, typically bringing service users together to shape or provide services, to differing degrees. An example of such an approach might be the custody and community councils run by User Voice (an 'ex-offender'–led third sector organization in England and Wales) (www.uservoice.org/our-work/our-services/councils/) or mutual and peer support groups. Collective forms are those strategies that 'benefit the whole community rather than just groups of users' (Needham, 2008, p. 224) and which include a diverse group of co-producers, for example, including community volunteers. Examples of such approaches could conceivably include Circles of Support through to more large-scale co-productive endeavours such as the Serenity Café (a recovery café and community hub run by and for people in recovery in Edinburgh: see www.serenitycafe.co.uk). As Needham (2008) observes, these different forms of co-production may be distinct categories in a conceptual sense, and perhaps in terms of scale and process, but not in terms of the outcomes or benefits that the different strategies potentially produce where we may find considerable overlap.

Slay and Stephen's (2013, p. 3) review of the literature on co-production in a mental health context identified six inter-related general principles that characterize co-productive practices:

1. Taking an assets-based approach: recognizing people who use services as partners in designing and delivering services.

2. Building on people's existing capabilities: moving beyond a deficit approach to one that provides opportunities to recognize and grow people's capabilities and actively support them to put these to use at an individual and community level.

3. Reciprocity and mutuality: offering people a range of incentives to work in reciprocal relationships with professionals and with each other, where there are mutual responsibilities and expectations.

4. Peer support networks: engaging peer and personal networks alongside professionals.

5. Blurring distinctions: between professionals and service users by reconfiguring the way services are developed and delivered.

6. Facilitating rather than delivering: enabling public service agencies to become catalysts and facilitators rather than being the main providers themselves.

While there are a number of illustrative case studies of co-productive community justice initiatives (see, for example, Graham and White, 2013), a recent systematic review of empirical research conducted by Voorberg et al. (2013) concluded that across the literature the objectives underpinning co-productive practices were rarely developed or articulated. Most studies seek to identify the influential factors – that is those factors that influence the process and practices of co-production on the organizational side and on the citizen/service user side. Resultantly, there is a dearth of systematic evidence on both the experience of co-production (Parrado et al., 2013) and the effects of co-production – both in terms of the process of participating in co-productive practices and in the outcomes of co-productive practices, for organizations and for service users (Voorberg et al., 2013). Gains from participation in the process can be considered an outcome and in turn may influence perceptions of outcomes. Indeed, they may be interdependent. Voorberg et al. (2013) conclude that, given this evidence gap, the impetus behind co-production often resides in its symbolic or normative value; put simply, it represents a virtue in and of itself. They advocate for further research into outcomes and the conditions or circumstances under and through which these outcomes occur (see also Parrado et al., 2013).

Despite this gap in evidence, co-production is widely claimed to offer 'intrinsic benefits' for individuals (Carr 2004, p. 8). Intrinsic benefits are those individual personal gains acquired through participation. These include, for example, gains in self-efficacy, self-esteem and increased social capital, factors which are also widely understood to be enablers to desistance. While intrinsic benefits are important, there is no significant evidence base testifying to the efficacy or otherwise of such processes in promoting change, enhancing social integration or substantially influencing service provision, policies or practice (Weaver and McCulloch, 2012). This does not mean that these changes and improvements are not occurring, just that they are not systematically evidenced.

Mutual aid groups: An unfinished alternative

The evidence base for co-production, let alone co-productive approaches to enabling desistance and social integration, is thus far limited and largely dependent on case studies. In similar vein, we discuss our experiences of supporting the development of a mutual aid group, which we propose is one approach to 'co-producing desistance', with the caveat that this approach has not, as yet, been subject to empirical testing – although there is wider empirical evidence supporting the theoretical frameworks on which mutual aid is based (see particularly Steinberg, 2014). Rather, in the spirit of Mathiesen's (1974) concept of the unfinished, which refers to the provisional nature of all reformist strategies whose outcomes are, by definition, uncertain, it is our intention to encourage practitioners to be open to unfinished alternatives, to work imperfectly in transitional and unfinished reformist efforts that seek to alter the status quo. 'The alternative is "alternative" in so far as it is not based on the premises of the old system, but on its own premises which at one or more points contradict those of the old system ... in terms of goals, or in terms of means together with goals' (Mathiesen, 2014, pp. 47–8); it has a distinct framework of understanding. An unfinished alternative is 'an attempt to change the existing state of affairs through an intervention that is partial, incomplete and in process' (McLeod, 2013, p. 120). The unfinished alternative emerges when we refuse 'to remain silent concerning that which we cannot [yet] talk about' (McLeod, 2013, p. 121). We hold that the relational paradigm, rooted in the rationalities of civil society and, in that, underpinned by a politics of fraternity (in the form of collective action, cooperation and mutual aid) (see Donati, 2011) represents such an alternative to the established 'risk paradigm', underpinned by the atomized individualism characterizing contemporary society (see Robinson, this volume). Here, then, we present an unfinished and alternative mechanism for co-producing change on the understanding that it alone is not sufficient to promote social integration but which, in our view, represents an alternative to existing arrangements and which might inform the development of innovative practices that seek to move 'beyond the risk paradigm'.

As noted in Weaver (2013c), a desistance focused and co-productive approach to working with groups may have more of an appreciative and collaborative, rather than correctional, focus and should be oriented to facilitating the development of new supportive social networks. Mutual aid groups are one such approach. While mutual aid manifests in a range of peer-to-peer activity, mutual aid groups can also function collaboratively with practitioners in the public and voluntary sectors to co-produce support (Burns and Taylor, 1998). In groups, mutual aid is premised on the reciprocal exchange of help; the group member is both provider and recipient of help for the purpose of co-producing mutual/collective and individual goals. In this sense, mutual aid is both a process and an outcome (Steinberg, 2004). It is also underpinned by the co-productive principles for practice delineated by Slay and Stephen (2013) outlined above.

Mutual aid-based groups can operate in a whole range of different ways – single-session, short or long term, open or closed, small or large, face-to-face or through the Internet (Steinberg 2004) – but they all prioritize and address the issues that matter to group members. The role of the worker is that of facilitator of learning in the mutual aid process in terms of 'not only helping people help themselves, but to help each other as well' (Schwartz, 1976, p. 194). As group members 'become involved with one another, they develop helping relationships and become invested in each other and in participating in the group' (Gitterman, 2006, p. 93). What is distinctive about this approach is that the sense of community and mutual support are co-produced insomuch as 'the practitioner brings his or her expertise to the group, but so does every other participant in some unique way, and it is those areas of expertise that form the basis of mutual aid' (Steinberg, 2014, p. 4).

Developing a sense of community is critical to the success and longevity of a mutual aid group. 'Only through a sense of community or we-ness will members come to acknowledge and accept one another as potential sources of help' (Steinberg, 2014, p. 4). This sense of community is enabled and encouraged, particularly in the early stages, by the identification of a shared purpose or common cause that connects members' individual goals through a collective purpose (Steinberg, 2004), which, in our experience (discussed below), can change in the life course of a long-term group with its changing membership or in accordance with the changing needs of the group.

Another distinctive feature of this approach is the emphasis placed not just on outcomes but also on processes of engagement and their impact on those engaged. There is some evidence to suggest that mutual aid-based groups can generate social capital and enhance feelings of individual and collective self-efficacy (Mok, 2005; Parsons et al., 1998; Riessman et al., 1993; Simon, 1994). Further benefits of participation include reinforcement of personal learning; social approval and acceptance, a sense of meaning, purpose and accomplishment; and improved self-worth and self-esteem (Burns and Taylor, 1998) – all of which are crucial to the desistance process (i.e. Barry, 2006; Farrall et al., 2011; Maruna and LeBel, 2009; Perrin and Blagden, 2014). Being part of such a group can also offer a vital source of hope and encouragement, of advice and guidance, and an opportunity for both sharing and learning.

As previously discussed, mutual aid groups can enable the development of the kinds of assets and reflexive relational networks that can facilitate not just desistance but also social integration. Maruna and LeBel (2009, p. 66), for example, suggest that when a person is voluntarily involved in a helping collective, he or she is 'thought to obtain a sense of belonging', or solidarity, through the 'sharing of experience, strength and hope', which is both a fundamental strength of mutual aid collectives and critical to their success. In turn, successful reintegration efforts need to foster a 'we' feeling and a 'strong sense of belonging to one group' (Cressey, 1995, p. 118, quoted in Maruna and LeBel, 2009, p. 64). Moreover, there is some empirical evidence to suggest a positive relationship between generativity, help-giving behaviours, advocacy and desistance (LeBel, 2007, 2009); 'research suggests that engagement with helping behaviours can send a message to the wider community that an individual is worthy of further support and investment in their reintegration' (Maruna and LeBel, 2009, p. 69). Engagement in generative, mutual aid and advocacy behaviours could, then, help to mitigate some of the stigma and exclusion that many experience, help to augment or maintain a person's prosocial identity and help to support people's social integration.

The Thistle Mutual Aid Group (MAG)

The Thistle MAG, named by its members, stands for *This Hand Is Support Through Learned Experience*, although the group is usually referred to by its members as 'The MAG'. The idea of the MAG was informed by the study reported on earlier in the chapter (Weaver, 2015) and its early development was underpinned by the work of Steinberg (2004), an expert in mutual aid-based group work. The quotes that follow come from interviews conducted by a member of the Thistle MAG, who, along with the interviewees, has kindly given his permission for their inclusion here. This informal peer-to-peer or 'cooperative inquiry' was undertaken approximately six months into the establishment of the group to explore what was working, why and how, to inform its continuing development. A participatory evaluation project is also underway (for details, see www.coproducingdesistance.org.uk/related-projects/).

The MAG meets weekly in a community facility; we wanted to create an informal environment that was both conceptually and physically distinct and distant from a criminal justice social work office. The MAG, which is a long-term, semi-open group, is supported or 'facilitated' by two criminal justice social workers (one of whom is the second author) and includes 10 service users. There is also a satellite support team comprising four other social workers and the first author – but increasingly, families of participants are also engaging in certain group activities and are highly supportive of the MAG. In this sense, the MAG is a truly co-productive initiative, not least in terms of its democratic approach; all decisions about the group are made by the group.

> **Gary:** There's no order of charge ... nobody claims rank or throws down authority.

On paper, the MAG members are considered to be at high risk of re-offending and are generally classed as 'hard-to-reach' service users. The ages of the members, all of whom are male, range from 26–54 and all of them have a substantial history of persistent offending, primarily comprising violent and drug-related offending for which many of them have served long-term prison sentences. This is a gender-specific group to enable men to explore the issues that matter to men. Across the MAG, members are dealing with considerable challenges, which variously include physical and mental health issues, addictions, the psychological and social effects of years in prison, and the effects of contemporary welfare reforms, inadequate housing, long-term unemployment and poverty.

The membership of the original group has altered since its inception in December 2013. Some members have left and new members have joined. The selection and recruitment of members is now undertaken by both the workers and the MAG members together. The MAG members have the final decision. The original members, however, were carefully selected by the facilitators and satellite supporters on the basis of similarity and difference to and from each other, in terms of age, offending histories, stages of change and personal characteristics. This is because we learn from people we can identify with, but also we learn from people who are different to us, who have different views, different experiences and different ways of doing things (Steinberg, 2004). The members worked with the social work facilitators and satellite supporters on an individual basis before coming together as a group. In these semi-structured individual preparatory sessions, informed by Steinberg (2004), facilitators communicate the techniques and principles of mutual aid, the mutual aid culture and process, while exploring individual strengths and aspirations for the group.

Participation in the group for both facilitators and members is entirely voluntary, and this has been critical in shaping the relational dynamics and the character of the relationships between everyone involved. As per Slay and Stephen (2013), the distinction between workers and members has since blurred, and we would all consider ourselves members, rather than facilitators, members or satellite supporters, with reciprocal commitments to the group and with shared roles, responsibilities and expectations. Everyone is there on an equal basis – there is no one person in charge – and this has engendered a real sense of inter-dependency, a genuine sense of shared concern for each other and an intense bond between everyone involved, and this sense of community and co-ownership is what makes it distinct from other groups in criminal justice.

Donald: I've never came across a group like this – in other groups there's always people not bonding and there's always something whereas this one, everyone is on the same level. We all know what we want to do ... [and] being with all the boys, we're all gelling together and its helping people. We're all just trying to better ourselves.

Gary H: Its excellent here. It's the interaction with people. I can be who I am here.

Colin: It's given me so much confidence and I've met a whole group of new people and I'm getting more involved in things.

Kathleen (social worker): The guys themselves set their own agendas. It's not prescriptive, there's no specific topics that have to be covered. It's the guys' group. They decide what they are going to be talking about. There's no taboo subjects; its open and honest discussion.

As Kathleen suggests, another distinctive feature of the MAG is that the issues that matter to and that are identified by members are prioritized and to date these have included a diverse range of topics including but not limited to masculinities, parenting, experiences of imprisonment, managing relationships, managing and overcoming addictions, inequality, stigma and discrimination. The MAG is united by a common cause, or a shared focus, which is about supporting each other with life after prison. Having this common objective is a basis for developing a sense of identification with each other; it encourages members to take ownership of the group; and it opens up lines of communication. Sharing experiences, aspirations and challenges; supporting each other; never judging each other; and being there for each other – these are the values and qualities that have led to a sense of community and co-ownership on which the ethos of the group – if not the group itself – depends.

In the MAG, members use their own experience, what they know about themselves, to shed light on the issues that other members bring up and to help them reach their own decisions about what might work for them. We work on the understanding that members do not have to agree with each other's ways of thinking, being and doing. We don't have to agree with someone to 'get' where someone's been – or where they are coming from. All that is being asked is that group members try to understand each other. For many of the members, it is just liberating to be able to discuss things that they have long felt a need to talk about and didn't have the chance to.

Gary: I learned a lot off yous [the other MAG members] and can take advice off yous. That's what I look forward to. As much as I have a hard week like everyone else when I come here I can lay it all out on the table, get support from the rest of the boys. It's a safe haven. I don't need to get uptight – I can actually sit, share my problems, whatever, have a chat with the group and off load, be at ease, and I don't feel under pressure.

Garry: The MAG is a place I can go and offload any of the challenges I've faced during the week without being judged. I was recently released from prison and it can be very daunting, stressful and it can seem at times there is no light at the end of the tunnel. I naively thought that getting released from prison meant my troubles were over but they were only just beginning. If it wasn't for the support element of the group, I would have struggled. There is other support out there but so much of it is disjointed and invisible. Some people feel like they've got nowhere to turn.

In addition to, or as an extension of, the mutual aid meetings, the MAG is a forum for sharing personal and social resources and for providing each other with different forms of practical help, and one of the members has recently established a closed online space for members to engage out-with the weekly meeting. As a group, we also participate in social activities and events together, which to date have included going to a stand-up comedy performance at a local arts centre, going out for meals in the local community, a day trip to a nearby island and forming a regular five-a-side football team that competes against other teams and community groups. We also hosted a five-a-side fundraising football event, including 16 teams comprising a range of criminal justice professionals and service user groups; the event raised funds for our local neonatal unit.

What the group ultimately becomes, what shape it takes, is for the members to decide. What seems to be emerging, which we had not expected, is the fact that not only does it have benefits for the members; everyone involved has learnt so much about the possibilities and potentials of a different way of working and a different manner of relating with each other. It has had a knock-on effect for how the practitioners involved work with, communicate and relate to other people who use services, and it has given all of us a renewed sense of why we came into the job.

Allan: The MAG motivates me, it inspires me and it reminds me of why I went into social work in first place – to assist and help people improve their situations and I feel as if the group in a lot of ways has allowed me to contribute to that.

Karen: I am seriously invested in this group as a participant and if you are going to be involved in it you have to leave that part of your [professional] role – not entirely – at the door, you can't do that obviously, but it's definitely about breaking down traditional barriers. You are the same as me; we just lived different lives. I know for a fact my life could have gone down a similar path so we can't judge, we need to get to know people. As social workers, we'll talk about relationships but what's that when you're sat behind a desk with a bit of paper?

Gordon: We have a lot of policies and procedures [in criminal justice] to follow – that will never go ... but I think we can do more of what we are doing just now and build on the Thistle MAG group to try and show that there's something a wee bit different we can try and do for people.

Conclusion

As previously suggested, and as Karen infers above, it is this relational WE, the 'we-in-relation' (Donati, 2014, p. 171), that has much to inform not just *how* we support people but the *nature* of that support. Engaging and working alongside others in relation with whom these relational goods can emerge can provide a relational network within and through which constructive aspects of people's identities and characters can be reinforced, and a sense of belonging and recognition established. We are not suggesting that mutual aid groups are the only way, nor are they sufficient to support desistance and social integration – nor is this kind of approach right for everyone. The MAG may not be transformative in the sense of overcoming the structural impediments to social integration and mitigating the lived realities of struggle not only to change but to be accepted after one has changed – but it is a space in which acceptance is given and recognition of those realities afforded, and it can ameliorate the pains of re-entry. We are suggesting, therefore, that the principles of solidarity, mutuality and subsidiarity (and the manner of relating they imply) can inform a range of practices that can enhance social integration (see, for example, Weaver and Nicholson, 2012). At the very least, this implies the need for services to become more relationally informed, more community facing and more community engaging in the recognition that, like people, communities have assets and networks that can enable and support change and social integration. Local communities are often a neglected resource, and yet they have so much to offer service users either as volunteers or in terms of using the various groups on offer or even just in terms of attending local events. Participating in these activities can offer a sense of structure to an otherwise unstructured lifestyle and provide opportunities to develop new relationships or vocational experiences. It is these less visible resources that inhere in civic groups that can add to the repertoire of resources and networks that service users can access and enables them to participate more fully in the life of their communities.

To conclude, we continue with a plea made by Weaver (2011). In standing between the pillars of reform and revolution – a position which Mathiesen (1974, p. 23) warns carries risks of being respectively 'defined in' by the current system and therefore neutralized or 'defined out' as 'irrelevant' – our task as practitioners is to defy being defined by any one position; to resist the pressures of working only for short-term goals that may be more ameliorative than transformative; to commit to being part of an ever-unfinished process of learning, but always on the way, cumulatively, towards a higher ideal of transformative change. In this vein, 'let clients take as their point of departure reforms which are closest to them and will change their lives now' (Cohen, 1975, p. 93). In so doing, as practitioners, we should work at what is close at hand but always in the openness of the unfinished, and in the direction of that which supports solidarity and integration.

References

Archer, M. (2007a) *Making Our Way Through The World: Human Reflexivity and Social Mobility*. Cambridge: Cambridge University Press.

———. (2011) 'Critical realism and relational sociology: Complementarity and synergy' *Journal of Critical Realism* 9(2): 199–207.

Barry, M. (2006) *Youth Offending in Transition: The Search for Social Recognition*. Abingdon: Routledge.

———. (2013a) 'Desistance by design: Reflections on criminal justice theory, policy and practice', *European Journal of Probation* 5(2): 47–65.

———. (2013b) 'Rational choice and responsibilisation in youth justice in Scotland: Whose evidence matters in evidence-based policy', *The Howard Journal* 52(4): 347–64.

Bovaird, T. and Loeffler, E. (2008) 'User and community co-production of public services: Fad or fact, nuisance or necessity', Briefing Paper 12, Third Sector Research Centre. Accessed online at: www.tsrc.ac.uk/Research/ServiceDeliverySD/Userandcommunitycoproduction/tabid/617/Default.aspx. (accessed 21 January 2013).

———. (2013) 'The role of co-production for better health and wellbeing', in Loeffler, E., Power, G., Bovaird, T. and Hine-Hughes, F. *Co-production of Health and Wellbeing in Scotland*. Governance International.

Brudney. J. L. and England, R. E. (1983) 'Towards a definition of the coproduction concept', *Public Administration Review* 43(1): 59–65.

Burns, D. and Taylor, M. (1998) *Mutual Aid and Self-Help: Coping Strategies for Excluded Communities*. Policy Press: Bristol.

Carr, S (2004) 'Has service user participation made a difference to social care services?' *Social Care Institute for Excellence*. Available online: www.scie.org.uk/publications/positionpapers/pp03.pdf. (accessed 31 July 2015).

Cohen, S. (1975) 'It's all right for you to talk: Political and sociological manifestos for social work action', in R. Bailey and M. Brake (eds) *Radical Social Work* (pp. 76–95) London: Edward Arnold.

Cooley, C. H. (1902/1922) *Human Nature and the Social Order*. New York: Scribner.

Donati, P. (2009) 'What does "subsidiarity" mean? The relational perspective', *Journal of Markets and Morality* 12(2): 211–243.

———. (2011) *Relational Sociology: A New Paradigm for the Social Sciences*. Routledge.

Farrall, S., Bottoms, A. and Shapland J. (2010) 'Social structures and desistance from crime', *European Journal of Criminology* 7(6): 546–70.

Farrall, S., Sharpe, G., Hunter, B. and Calverley, A. (2011). 'Theorizing structural and individual level processes in desistance and persistence: Outlining an integrated perspective', *Australian & New Zealand Journal of Criminology* 44: 218–34.

Gitterman, A. (2006) 'Building mutual support in groups', *Social Work with Groups* 28(3/4): 91–106.

Habermas, J. (1987) *The Theory of Communicative Action: Vol. II: The Critique of Functionalist Reason.* Cambridge: Polity Press.

LeBel, T. P. (2007) 'An examination of the impact of formerly incarcerated persons helping others', *Journal of Offender Rehabilitation* 46(1/2): 1–24.

———. (2009) 'Formerly incarcerated persons use of advocacy/activism as a coping strategy in the reintegration process', in Veysey, B., Christian, J. and Martinez, D. J. (eds) *How Offenders Transform Their Lives.* Willan Publishing.

McLeod, A. (2013) *Confronting Criminal Law's Violence: The Possibilities of Unfinished Alternatives.* http://scholarship.law.georgetown.edu/facpub/1279.

McNeill, F. (2006) 'A desistance paradigm for offender management', *Criminology and Criminal Justice* 6(1):/ 37–60.

———. (2012) 'Four forms of "offender" rehabilitation: Towards an interdisciplinary perspective', *Legal and Criminological Psychology* 17: 18–36.

———. (2014) 'Desistance and criminal justice in Scotland', in Croall, H., Mooney, G. and Munro, M. *Criminal Justice in Scotland*, 2nd edn London: Routledge.

Maruna, S. and LeBel, T. P. (2009) 'Strengths-based approaches to reentry: Extra mileage toward reintegration and destigmatization', *Japanese Journal of Sociological Criminology* 34: 58–80.

Mathiesen, T. (1974) *The Politics of Abolition.* London: Martin Robertson.

———. (2014) *The Politics of Abolition Revisited.* Routledge.

Mok, B. H. (2005). 'Organizing self-help groups for empowerment and social change: Findings and insights from an empirical study in Hong Kong', *Journal of Community Practice* 13(1): 49–67.

Needham, C. (2008) 'Realising the potential of co-production: Negotiating improvements in public services', Social Policy and Society 7(2): 221–31.

O'Malley, P. (1992) 'Risk, power and crime prevention', *Economy and Society* 21(3): 252–75.

———. (1996) 'Risk and responsibility', in A. Barry, T. Osborne and N. Rose (eds) *Foucault and Political Reason.* Chicago: Chicago University Press.

Parrado, S., van Ryzin, G., Bovaird, T. and Loeffler, E. (2013) 'Correlates of co-production: Evidence from a five-nation study of citizens', *International Public Management Journal* 16(1): 85–112.

Parsons, R. J., Gutierrez, L. M. and Cox, E. O. (1998). 'A model for empowerment practice', in Gutierrez, L. M., Parsons, R. J. and Cox, E. O. (eds) *Empowerment in Social Work Practice: A Source Book* Pacific Grove, CA: Brooks/Cole.

Perrin, C. and Blagden, N. (2014) 'Accumulating meaning, purpose and opportunities to change "drip by drip": The impact of being a listener in prison', *Psychology, Crime & Law* 20(9): 902–20.

Pestoff, V. (2012) 'Innovations in public services: Co-production and new public governance in Europe', in Botero, A., Paterson, A. and Saad-Sulonen (eds) *Towards Peer Production in Public Services: Cases from Finland.* Aalto University publication series Crossover 15/2012. Helsinki, Finland, accessed online at: http://p2pfoundation.net/Co-Production_and_New_Public_Governance_in_Europe. (accessed 31 July 2015).

Riessman, F. B., Bay, T. and Madara, E. J. (1993) 'The politics of self-help', *Social Policy* 23(2): 28–38.

Rose, N. (1996b) 'The death of the social? Refiguring the territory of government', *Economy and Society* 25(3): 327–34.

Schwartz, W. (1976) 'Between client and system: The mediating function', in Roberts, R. and Northen, H. (eds) *Theories of Social Work with Groups.* pp. 44–66. New York: Columbia University Press.

Simon, B. L. (1994) *The Empowerment Tradition in American Social Work: A History.* New York: Columbia University Press.

Slay, J. and Stephens, L. (2013) *Co-Production in Mental Health: A Literature Review.* London: New Economics Foundation.

Steinberg, D. M. (2004) *The Mutual-Aid Approach to Working with Groups: Helping People Help One Another.* Abingdon: Routledge.

———. (2004) *A Mutual-Aid Model for Social Work with Groups.* Abingdon: Routledge.

Voorberg, W., Bekkers, V. and Tummers, L. (2013) 'Co-creation and co-production in social innovation: A systematic review and future research agenda'. Paper presented at the EGPA – conference, Edinburgh 11 September–13 September 2013.

Weaver, B. (2011) 'Co-producing community justice: The transformative potential of personalisation for penal sanctions', *British Journal of Social Work* 41(6): 1038–57.

———. (2012) 'The relational context of desistance: Some implications and opportunities for social policy', *Social Policy and Administration* 46(4): 395–412.

———. (2013a) *The Story of the Del: From Delinquency to Desistance,* PhD thesis, Glasgow: University of Strathclyde.

———. (2013b) 'The importance of social relations in personal change', *Scottish Justice Matters* 1(2): 12–14.

———. (2013c) 'Co-producing desistance: Who works to support desistance?', in I. Durnescu and F. McNeill, *Understanding Penal Practices.* Abingdon: Routledge.

Weaver, B. and Nicholson, B. (2012) 'Co-producing change: Resettlement as a mutual enterprise', *Prison Service Journal* 204, available online at www.crimeandjustice.org.uk/opus1972/PSJ_November_2012_No._204.pdf. (accessed 31 July 2015).

Weaver, B. and McCulloch, T. (2012) *Co-producing Criminal Justice: Executive Summary.* research report no. 5/2012 The Scottish Centre for Crime and Justice Research: Glasgow. www.sccjr.ac.uk/wp-content/uploads/2012/11/Co-producing_Criminal_Justice.pdf. (accessed 31 July 2015).

Weaver, B. and McNeill, F. (2014) 'Life lines: Desistance, social relations and reciprocity', *Criminal Justice and Behavior,* online version doi.0093854814550031.

14

CHANGING RISKS, RISKING CHANGE

Chris Trotter
Monash University

Gill McIvor
Stirling University

Fergus McNeill
Glasgow University

Introduction

There are a number of themes which emerge from the chapters of this book. First, the authors have a common conception of the risk paradigm. It refers to the practices which have developed in probation and institutional settings of using actuarial risk assessment instruments to assess levels of risk of offenders. These instruments then help workers to identify criminogenic needs, in other words, factors such as unemployment, criminal peer groups or poor family relationships which appear to be related to the offending behaviour of particular individuals. These criminogenic needs then become targets for intervention either through structured group programmes or individual discussion with a probation officer. Sometimes the offenders might be referred to another agency to address the risk factor (e.g. drug use, violent disposition, psychiatric problems).

The theme that emerges most strongly through just about every chapter is that the risk paradigm, including both risk assessment and risk-driven interventions, has serious limitations as a method of dealing with young and adult offenders. This applies to institutional and community-based interventions, although for the most part the book is concerned with probation and parole supervision and other community-based interventions. There are varying views around this theme, with some saying that risk assessment and risk-driven interventions have virtually no value and others saying that they have a place despite their limitations.

There is a consistency across the chapters in terms of the limitations of the risk paradigm. The practice of risk assessment and risk-driven interventions is often compromised. Risk-based approaches deskill staff. There is confusion regarding the purpose of risk assessment. The risk paradigm does not cater for structural factors such as poverty or class. It translates disadvantage into individual deficits. Communicating risk levels to individual offenders is problematic. Risk assessment instruments often don't work for minority groups. Staff are resistant to actuarial models. It leads to an authoritarian model of rehabilitation which does not work. Risk factors may have little to do with what motivates offenders to choose more prosocial lives. Addressing what got someone into trouble might not get them out of it. The very concept of the risk principle, that high-risk offenders benefit most from intensive interventions, may be incorrect. Low-risk offenders may benefit from effective interventions just as much if not more than high-risk offenders.

On the other hand, some of the authors argue that risk assessment in particular has a place in criminal justice. There is value in allocating scarce resources to those who are likely to do the most harm. Reduced scores on actuarial risk scales are related to reduced offending and this can be measured. While actuarial risk assessment tools may not work for all groups, new tools have been developed and modified for different groups such as sex offenders. Protective factors can be included in the risk assessment process and risk-driven interventions to address some of the perceived deficit focus.

The second theme which runs through the book relates to the broader concept of the risk society and role of the media. Risk may have always been there; however, the focus on risk in corrections in English-speaking countries has developed progressively over recent decades. It has been driven in part by a media which is prone to focus on one-off high-profile failures, often in the form of a murder in horrific circumstances by an offender who is under community-based supervision. This has led in turn to a need for probation services and others to be accountable, to be seen to be able to assess risk.

The third theme which emerges time and time again from the authors is that there is a way 'beyond the risk paradigm'. This includes strengths-based work, a focus on relationship and community and a greater focus on what we have learnt from desistance theory and research and models such as Good Lives. We can also learn from the concepts of resilience and recovery used in fields such as child protection and mental health, and from an understanding that domestic violence, sex offending or any other type of offending cannot be explained in simple terms and by addressing one or two specific issues. Offenders may be motivated by factors seemingly unrelated to risk as they develop goals for a better life – for example, single status may not be a risk factor, but marriage or a partner can have a strong influence towards a prosocial lifestyle.

Limitations of the risk paradigm

Gwen Robinson, in the first chapter, gives us some of the history of the development of the risk paradigm. She argues that while the concept of risk may have always been there, justice departments have over recent decades moved, in the United Kingdom in particular, from welfare to what works to risk management. This has been done under the guise that managing risk leads to rehabilitation; however, it has led to a focus on risk assessment and risk-driven interventions, often at the expense of rehabilitation – a focus on the risks posed by individuals rather than the risks faced by them.

Gwen Robinson, Kevin Haines and Stephen Case, Craig Schwalbe and several other authors have pointed out the stated intention of the proponents of the risk paradigm in criminal justice is clearly to reduce re-offending. The late Don Andrews and Jim Bonta (e.g. Andrews and Bonta 2010) argued, along with their colleagues, that numerous meta-analyses of relevant criminal justice literature have shown that a focus on high and medium-risk offenders leads to lower reoffending; that actuarial methods of assessing risk are more effective than professional or clinical judgements; and that addressing criminogenic needs as revealed through risk assessment leads to reduced rates of reoffending.

The authors in this book have argued, however, that in practice risk-based approaches to criminal justice do not achieve their stated aim of reducing reoffending. In fact, they see the risk paradigm as managing risk at the expense of rehabilitation.

Craig Schwalbe perhaps takes the most favorable position of any of our authors in relation to the value of risk assessment tools and processes. He acknowledges that risk has a place in criminal justice work despite its shortcomings. He argues, for example, that risk assessment tools can in fact reduce over-classification and lead in turn to less institutionalization in comparison to purely clinical assessment processes. On the other hand, he suggests that risk assessment inherently contains structural biases – for example, disadvantaged young people are more likely to be expelled from school. He also points out that in practice the risk tools are rarely tested for reliability and often the services to meet criminogenic needs are not available. He also raises the issue of labelling and the dilemma faced by practicing probation and parole officers in terms of how you can discuss negative risk assessments with clients and how you integrate risk assessment with problem-solving and case planning.

Chris Trotter identifies research which suggests that risk assessments are often not undertaken in practice the way they were intended. He points out that numerous studies have found slippage or poor implementation of the risk assessment instruments. He indicates that some research found that the instruments were no more effective in practice than simply identifying a few key risk factors such as prior convictions and age. On a similar theme, Keven Haines and Stephen Case refer to research in youth justice in Wales which suggests that while workers may identify criminogenic needs through the risk assessment process these needs were not actually linked to the interventions that followed. They refer to research which found that outcomes for one-third of young people were incorrectly predicted by the risk assessment tool, and as a result large numbers of young offenders were subject to disproportionate and unnecessary criminal justice interventions.

Several of the authors discuss the confusion regarding what risk assessment is for. Is it for the purpose of providing additional services to offenders, or is it also for the purpose of informing sentencing? Peter Raynor refers to the practice in some jurisdictions of including risk assessments in court reports. Kevin Haines and Stephen Case also raise this issue. They refer to research in Wales which found that comprehensive risk assessment material was provided to courts and that the courts generally followed the risk-related recommendations. The argument is presented that risk assessments may lead to additional penalties and, given that the risk assessments include many factors over which the young person has no control – family issues or school failure, for example – this is unfair. It is even more unfair if the risk assessment is completed poorly and young people are incorrectly classified. Peter Raynor discusses research which suggests that risk assessment has led to pre-sentence reports becoming more negative.

Others talk about the general resistance from staff to the use of the risk assessment instruments. Peter Raynor suggests that workers find them too computer focused and that they are seen as part of managerialism. Kevin Haines and Stephen Case point out that staff find them deskilling and that they rob workers of important discretionary capacity. Workers become form completers rather than professional caseworkers.

Perhaps one of the strongest arguments against the risk paradigm, and one which comes through strongly throughout most of the chapters of the book, is that it perpetuates disadvantage. Peter Raynor, Kevin Haines and Stephen Case, Gill McIvor and others argue that the risk factors identified in risk assessment tools are socially structured. Offenders are defined as high risk because they have minimal family support, low educational achievement, unemployment and inadequate housing, for example. It is argued that social issues such as poverty, unemployment and social disorganization are turned into individual deficits.

In addition to this, Gill McIvor and others argued that the reconceptualization of 'needs' and structural disadvantages as risk factors further disadvantages minority groups who are over-classified by the risk assessment tools. McIvor argues that different factors lead to crime by women compared to men. She points to mixed research about the effectiveness of risk assessment tools for women, particularly given that they have been developed predominantly with male samples. Similarly, indigenous offenders may be over-classified. Even if tools can be adapted to disadvantaged groups, they decontextualize, individualize and pathologize individuals, and considerations of risk may outweigh concerns about due process and proportionality.

David Rose discusses the risk paradigm in relation to mental illness and domestic violence. There is an increasing focus on risk management in mental health, yet the research points to the importance of strengths-based work and recovery-based approaches.

In the field of domestic violence, Dave Moran suggests that the programmes have often been based on addressing the perpetrator's sense of entitlement. They engage with men almost entirely in terms of their abusive behaviour in a one-size-fits-all approach. Rather than addressing the complex needs of men, they focus on the violence itself. It is not argued that there is not a place to specifically address violent behaviour, but that there are multifactorial explanations for domestic violence, and that focusing solely on men's negative characteristics and deficits is likely to be less effective than more systemic approaches which acknowledge diversity and individual strengths and needs.

In a similar vein, Anne Marie McAlinden argues that risk-based responses to sexual offending are at best uncertain in their effects and at worst counterproductive, in that they often reduce the potential for successful reintegration. She discusses the range of measures which have been put in place to manage the risk posed by sex offenders in the community, including offender notification and pre-employment vetting. She suggests that these approaches ignore the family as a dangerous place and respond to media portrayal of sexual assaults and murders. The isolation and stigmatization does little to help perpetrators or victims.

Media

Wendy Fitzgibbon ties together a lot of the themes in this book in her discussion of the media. As Gwen Robinson suggested in her chapter, it is difficult to separate the increasing dominance of the risk paradigm in criminal justice from wider social influences, the media in particular. Critical incidents including brutal murders committed by offenders on probation or parole have often attracted a large amount of media attention. The media presentations ignore statistical probabilities and generate unreasonable fear in communities. The response is to develop more and more sophisticated methods of risk assessment despite the fact that it not possible to say what someone will actually do from their risk score. Wendy Fitzgibbon argues that this has led to progressive deskilling and declining professional status of probation and social work in the United Kingdom. Like many others in this book, she argues for a move back to a focus on the relationship between individual client and practitioner.

Beyond the risk paradigm

The third theme which comes through loud and strong in this book is that there is an alternative and preferable approach to working with offenders. There is a way beyond the risk paradigm.

Fergus McNeill discusses desistance and argues that offenders are likely to desist from crime as they develop social capital (particularly in the form of reciprocal relationships). Supporting desistance involves not a focus on risks and deficits, but on supporting relationships and building strengths and hope.

Chris Trotter argues that what gets people out of crime may be very different to what gets them into crime. He outlines research which suggests that reoffending can be reduced when supervisors of offenders purposefully focus on offenders' prosocial comments and actions, and when they help offenders with issues which the offenders themselves define, which are of concern to them, rather than focusing on criminogenic needs defined by supervisors. In other words, a focus on collaboration and strengths can take offender supervision beyond the risk paradigm with benefits for the offenders and the community.

Tony Ward and Imogen McDonald argue that rather than focus on risk we should focus on agency. *Agency* refers to a person's capacity to plan action and control their behaviour. They argue that the commission of an offence requires the presence of *both* an agent(s) and an external context that supports criminal actions. They argue, consistently with the arguments presented by Fergus McNeill and Chris Trotter and others in the book, that individual strengths rather than risks can be supported as motivating and protective influences.

Beth and Allan Weaver suggest that the way forward is not about risks, but about a greater focus on supporting social integration with the development of networks which can support desistance. At a community level this can involve circles of support through to large-scale co-productive endeavours such as the Serenity Cafe (a recovery café and community hub run by and for people in recovery in Edinburgh), peer support networks and mutual aid-based groups.

Conclusion

This book grew out of a workshop held at the Monash University Centre in Prato, Italy. The authors, mostly academic social workers, joined with experts in mental health and child protection to discuss our concerns about the rise of, and dominance of, the risk paradigm in our respective disciplines. We agreed that the prevalence of risk assessment and risk-driven interventions has led to a situation where the client is largely left out of planning their own interventions. We talked about rehabilitation, desistance, recovery, resilience and collaboration, and we agreed that there is a way forward which would benefit our clients and our communities. This is not a return to the often flawed, relationship-driven case-work of the 1970s but a focus on new knowledge, including worker skills and strengths-based models of intervention, which have been shown to improve outcomes for our clients. In this volume we have presented what we believe is a fair critique of risk-based work in corrections, particularly in community-based interventions and supervision. And we have pointed to a way beyond the risk paradigm which focuses on strengths rather than deficits, on skills rather than formulaic approaches and on collaboration rather than direction.

INDEX